ECONOMICS IN RUSSIA

Modern Economic and Social History Series

General Editor: Derek H. Aldcroft

Titles in this series include:

The Popularization of Malthus in Early Nineteenth-Century England
Martineau, Cobbett and the Pauper Press
James P. Huzel

Taste, Trade and Technology
The Development of the International Meat Industry since 1840
Richard Perren

Alfred Herbert Ltd and the British Machine Tool Industry, 1887–1983
Roger Lloyd-Jones and M.J. Lewis

Rethinking Nineteenth-Century Liberalism
Richard Cobden Bicentenary Essays
Edited by Anthony Howe and Simon Morgan

Governance, Growth and Global Leadership
The Role of the State in Technological Progress, 1750–2000
Espen Moe

Triumph of the South
A Regional Economic History of Early Twentieth Century Britain
Peter Scott

Aspects of Independent Romania's Economic History with
Particular Reference to Transition for EU Accession
David Turnock

Estates, Enterprise and Investment at the Dawn of the Industrial Revolution
Estate Management and Accounting in the North-East of England, c.1700–1780
David Oldroyd

Across the Borders
Financing the World's Railways in the Nineteenth and Twentieth Centuries
Edited by Ralf Roth and Günter Dinhobl

Mining Tycoons in the Age of Empire, 1870–1945
Entrepreneurship, High Finance, Politics and Territorial Expansion
Edited by Raymond E. Dumett

Economics in Russia

Studies in Intellectual History

Edited by

VINCENT BARNETT
Bedfordshire University, UK

JOACHIM ZWEYNERT
Hamburg Institute of International Economics, Germany

ASHGATE

Published by
Ashgate Publishing Limited
Gower House
Croft Road
Aldershot
Hampshire GU11 3HR
England

Ashgate Publishing Company
Suite 420
101 Cherry Street
Burlington, VT 05401-4405
USA

www.ashgate.com

British Library Cataloguing in Publication Data
Economics in Russia : studies in intellectual history. – (Modern economic and social history)
1. Economics – Russia 2. Economics – Soviet Union 3. Economics – Russia (Federation)
I. Barnett, Vincent, 1967– II. Zweynert, Joachim
330.9’47

Library of Congress Cataloging-in-Publication Data
Barnett, Vincent, 1967–
Economics in Russia : studies in intellectual history / by Vincent Barnett and Joachim Zweynert.
p. cm. – (Modern economic and social history)
ISBN 978-0-7546-6149-8 (alk. paper)
1. Economics–Russia. 2. Economics–Soviet Union. 3. Economics–Russia (Federation)
I. Zweynert, Joachim. II. Title.
HB113.A2B345 2008
330.0947–dc22

2007052264

ISBN 978-0-7546-6149-8

Mixed Sources
Product group from well-managed forests and other controlled sources
www.fsc.org Cert no. SA-COC-1565
© 1996 Forest Stewardship Council
FSC

Printed and bound in Great Britain by
MPG Books Ltd, Bodmin, Cornwall.

Contents

List of Figure and Tables

Figure

Tables

Notes on Contributors

Vincent Barnett, Creative Arts, Technology and Science, University of Bedfordshire, England.

William Coleman, School of Economics, Australian National University, Australia.

Michael Kaser, St Antony's College, Oxford, England.

Shuichi Kojima, Department of Economics, Konan University, Japan.

Natalia Makasheva, Institute of Scientific Information on Social Sciences, Moscow Higher School of Economics, Russia.

Danila Raskov, St Petersburg State University, Russia.

Alla Sheptun, Moscow Finance Academy, Russia.

Leonid Shirokorad, St Petersburg State University, Russia.

Pekka Sutela, Helsinki School of Economics, University of Helsinki, Finland.

Anna Taitslin, Faculty of Law, University of Canberra, Australia.

Andrey Zaostrovstev, University of Finance and Economics, St Petersburg, Russia.

Joachim Zweynert, Hamburg Institute of International Economics, University of Hamburg, Germany.

Modern Economic and Social History Series General Editor's Preface

Economic and social history has been a flourishing subject of scholarly study during recent decades. Not only has the volume of literature increased enormously but the range of interest in time, space and subject matter has broadened considerably so that today there are many sub-branches of the subject which have developed considerable status in their own right.

One of the aims of this series is to encourage the publication of scholarly monographs on any aspect of modern economic and social history. The geographical coverage is world-wide and contributions on the non-British themes will be especially welcome. While emphasis will be placed on works embodying original research, it is also intended that the series should provide the opportunity to publish studies of a more general thematic nature which offer a reappraisal or critical analysis of major issues of debate.

Derek H. Aldcroft
University of Leicester

Foreword

Many scholarly (and also some popular) books have appeared since the collapse of the USSR, dealing with various aspects of the transition from communistic or Soviet-style economic systems to capitalism or market-control forms of economy. Yet very few books have appeared in the same period dealing with the long but often overlooked tradition of Russian economics itself, and how this tradition has grown and developed over a significant period of time. In fact, in order to fully comprehend the current position of the Russian economy, some understanding of its *alter ego* in the intellectual realm (Russian economics) is certainly necessary. This volume, although in no sense a comprehensive guide to this neglected topic, aims to introduce the reader to some significant currents and features of Russian economic ideas broadly considered, and thus to complement the many available accounts of the very recent development of capitalism in Russia.

Timeline: The Main Events of Russian History

862–79	Rurik, founder of Kievan Rus'
Late 10th century	The Christianisation of Russia
1147	Moscow founded by Yuri Dolgoruky
1237	Tatar Invasion begins
1240	Tatars capture Kiev; Alexander Nevsky defeats Swedes on River Neva
1299	Metropolit Maksim moves from Kiev to Vladimir
1362	Dmitrii Ivanovich becomes grand prince of Vladimir
1453	Constantinople falls to the Turks
1462	Ivan III becomes grand prince of Muscovy; territorial expansion of Muscovy begins
1547	Ivan IV ('The Terrible') given the title of 'tsar'
1560s	Edition of *Domostroi*, a book of principles of family life
1589	Russian patriarchate established
1598–1613	Times of Troubles; Moscow occupied by Poles; Novgorod occupied by Swedes
1613	Michael Romanov becomes tsar
1654	Beginning of schism (*raskol*)
1689–1725	Peter I (The Great)
1700–21	Great Northern war with Sweden
1703	Founding of St Petersburg
1711	Establishment of Senate
1711–65	Mikhail V. Lomonosov
1722	Creation of the Table of Ranks
1726	Foundation of the Academy of Sciences in St Petersburg
1755	Foundation of Moscow University
1762–96	Catherine II
1767	Catherine's *Nakaz* and Legislative Commission
1773–75	Pugachev's rebellion
1796–1801	Paul I
1801–25	Alexander I
1801	The first chair of political economy established at Moscow University
1802	Creation of Ministries
1804	University Statute
1807–11	Speransky's reforms
1812	Napoleon invades Russia
1813–14	Alexander's pursuit of Napoleon to Paris

1816–19	Emancipation of the serfs in the Baltic provinces
1818	Karamzin's *History of the Russian State*
1825	Decembrists' uprising
1825–55	Nikolai I
1830	Alexander Pushkin (1799–1837) finishes *Eugen Onegin*
1836	Chaadaev's *First Philosophical Letter*
1842	Nikolai Gogol's *Dead Souls*
1851	Railway between St Petersburg and Moscow opened
1853–56	Crimean War
1855–81	Alexander II
1857	First number of Alexander Herzen's *Kolokol* (The Bell)
1860–73	First railway boom
1861	Emancipation of the serfs
1863	New liberal University statue
1864	Local government and judicial reforms
1865–66	Publication begins of Tolstoy's *War and Peace*
1866	Karakozov's attempt to assassinate Alexander I; Dostoyevsky's *Crime and Punishment*
1873–74	'To the People' movement reaches its peak
1878	Formation of 'Land and Freedom' revolutionary group
1881	Assassination of Alexander II
1881–94	Alexander III
1881	Introduction of law on 'states of emergency'
1889	Introduction of Land Captains
1891	Construction of the Trans-Siberain railway begins
1894–1917	Nikolai II
1898	First congress of the Social Democratic Party
1901	Formation of the Socialist Revolutionary Party
1902	Lenin's *What Is to Be Done?*
1904–05	War with Japan
1905	'Bloody Sunday' starts two years of revolution; a new Constitution is promised
1906	First Duma (parliament) meets
1906–11	Stolypin's agrarian reforms
1907	Second Duma meets and is dissolved
1907–1911	Third Duma
1911	Assassination of Stolypin
1912	Lena goldfields shootings: worker radicalism re-emerges
1913	Stravinsky's *The Rite of Spring*
1914	Outbreak of First World War
1917	Overthrow of the monarchy; Lenin returns from exile and publishes 'April theses'; 'October Revolution' establishes Soviet power
1918–24	Vladimir Ilich Lenin in control of Soviet Russia

1918	Constituent Assembly is dissolved; Nikolai II and his family murdered by the Bolsheviks who then launch a systematic terror against their enemies
1921	Revolt of the sailors at Kronstadt
1921–29	New Economic Policy
1922	Treaty of Rapallo signed with Germany; the Soviet Union is officially created
1923	A stroke incapacitates Lenin; triumvirate of Stalin, Zinoviev and Kamenev formed
1924	Stalin and Bukharin promote the idea of 'Socialism in One Country'
1927	15th Congress of the VKP calls for a five-year plan
1928	*Shakhty* trial; Bukharin's 'Notes of an Economist' is published in *Pravda*
1929	Bukharin, Rykov and Tomsky are condemned by the Politburo; Plenary Session of the CK decides for collectivisation; Fifth Soviet Congress accepts five-year plan
1930	Trial of the 'Industrial Party'
1938	Peak of the Stalinist terror; 'show trial' of Bukharin and Radek
1939	Soviet troops invade Poland; Russian–Finnish war
1941	German troops invade the Soviet Union
1942	The Battle of Stalingrad
1945	Yalta Conference; Second World War ends
1953	Death of Stalin
1953–64	Nikita S. Khrushchev
1962	The Cuban Missile Crisis
1964–82	Leonid Brezhnev
1965	Kosygin reforms
1968	The Soviet Union occupies Czechoslovakia
1969	Solzhenitsin wins Nobel Prize for Literature
1979	Soviet troops invade Afghanistan
1982–84	Yuri Andropov
1985–91	Mikhail Gorbachev
1986	Chernobyl nuclear accident
1987	Yeltsin is demoted after he criticizes the party leadership
1988	The crisis over Nagorno-Karabakh erupts
1989	The Berlin Wall crumbles
1990	Gorbachev wins the Nobel Prize
1991	Yeltsin elected president of the Russian Federation; Gorbachev resigns as president of the Soviet Union; the demise of the Union of Soviet Socialist Republics
1992	Yegor Gaidar launches 'shock therapy' economic reform

1993	Yeltsin dissolves the Russian parliament and calls elections to a State Duma, which support nationalists and former Communists; ratification of new constitution
1994	Russian troops invade Chechnya
1996	Yeltsin re-elected as president
1998	Russian financial crises erupts
1999	Yeltsin resigns as president; Vladimir Putin becomes acting president
2000	Putin elected president of the Russian Federation
2004	Putin re-elected president of the Russian Federation

Chapter 1

Introduction

Vincent Barnett and Joachim Zweynert

In Russia over the last hundred years, it is possible to observe two rather different evaluations of the development of Russian economic thought. One group of authors, beginning with Vladimir V. Svyatlovsky and including Jack F. Normano, argued that at least up until the 1890s, Russian economists in the main followed (if not imitated) their Western counterparts. This view dominated in Russia and the Soviet Union up until the XV Party Congress of the CPSU, at which the dogma of world revolution was abandoned and replaced with that of building 'socialism in one country'. From this time onwards, national historiography had to prove that Russia was ahead of the rest of the world on the road to the communist utopia. Accordingly, the thesis that Russian 'bourgeois' authors had done nothing but slavishly imitate Western 'vulgar' economists was often propagated. At the same time, much effort was devoted to proving that Russian 'progressive' authors had always been closer to Marxism-Leninism than their Western contemporaries and hence had been leading the way as the vanguard of change. This type of tendentious Soviet historiography contributed to denigrating the indigenous history of Russian economic ideas in the eyes of many post-Soviet economists and has also downgraded its significance amongst Western historians.

After the collapse of the USSR, in the 1990s there was a relative de-coupling of ideology from the history of Russian economic thought. Ignored by many of their Russian colleagues, a small group of experts in this field tried to reinvigorate the memory of the Russian scientific community regarding the contributions of native economists and re-issued some long-forgotten books and articles, including the contributions of Russian émigré economists. Most of these researchers were particularly interested in 'bourgeois' and anti-communist economists and hence they showed relatively little interest in the contributions of official Soviet thinkers. Since the turn of the millennium, the situation has changed once again. Being critical of both the outcome of Russia's transition to the market and of the increasing influence of Western mainstream economics in Russia, a group of scholars around the economist Leonid I. Abalkin have initiated a discussion about the existence of a so-called 'Russian school of economists'.

Arguing in the spirit of the Slavophile and Eurasian idea of the existence of a Russian national character, these authors hold that almost all Russian economic thinkers started not from an individualistic methodology, but from a consideration of the collective forms that the individuals invariably had to subordinate themselves to. This Russian tradition of economic thought, Abalkin and his followers have argued, offers a much more relevant foundation for Russian economic policy than those which have been imported from the West. At about the same time, another group of scholars started to undertake attempts to revive old-style Soviet political economy. This found an expression in a number of publications from the so-called 'Tsagolov school', named after Nikolai A. Tsagolov, the author of the standard Soviet textbook on political economy. In both of these recent developments there is a clear tendency to oppose Western and Russian economic thought and to claim the superiority of the latter.

However, the extensive presence of ideology in the history of Russian economic thought, and its ambiguous relationship to Western influences, is perhaps not due to the features of a 'Russian character', however this might be defined. Rather, it reflects more the fact that, since the time of Peter the Great, the issue of precisely what developmental path the country should take has been the subject of heated and controversial debates that still have not come to an end. Economics in Russia has been directly concerned with this issue and this might explain (in part) why economics was more strongly politicized than it was in many Western countries, especially since the issue of choosing the 'correct' developmental path has always been connected with the exchange of ideas with the West. This in turn suggests the need for joint research efforts between Russian and Western experts in the area of the history of Russian economic thought, thus allowing for a combination of internal and external perspectives that will contribute to a more balanced evaluation of its true significance.

Today, almost 20 years after the fall of the Berlin wall, not nearly enough is known about the history of Russian economic thought (in its broadest sense) in the West. Hence the basic aim of this volume is to provide a collection of original and revealing accounts of aspects of the development of Russian economic ideas from the very early period to contemporary times. There is only one chapter in the book devoted to the economic thought of a certain epoch (the Enlightenment). Instead, chapters deal with key figures, issues, or concepts typical of certain periods or prevalent among certain groups. Moreover, no claim for a comprehensive or complete coverage of all periods or all economists will be made. Rather the goal of the volume is to stimulate a renewed consideration of the rich heritage of Russian economic thinking (widely considered) across a number of centuries. Another basic aim is to bring Western and Russian scholars together in a constructive way that is not always done successfully in the academic literature.

Contributions in the tradition of Mark Blaug and Joseph Schumpeter that focus on economic analysis in a narrower sense and contributions that, in line with authors like Karl Pribram or Mark Perlman and Charles R. McCann Jr, deal with economic thought in the context of history and culture, are both represented in the volume. Due to the nature of the intellectual environment under investigation, the latter approach tends to dominate more in the earlier historical periods under consideration. In terms of individual content, historians that utilize approaches from all different traditions in economics, including mainstream and heterodox views, were invited to participate. No preconceived attitude or framework thus dominates the volume, except to say that both editors believe that history remains a vital component of any relevant economic understanding. The remainder of the introduction will provide a short overview of all the chapters that follow. It should be stated clearly that the specific arguments presented by the individual contributors in each chapter are their own and are not necessarily endorsed in full measure by the editors, or indeed by any of the other contributors.

Pre-1917 Chapters

The volume is rich in chapters that explore Russian economic thinking a long time before the Bolsheviks were even formed as a political force. The main question that Danila Raskov asks in his contribution 'Economic Thought in Muscovy: Ownership, Money and Trade' is whether in the sixteenth and seventeenth centuries 'economic thought' existed in Russia as a separate entity, or whether economic considerations remained subordinated to religious, legal and political discourses. A key feature of Muscovy in the period under review was a vast fusion between the state and the church, and the power of both institutions strictly limited the range in which independent scientific thought could develop. However, as Raskov's analysis shows, in debates on issues of ownership, money and trade, the arguments deployed sometimes did go beyond the borders of religion or politics and followed their own unique economic logic. However, this was the exception rather than the rule. All in all, Raskov argues that Russian economic thought in the sixteenth and seventeenth centuries still oscillated 'between mercantilism and the Middle Ages', with written texts usually being part of religious discourse, while political practice was strongly influenced by mercantilist concepts.

The contradiction between Peter the Great's radical economic reforms and the fact that the social structure of Russia remained close to that of the Middle Ages, was characteristic for the Russian 'Age of Enlightenment', suggests Leonid Shirokorad. By stimulating its emancipation from religious doctrines, both Peter the Great and Catherine II gave economic research in Russia a significant boost. However, Shirokorad argues that in the eighteenth century, there had not yet emerged anything that could really be called 'economic science' in Russia. This was mainly for two reasons. Firstly, as soon as the considerations of economic thinkers came into conflict with the claim for absolute power of Russian autocrats, much of their liberal rhetoric fell silent. Thus, a number of thinkers who had been encouraged to contribute to economic reforms by highlighting the social conditions in the Russian Empire met their fates in prison or in banishment. Secondly, in the poorly developed system of Russian university education, economic research and teaching was not properly institutionalized until the nineteenth century.

In her contribution on 'Russian Monetary Reformers', Alla Sheptun analyses the contributions made by three outstanding Russian economic thinkers and statesmen to the development of the Russian system of finance and banking. In the period of Russian proto-industrialization, the ideas of Mikhail M. Speransky, Nikolai S. Mordvinov and Nikolai Kh. Bunge played a decisive role in establishing the institutional foundations for the take-off into Rostow-type growth of the Russian economy at the end of the nineteenth century. The three men, Sheptun relates, were all deeply influenced by liberal ideas, but at the same time were convinced that for Russia to develop, the state had to act as the locomotive of economic modernization.

In this way they contributed to the formation of what Chris Monday has called a 'bureaucratic direction in Russian economic science'. Sheptun's chapter is particularly welcome in that a serious analysis of the significant contributions made by nineteenth-century Russian economists to monetary theory has been lacking in Western literature, even though some of their names have been periodically recognized.

Academic political economy in Russia in the first half of the nineteenth century was involved in a conflict 'Between Reason and Historicity' suggests Joachim Zweynert. In particular, due to German influences, most Russian academic economists were aware that economic laws could not be formulated independently from the concrete conditions of time and space. However, when the Slavophiles used the argument of historical specificity in support of a 'special path' for Russian economic development, many liberal economists employed the rationalistic concept of a 'natural order' in order to defend the concept of an exchange economy. In this way, a conflict emerged between the liberals' methodological writings and their statements on economic policy. The fact that Marx's teachings claimed to reconcile reason and historicity, Zweynert concludes, may partly explain the great interest in his works in Russia within some sections of the academic community.

Natalia Makasheva argues in her chapter 'Searching for an Ethical Basis of Political Economy' that Sergei N. Bulgakov and Mikhail I. Tugan-Baranovsky had much in common, and yet they also greatly differed from each other. Their work developed in the context of the challenge of the spread of neo-Kantian philosophy and its demand to draw a clear borderline between positive and normative knowledge. As with the majority of their Russian colleagues, Tugan-Baranovsky and Bulgakov remained true to the idea that economics should be based on ethical foundations. Referring to the Kantian idea of the 'supreme value of the human personality', Tugan-Baranovsky arrived at the political economy of socialism, whereas Bulgakov turned from Marxism to religion and developed a doctrine of Christian socialism. Their names thus stand for two opposite versions of normative economics.

Post-1917 Chapters

The volume is similarly rich in chapters that explore the development of Russian economic ideas after the Bolshevik revolution in 1917. William Coleman and Anna Taitslin provide a rather controversial account of some of the economic ideas of Alexander V. Chayanov, in which Chayanov's penchant for radical utopian projection is critically examined. They also attempt to locate Chayanov within the range of agrarian theorists who proliferated in Russia at this time and to document his rise and fall from intellectual fashion as the twentieth century progressed. For a long time Chayanov has been a 'hero' of Western left-orientated economists and anthropologists engaged in issues of rural development in less developed countries. From a very different perspective, Coleman and Taitslin set themselves the task of demystifying the contributions of the author of *The Theory of Peasant Economy*. Although in this account Chayanov comes off quite badly when considered as a technical economist in the neoclassical style, and a different evaluation of Chayanov's significance could easily be made, this chapter does indicate very well the extraordinary and unique nature of the immediate post-revolutionary period in Russia. Fantastic visions of social harmony co-existed alongside political puppetry and horrific executions of the cruellest sort. It seems likely that Chayanov came to regret that he lived in such interesting times.

One pair of chapters that document two aspects of the same phenomenon have been provided by Vincent Barnett and Shuichi Kojima, who explore the ideas and experience of Russian émigré economists after leaving their land of origin. Kojima examines the work of Boris D. Brutzkus and Sergei N. Prokopovich; Barnett that of Simon S. Kuznets, Jacob Marschak and Wassily W. Leontief. Barnett argues that the Russian émigré economists who ended up in the USA took with them some underlying approaches to economic analysis that could well have been influential within American economics itself and hence that, in the early post-Soviet period, there was no insurmountable methodological chasm between Russian and Western traditions. Although many of the Russian economists who settled in the USA were relatively young at the time of their initial emigration, an individual's early educational environment is often crucial for comprehending their later development. Barnett consequently argues that the trans-national movement of Eastern economists in the early part of the twentieth century was thus of some significance for the development of the approaches and themes of mainstream Western economics in both Europe and the USA.

Following Barnett, of particular importance is Kojima's argument that some exiled Russian economists were among the first scholars to provide an analysis of the Soviet economy for Western audiences, which meant that their approaches and assumptions may have been very significant for early Western conceptions of the nature of the USSR itself. Today the question of the nature of the Soviet system is of only academic interest, but in the 1920s and 1930s, this question was one of the most important political topics of the day. In his chapter Kojima also documents some key differences in approach to economic understanding between Brutzkus and Prokopovich, for example that the former took a mainly theoretical approach to analysing the Soviet system, the latter a more empirical one. This distinction also has some relevance to tracing how an understanding of the characteristic structure of the USSR grew out of specific conceptions of the nature of socialism itself, in that precisely what version of socialism was to be implemented was (and remains today) an essentially contested concept. The two chapters by Barnett and Kojima add to recent literature on the emigration of economists from (for example) Germany and Austria, and taken together they demonstrate the rich variety of exiled Russian economists in the immediate post-Soviet period. And as Barnett has argued elsewhere, the quality of Russian economics in the immediate post-Soviet period was rather high.

Another pair of chapters that can usefully be considered together has been provided by Michael Kaser and Pekka Sutela. Both are highly respected experts in the political economy of Soviet socialism and in analyzing ongoing economic reforms, and they have contributed enlightening accounts of aspects of Soviet economic debates in different stages of development. Kaser focuses on the late Stalin era and his chapter clearly indicates how political factors totally dominated the development of economics in the USSR in this period. The specific ideas and processes under consideration may appear rather antiquated from today's perspective, but it is as well to be reminded of exactly how artificial and coded Soviet economic debates were under such a totalitarian corporate political dictatorship, as was presided over by what has recently been designated as 'Team Stalin'. 'Doing economics while treading on eggshells' might be one way of describing it, with the consequences of putting a foot (or a comma) wrong in some cases being a swift and inglorious death. It is also clear from comparing Kaser's account with the chapters that precede it of the extent of the decline in Russian economics that occurred after 1929. In terms of the quality and the international significance of economic ideas, it could reasonably be argued that 1929 was much more of a structural break than 1917 was.

Sutela's chapter continues the story of Soviet economics across the post-Stalin era and into *perestroika* and beyond. The death of Stalin in 1953 paved the way for the (re-)employment of mathematical methods in Soviet economics in tandem with various reform efforts, but throughout the 1960s and 1970s there was a constant struggle between the old-style political economy of socialism and modernization along proto-neoclassical lines. Political factors were still crucial to understanding the development of economic reformers in the Khrushchev and Brezhnev periods – people such as Leonid Abalkin and Stanislav Shatalin – although under Gorbachev the influence of Western economists (like Sutela himself) on Russian thinking grew substantially. However, Sutela suggests that even in the post-*perestroika* period, the ghosts of outmoded economic methodologies from the past still haunt the Russian intellectual landscape. A more general point to be made here is that after the prevalent post-Soviet euphoria of the immediate transition to the market in the early 1990s, some disillusionment with simplistic neoclassical conceptions of the nature of economic behaviour began to creep into Russian economic thinking as the 1990s progressed, especially after the major financial crisis that broke out in 1998. This may have opened the gates to allowing a wider variety of economic thinking to gain a foothold.

Consequently the final chapter by Andrey Zaostrovstev provides a revealing account of the development of economic ideas in post-Soviet Russia. The resurgence of Russian nationalism under Vladimir Putin is a political development of international significance, and Zaostrovstev's chapter provides a glimpse into some aspects of how this recently regained national pride is impacting upon the development of economic ideas and government policies. He highlights a few examples of (perhaps surprising) continuity in the underlying attitudes of some Russian economists to the relationship between Russia and the West in the Soviet and the post-Soviet eras, and also in their understanding of the significance of the Russian nation itself as a bearer of non-Western culture. If the new political realities of the post-Soviet period are to be fully understood by politicians in the West, then engagement with long-standing Russian intellectual traditions is essential to engender both in the academic community and in wider circles. It is hoped that this volume will contribute in a small way to this important endeavour by providing a wider perspective from which to appreciate the multi-faceted development of economic ideas in Russia over many centuries.

Chapter 2

Economic Thought in Muscovy: Ownership, Money and Trade

Danila Raskov

Pre-Petrine Russian thought is usually viewed as standing in the shadow of the Enlightenment.[1] However, it has become clear to historians that the 'Window to Europe' had been opened well before Peter the Great (Kliuchevsky [1907] 1994; Kotilaine 2004). The 'Window to Russia' dated back at least to the establishment of an English trading company in Moscow in the reign of Ivan IV. The first direct encounter with European institutions may have occurred with the inclusion of part of the Ukraine and especially of Kiev into Muscovy (Okenfuss 1995). Consequently the historic period commonly termed as Muscovite Russia was very important in forming the legal institutions of land ownership, taxation, the monetary system and also to developing the processes of foreign and domestic trade.

Economic thought in this period was pioneering in many ways. It witnessed the first Russian economic thinkers, the first Russian mercantilists, the first treatises on monetary thought and the development of the first theories of ownership. However, these advances in economic thought were by no means universally recognized. Instead, their importance remains an open question even today. Did Russian economic thought, separate from religious and political ideas, really exist in the sixteenth and seventeenth centuries? Were developments in economic thought limited to specialist publications and academic treatises, or were they also found in legal documents, decrees and reform drafts? Was there such a phenomenon as Russian mercantilism and did the dispute over church landownership go beyond religion? And finally, how did Russian economic thought in this period compare with Western thinking?

The history of Russian economic thought is obviously dependent on historical sources. However, problems emerge in this area due to the fact that authors from this early period seldom wrote specifically on economic topics. Texts were produced in monasteries, in *prikazy* (chancelleries) and more rarely by publicists. In the absence of purely economic texts, the importance of studying legal documents such as *Stoglav* (the Hundred Chapters Church Council), *Ulozhenie* (the Code of Law) and *Novotorgovyi ustav* (the New Commercial Code) cannot be overestimated. A further issue is that a discussion of Russian economic thought cannot avoid evaluating its originality in comparison to Western Europe. It is particularly important to ascertain

1 The author is grateful to Leonid Shirokorad for initial encouragement, and to Ludovic Desmedt, Jérôme Blanc, Vincent Barnett, Joachim Zweynert, Jeremy Meiners and José Luis Cardoso for comments on the manuscript.

the relation of Russian thought to medieval and/or mercantilist principles. According to Eli Heckscher, it was exactly 'in the domain of the ethical' that the main difference between the two artificially distinguished epochs occurred (Heckscher [1931] 1935, vol. 2, 285).

Thus this chapter examines the most significant discussions, treatises and legal documents of the sixteenth and seventeenth centuries relating to the problems of ownership, money and trade, in order to determine their originality and proximity to mercantilism and to medieval economic thought. The chapter consists of four main parts. The first part offers a brief overview of the historical and institutional development of Muscovy and introduces the main sources that will be used. The second considers a heated discussion that occurred in the sixteenth century dealing with monastic landownership. The third is devoted to economic thought on trade-related issues and the fourth considers the specific monetary problems of this period. Finally, the question of the proximity of Russian economic thought to mercantilism and to the Middle Ages, as two special epochs in Western Europe, will be evaluated in the conclusion.

The Epoch of Muscovy

Economic thought in the Muscovy period was mainly focused on two major issues, the moral assessment of economic phenomena and government economic policy. However, the separate discipline of economics did not really exist at this time. As a result, the following brief description of the historical context will concentrate on revealing the peculiarities of the political, legal and religious institutions of Muscovy. The main written sources of this period, along with their authors, will also be considered.

The state structure of Muscovy took shape at the turn of the fifteenth to sixteenth centuries and its development differed from that of both Kiev and Novgorod. By the end of the fifteenth century, Moscow did not just perceive itself as one of a number of appendages, but instead as the national centre of 'All Russia'. Under Ivan III, Muscovy began to become independent from Tartar subjugation. Without the imposition of a strong will and the use of repression, the unification of Russian lands under the authority of Muscovy would not have been possible, and thus the interests of the state occupied a central position in the social and economic domains at this time. Thanks to the existence of a special type of authoritarian power, military strength could be concentrated, external threats resisted, and the borders of the kingdom expanded. In the beginning of the sixteenth century, the Principality of Moscow covered over 1 million square kilometers. By the end of the Muscovite period, 200 years later, the state had expanded to over 12 million kilometers (Kulisher [1925] 2004, 254–55). During this time, Siberia and the left bank of the Ukraine had been acquired and Kazan and Astrakhan conquered. By the seventeenth century, Russia bordered the Kingdom of Sweden, the Livonian Order, the Grand Duchy of Lithuania and Rzeczpospolita.

In the presence of such a strong centralized power, no absolute rights could exist. Under the Muscovite system of governance, any ownership was relative, as the absolute right of ownership belonged only to the tsar. However, outside of special circumstances, such as confiscation or disgrace, private property rights could be considered as existing at the local level and an abundance of land not under private control resulted in the prevalence of the free seizure of land.

Serfdom was the foundation of Muscovite agriculture and it also supported the structure of the state. Serfdom was formally established with the *Ulozhenie* code of 1649, but the buying and selling of serfs did not develop until the end of the seventeenth century. The country was ruled by means of *prikazy* or the so-called 'chancellery system'. A *prikaz*, which meant 'command' or 'order', was the central governmental body in Muscovite Russia and it had both administrative and judicial power. The system of *prikazy,* which had emerged in the late fifteenth century, grew into the early modern state bureaucracy.

The political and economic organization of Muscovy cannot be understood outside the context of religious life. The adoption of Byzantine Christianity was a government affair from the very beginning and it was implemented 'from above' (Chmeman 1954, 342–43). However, this top down conversion to Christianity did not completely replace previous attitudes, resulting in the existence of the phenomenon of 'dual belief'. In part, this explained why Russian Orthodoxy was biased towards divine service and rituals, rather than bookish rationality and reason. Learning and an orientation toward science did not emerge from church institutions, but instead appeared later under strong government influence and as a result of top down implementation.

Nevertheless, Russian Orthodoxy had a deep impact on the world outlook of Muscovy. It found an expression in the 'Moscow – the Third Rome' concept. The first was the Roman Empire, the second the Byzantine Empire. Through the use of historical and Biblical arguments, this concept dominated the national consciousness of Muscovites (Stremoukhov [1953] 2002, 440–41). The idea took shape in a message addressed by a monk called Philotheus from the Yelizarov Monastery in Pskov to Vasily III. The monk argued that: 'All the Christian Orthodox realms have been transformed together into your single tsardom: you are the only tsar for the Christians … Two Romes have fallen, but the third stands' (Philotheus [16 c.] 2000, 301, 305). Thus, the historical context of this period meant that any thought would develop either in monasteries and within religious disputes, or in a general political context.

Historical studies of the economic thought of Muscovy started in the middle of the nineteenth century. In 1840 a work by Grigory Karpovich Kotoshikhin (1630–67) entitled *On Russia During the Reign of Aleksey Mikhailovich* was published. *The Book of Poverty and Wealth* by Ivan Tikhonovich Pososhkov (1652–1726), who is seen by many as the first Russian economist (Shirokorad 2008), was published in 1842 (Pososhkov [1724] 1987). In 1849 *Domostroy*, a 'housekeeping encyclopedia' dating back to the sixteenth century, was printed, and the *Political Thoughts* (or *Politics*) by Yuri Krizhanich (1617–83) ([c. 1666] 1985) was published in 1859.

Perhaps the first survey of the history of Russian economic thought was a brief essay by a professor of Moscow University, V. Leshkov, entitled *The Ancient Russian Science of Public Economy and Welfare*. It was devoted to the hundredth anniversary of Moscow University and it offered a comparative analysis of three of its great literary works, the *Domostroy,* I.T. Pososhkov's *Book of Poverty and Wealth* and the *Instructions* by A. Volynsky (Leshkov 1855). Other surveys, for example *A History of Economic Ideas in Russia* by Vladimir Svyatlovsky ([1923] 2003) and the first part of volume I of *A History of the Russian Economic Thought* edited by Anatoly I. Pashkov ([1955] 1964), should be mentioned. Both publications appeared in Soviet times but differed significantly in terms of the thoroughness of the research and their general assessment. In both books, Russian economic thought was compared with European mercantilism. While Svyatlovsky demonstrated the secondary nature of Russian thought, Pashkov strove to illustrate the independent development of Russian ideas and interpreted backwardness as originality.

In addition to these surveys, much has been done to study separate periods, individual authors and sources in the seventeenth century. In particular, studies have been conducted on mercantilism in economic policy (Bazilevich 1940; Kotilaine 2004), on the social and economic views of A.L. Ordin-Nashchokin (c. 1605–80) (Chistyakova 1950; Baron 1991) and on Yurii Krizhanich (Mordukhovich 1962; Baron, 1987). The works of such sixteenth-century publicists as Ivan Peresvetov and Ermolai-Erazm (Rzhiga 1908, 1926) have been published and analyzed. In these analyses, reference was often made to a controversy of the sixteenth century over the right of monasteries to own land with peasants and villages, the disputes between the Non-Possessors (the 'Transvolgan elders' like Nil Sorsky (c. 1433–1508) and Vassian Patrikeyev (?–1545)) and the Josephites (Iosif Volotsky (1439–1515)) (Pavlov 1871; Budovnits 1947; Sinitsyna 1977; Pliguzov 2002).

Ivan Tikhonovich Pososhkov lived in late Muscovite Russia. It was noted by a historian of feudalism that:

> In terms of his erudition and main intellectual interests, Pososhkov was a typical person of pre-Petrine Russia, a remarkable self-taught dogmatist in the realm of Muscovite ecclesiastic literature. He read a great deal, but these were the Holy Scriptures and theological writings, excluding arithmetic and grammar textbooks. When teaching his son to 'respect the book as the sacred icon,' the word 'books' he attributed to holy books only (Pavlov-Silvansky 1897, 80)

Pososhkov struggled for the preservation and development of the old spiritual culture, although he recognized the necessity of governmental and economic reforms. Even in his work with the most economic content, *The Book of Poverty and Wealth*: *An Exposition Showing How Needless Poverty Arises and How Wealth may be Caused to Increase Abundantly*, Pososhkov treated wealth not only as a material but also as a spiritual category. The first chapter was dedicated to the clergy and the author did not separate out moral and economic behaviour, religious and civil values, or even the church and the state (Okenfuss 1995, 101–103). According to some historians, the writing of this book was protracted and it was written section by section. This is an additional argument in favour of the informal treatment of Pososhkov as a representative of not only Petrine but also of Muscovite Russia. He lived on the borderline between these two epochs, though in terms of spirit he was closer to the preceding one. Pososhkov is of further interest because, like the Old Believers, he struggled to preserve past times, while at the same time arguing that trade, money and state economy required reform.

It is necessary to consider precisely who the authors of Russian economic thought during the Muscovy period were and in what form their arguments were presented. Quite often, the primary records were messages and treatises addressed to ecclesiastical and royal authorities. In the case of legal documents and orders, the composers of these messages can be subdivided according to definite groups. Among the authors were: (1) priests and monks; (2) officials and executives in the tsar's service; (3) trades people and manufacturers who were eager to provide useful advice to the tsar; and (4) more rarely, independent scientists and publicists. Among the authors of the first type were: Iosif Volotsky, the abbot of the Volokolamsk Monastery; the Non-Possessor Nil Sorsky, the founder of many Transvolgan *sketes* (groups of hermits following monastic rule); Sylvester, the archpriest of the Annunciation Cathedral in the Kremlin; and Krizhanich, who received a Catholic education in Vienna and Rome. Authors of the second type included: Peresvetov, who had moved from Lithuania to Moscow to become a servant of the tsar; Ordin-Nashchokin, a statesman; and Kotoshikhin, the Pskov military leader involved in foreign policy. Among authors of the third type was Pososhkov, first a craftsman and later a governmental servant at a vodka distillery. Peresvetov and Krizhanich may also be attributed to the fourth type of scholars and publicists.

Disputes over Ecclesiastical Landownership

The issue of landownership occupied a special place in Muscovite debate. This was reflected in both the controversies over the right of monasteries to own land and villages and in numerous legal documents, including the *Ulozhenie* of 1649. The issue of monastic property became the subject of the first fierce economic dispute. To a considerable degree this dispute was a moral and religious issue (Pavlov 1871). Both Nil Sorsky and Iosif Volotsky opposed personal gain in this context. The principle of non-possession was a unifying one, because along with obedience and chastity, non-possession was a monk's virtue, a norm of the monastic life. But at the same time, the dispute was not purely religious. As noted by N.V. Sinitsyna, the disagreements were over social practice and the question of the sources of wealth (Sinitsyna 1977, 105).

The ideals of the two sides differed. For Iosif Volotsky, the goal was to create a strong, richly decorated monastery with an extensive and diversified economy, providing help to all those in need and offering a means of social insurance. 'Collective wealth accumulation' by a monastery helped individual monks to adhere closely to personal non-possession. According to Iosif Volotsky's *Monastic Rule*, he who sought divine favour 'must be an absolute non-possessor ... owning nothing and never dreaming of owing anything, the monastery being the owner' (Pavlov 1871, 13). Monastic property was believed to belong to no one in particular, but rather was provided by God for noble deeds. For Nil Sorsky the ideal was a solitary *skete* in which a monk could be secluded from the world and supported by his own labour. Upon returning from the Orient to the Kirillo-Belozersky Monastery, Sorsky retired to a *skete* on the Sora River. Monastic charity and almsgiving were not appreciated by the Transvolgans, as they led to vanity, vainglory and arrogance. Instead, the 'work of thought' and 'wise prayer' mattered the most to them.

At the *Sobor* (Church Council) of 1503 the Possessors, headed by Iosif Volotsky, had the upper hand but the dispute later intensified. The Non-Possessors were joined by such authors as Vassian Patrikeyev (a former prince and diplomat) and Maxim the Greek (a monk). In the 'Deliberations of monk Vassian on the impropriety of owning *votchinas* by monasteries', a disciple of Sorsky addressed not only the monks whom it befitted to support themselves 'by righteous labour, through their own sweat and force', but also the tsar, who was humiliating monks by treating them like warriors and granting land to them (Patrikeyev 1859, 2–7). Such grants were seen to corrupt the monks' souls. Thus a moral assessment was made of both the behaviour of monks and civil power, particularly that of the tsar. The history of ecclesiastic landownership illustrated the acuteness of the issue that combined the interests of the supreme power, the church itself, the middle class and the peasantry. Tsars quite often introduced restrictions relating to ownership, imposed bans on the purchase and transfer of ecclesiastic property, confiscated land and then returned land. In the end, representatives of Iosif Volotsky prevailed among the bureaucracy. But Ivan the Terrible preferred the followers of Maxim the Greek and Vassian Patrikeyev.

Ecclesiastic property was invariably protected by traditions. The Khans' *yarlyk* (Letter of Patent) guaranteed its inviolability. Anyone who encroached on ecclesiastical and monastic property was threatened with excommunication. However, Ivan III confiscated large pieces of land from the Novgorod clergy on two occasions. The rights of ownership, those of the monasteries included, were limited by the absolute power of the tsar, which conditioned the weak development of the institution of private ownership in Russia (Pipes [1999], 210–71). The land was considered as 'belonging to nobody' and any ownership was 'God-granted'. Possession of large land holdings became either hereditary (*votchina*) or conditional (*pomest'e*), granted by the supreme power in exchange for military service. The historical distinction between hereditary land and *pomest'e* had gradually disappeared by the end of the seventeenth century. In 1676–77 the old distinction was abolished. In reality, often both life and land ownership depended on the ruler's good grace. As Ivan the Terrible used to say, effective government required frequent 'shuffling of the humble people'.

The monasteries were provided with special *votchinas*, which kept growing thanks to new rewards, investments, testaments and, less frequently, by purchases. By the end of the sixteenth century, the Troitse-Sergiev Monastery possessed 2,500 villages and 60 per cent of arable land in the Moscow District belonged to monasteries (Kulisher [1925] 2004, 300–301). A conventional evaluation was that the land area owned by the Russian church in the sixteenth century was one third of all cultivated land (Pavlov 1871, 23). Richard Chancellor, who visited Muscovy in the middle of the sixteenth century, noted that 'the monks had twice as much land as the Great Prince himself' (Pliguzov 2002, 320–29).

This dispute over the right of churches and monasteries to possess villages and peasants was not purely theoretical, as it had many practical consequences. Supporters and critics of ecclesiastic landownership had sometimes to pay for their views with their lives, as a victory for one of the parties often led to the confinement of their opponents. The main arguments used in the dispute were religious, with the proofs offered being the Holy Scriptures, the *Kormchaya Kniga* (Book of Guidelines) and the Life of the Holy Fathers. In rare cases, the dispute turned to criticism of sources or attempts to identify weaknesses in the arguments of the opposition. Fundamentally, both parties shared the idea of personal non-possession, but their views differed over the ability of a monastery to own property. Iosif Volotsky and his followers demonstrated a tendency to delegate social functions to monasteries, while Nil Sorsky and his followers used the example of the monasteries of Athon and even Catholic monasteries when defending the ideals of absolute asceticism.

These two positions developed along different paths in later Russian history. The disposition towards outward decoration and wealth, the establishment of social aid and social credit, found its reflection in the organization of the rich communities of the Old Believers. To some extent, the idea of personal non-possession, combined with the increasing power of a redistributing centre, found continuity in Soviet times. The spirit of the Non-Possessors, who used stronger and more independent theological argumentation and were noted for their more profound erudition, was preserved in a critical attitude towards the secular authorities and towards financial relations, and in the selfless pursuit of justice. Although this controversy was essentially religious and belonged to the Middle Ages, the questions raised over the right of the Church to own land paved the way for the secularization that occurred during the reign of Catherine II.

Trade

During the sixteenth and seventeenth centuries, Muscovy traded with the West by a land route passing through Novgorod. It was not until the expedition of Richard Chancellor in the beginning of 1550s that maritime trade through Archangelsk began. The English were granted a right of free trade and entrance and in 1567 this privilege was extended to include the cities of Kazan, Astrakhan, Narva and Derpt. The right to trade with Persia was also awarded in this year. However, England was not the only Western nation to trade with Muscovy, as the Dutch actively traded with Muscovy as well.

Since the 1620s Russian merchants had been writing *chelobitnye* (humble petitions) to the tsar requesting the revocation of privileges granted to foreign merchants. As a result, Aleksey Mikhailovich revoked these privileges and the English Yard in Moscow was turned into a 'large prison'. In accordance with the *Novotorgovyi ustav* of 1667, retail sales were forbidden and foreign traders were ordered to pay duties of 5 per cent in border cities and 10 per cent in the interior (Articles 40–41, 60–63). In the seventeenth century, these duties were to be paid to Joachimsthalers, Dutch merchants who held priority status among the foreign merchants. For many commercial activities in Muscovy, the tsar was the first and largest customer and his representatives were first to inspect the goods brought for exchange. In response, Russian economic thought reacted in various ways to the problems of granting privileges to foreign merchants, the right to carry out trade in cities and at fairs, the policy of levying duties and the eroding of geographic fragmentation.

With regard to the issue of foreign traders, there was a definite ambivalence in Muscovy. The practices and technologies of Westerners were imitated, but not to the degree that any original ways would be completely abandoned. Krizhanich's mantra, 'Know thyself! Do not trust foreigners!' revealed the belief that a difference did indeed exist between Russians and Westerners (Krizhanich [c. 1666] 1985, 7). Yet at the same time, Krizhanich advised people to learn about arithmetic, different occupations and legislation from foreign merchants. He reasoned that in all trades, people were guided by their own interests and in pursuit of their own benefit they will certainly cheat – buying cheap and selling at a triple price. With some reservations, the advice from Krizhanich can be termed mercantilistic. He stood for increasing the volume of foreign trade by means of developing new trade routes and access to the sea, for protecting the home market, for strengthening the tsar's monopoly in trade, for keeping prices at a lower level than that offered by private trade and for prohibiting foreign merchants to trade in the country (Krizhanich [c. 1666] 1985, 14–32). As regards the interests of local merchants, he argued for permission for tradesmen of all classes to create exchanges and pool funds for commercial purposes.

Pososhkov, through his praise of the merchant class, argued that no tsar could rule and no army could exist without them. Pososhkov considered it necessary to strengthen the status of merchants and protect them from competition with foreign traders as well as from members of other indigenous classes. 'If our Russian merchants were given freedom in their trade so that they suffered no kind of interference at the hands of either men of other callings or the foreigner, then his Majesty's revenue from trade would be of quite another order' (Pososhkov, [1724] 1987, 253). In some cases these views were expressed as proposals for policy reforms. The treatise entitled *Politics* called for a radical restructuring of society under the guidance of the monarch. For example Krizhanich considered it wrong to maintain the closed nature of monetary circulation in Russia:

> Foreign coins made from pure gold and pure silver should be accepted throughout the realm and should be used at all fairs in accordance with their proper price, corresponding to the value of gold and silver in Germany, Persia, and Turkey. They should be accepted and issued by the treasury at the prevailing price (Krizhanich [c. 1666] 1985, 222).

In this way, Krizhanich called for an end to the circulation of separate currencies inside and outside the country. This would mean the abandonment of the revenues from re-minting foreign coins for the sake of maintaining economic stability and reducing the amount of counterfeit money.

An episode that drew discussion at the time was of rising commodity prices during the monetary reform of Aleksei Mikhailovich, when he attempted to replace silver coins with copper ones. Copper was 60 times cheaper than silver, but through the reform, coins were to be accepted at the same value. As a consequence, confidence dropped sharply and silver money was gradually withdrawn from circulation. According to Kotoshikhin, a rise in prices occurred in the 1650s for the following reasons: the introduction of inferior money itself, the amount of counterfeit money in circulation and the lack of confidence in the new money (Kotoshikhin 1859, 82). Pososhkov remarked on the price rises as follows: 'A pud of copper formerly stood at three rubles but now stands at seven or eight … A ream of writing paper, formerly at eighty kopeks, now sells at two rubles. A crate of window glass could once be bought for three rubles but has now gone up to ten.' (Pososhkov [1724] 1987, 259). However, he did not associate such rises with the debasement of coinage, rather he explained it as the outcome of greedy foreign merchants who were setting prices too high. As a countermeasure, an administrative solution was proposed to allow the tsar and his representatives to fix uniform prices, 'a set price that would be the same in the first and in the last shop'.

S. Herberstein, the Austrian representative to Muscovy, provided a laconic yet informative description of usury in Russia as follows: 'Money lending at interest is common there, and although they say it is a black sin, almost nobody is withholding. To a certain extent the conditions are unbearable, namely always one per five, i.e. twenty per one hundred. The churches seem to be more generous, i.e. (as is said) they are taking ten per one hundred' (Herberstein [1557] 1968, 84). Regarding the interest rate, Krizhanich referred to the experience of the Roman emperor Augustus and placed great hope in a supreme ruler who would be able to provide interest-free loans with real estate backing. 'Emperor Augustus lent money to his subjects without interest or usury for good security … In this way he checked usury and theft and, surprisingly, also increased and developed trade' (Krizhanich [c. 1666] 1985, 30). Pososhkov also held the view that merchants should help each other and never let another be reduced to poverty. Pososhkov's opinion was that the treasury should offer credit for the needs of merchants and craftsmen, and that this fund should also collect interest depending on profitability (Pososhkov [1724] 1987, 367–68). The question of usury was never as acute in Russia as it was in medieval Europe, yet the idea of having interest-free loans in this later period still showed a connection with the ideals of Christianity.

Money

Russian economic thought paid close attention to issues relating to money from the very beginning. Yet as for many other countries, the disputes around money became more acute in times of crisis. The most famous crisis during this period was the monetary reform undertaken by Aleksey Mikhailovich, which ended in a fiasco. During the six years from 1658 through 1663, the silver to copper kopek ratio dropped from 1:1 to 1:15. Kotoshikhin, Krizhanich and Ordin-Nashchokin witnessed and commented on this failed reform. Problems such as the determination of the value of money, actions to stop counterfeiting, the search for sources of raw materials and the regulation of currency inflow and outflow became important at this time. Concerning the determination of the value of money, two tendencies were apparent. First, that the value of money was determined by the market in precious metals, and secondly, that the tsar would establish and guarantee the value of coins.

The authors in question were far from an agreement that money was a synonym for wealth, as their views on wealth differed on moral and utilitarian grounds. On the one hand, the love of money was strongly condemned as one of the sins of Christianity. Greed and avarice were opposed to the ideals of withdrawal from the world, wise prayer and the love for one's neighbour. On the other hand, money and wealth became an integral part of political, social and even ecclesiastic life and the idea that wealth should only be seen as a breeding ground for sin became outmoded.

The archpriest Sylvester's *Domostroy,* dated to the middle of the sixteenth century, offers a typically medieval exhortation of a father to his son.[2] According to *Domostroy*, wealth was a result of the right way of life and fair practice. Wealth was not an end in itself, more important was a regular, full life that conformed to the rules of social conduct. Wealth for the state was not measured in silver or gold, but rather in the number of its inhabitants: 'The king who has more people is rich, not the one who has more gold', noted Krizhanich ([c. 1666] 1985, 7). A state was considered rich when its subjects were rich and the laws were fair, not when the treasury was full. Money was compared by Krizhanich to blood inside an organism, which in the case of unskillful medical treatment (debased coinage) might drain away. In *The Book of Poverty and Wealth*, Pososhkov subdivided wealth into the material, which was contained in households, and into the immaterial, 'that is, for righteousness' (Pososhkov [1724] 1987, 154).

Traditionally, all monetary concepts were divided into nominalist and metallic views, though these conceptual differences did not always apply in reality. Did the market or the sovereign determine the value of money? Did money have intrinsic value, or was it just a medium used in exchange, its value being determined by royal power? In practice, supporters of the metallic conception opposed the exploitation of monetary symbols, while advocates of the 'tsar's will' were inclined to justify the debasement of coinage by the sovereign. However in the absence of a developed theory of money, the debate was often vague. A striking example was provided by Pososhkov's account of monetary value. As a rule, he is usually placed among the nominalists (Pashkov (1955) 350–53; Svyatlovsky [1923] 2003, 59). The following Pososhkov statement about copper coins is well known:

> Their face value shall not be, in the foreign manner, that of the actual value of the copper but as His Majesty shall decide … we are not like the foreigners; our concern is not the value of the copper but the glory of our Tsar. Therefore it is not the weight of copper in the coins that we take into account but His Majesty's superscription upon them … it is not the weight of the metal that decides but the Tsar's will … since our Monarch is absolute and all-powerful, and no aristocrat or democrat. Therefore it is not the silver that we value; it is His Imperial Majesty's word that bestows honour and authority (Pososhkov [1724] 1987, 376–77).

In this view, when the merchant class was powerful, the value of money was determined by its metal content, but when the monarch was omnipotent and the

2 This work, typical of the middle ages, was devoted to economy in its initial Greek sense, i.e. to the art of housekeeping. Christian moral commandments were combined with detailed descriptions of everyday matters. Comparable with *Trattato del governo della famiglia* A. Pandolfini, Menagier de Paris (Domostroi, [16c.] 1994).

merchant class was obedient, the monarch determined the value of coins. However, silver and gold were treated by Pososhkov differently. The purity of metal was compared with purity of faith: 'Just as the Christian faith has been preserved in Russia in its purest state, without any taint of heresy, so our coinage should also be the purest in the world, free of all debasement' (Pososhkov [1724] 1987, 375). For Pososhkov, it was the question of combating counterfeiters and the desire for purity in silver that were important. For a long time the fineness of silver coins had been very high, for example under Ivan the Terrible it was 92.5/100. But by the early eighteenth century it had fallen, to the disdain of some. Thus, it was the determination of the economic context by the political that was of importance for Pososhkov's account of monetary value. In addition, the rational comprehension of money was combined with a mystical attitude toward the purity of coinage, which in turn had an indirect relation to the purity of the sovereign's faith.

As a rule, the metallic concept separated the economy from politics and emphasized the special status of the market. It is problematic to strictly associate Krizhanich with one of these concepts. According to him, the correct hierarchy had God as the owner of everything on Earth. The monarch was the manager of God's domain with the right to coin money with the 'royal face'. Krizhanich placed his hope for the realization of reforms with the sovereign only, as the people were lazy, slow and unskilled, and foreign merchants were guided only by their own selfish interests. It seemed at one point as if Krizhanich had made a supposition that the king had the power to coin money and serve as the guarantor of its exchange, but his views were sometimes the opposite of this. Keeping the disastrous results of the monetary reform of Aleksey Mikhailovich in mind, Krizhanich argued that value of copper coins depended on the price that 'copper is sold at the market' (Krizhanich [c. 1666] 1985, 223). Krizhanich consequently believed that it would be in the interest of the tsar to let market forces determine the value of coins. This practical advice placed Krizhanich closer to the supporters of the metallic concept rather than with the nominalists. On the whole, the views of Krizhanich concerning the nature and value of money lacked detailed theoretical backing.

Directly related to the issue of the value of money was the issue of the debasement of the coinage. Krizhanich, the author of *Politics*, believed that a correct financial order, identified by the use of good-quality money that ultimately encouraged trade, was most important for a state (Krizhanich [c. 1666] 1985, 5–6). In the opinion of Krizhanich, poor methods of replenishing the treasury, alchemy, ruthless exactions and a poor organization of foreign trade were included in the revenue from coinage, which was as unreliable as anything obtained without labour. 'This method is not only unjust, but sinful and very deceitful as well. It appears beneficial, but actually is detrimental and harmful. No ruler can ever expect to obtain money from the debasement of currency without a hundredfold loss in the process … The coining of worthless money resembles this deadly *remedia desperata*' (Krizhanich [c. 1666] 1985, 9–10). Obviously, such a *remedia desperata* was undesirable, as excessive exactions led to monetary chaos.

The problem of the raw material for coins persisted in Russia until the middle of the eighteenth century. Spassky admitted that 'the main regulating factor of production of money was the receipt of silver from abroad', which arrived via the

Joachimsthalers (Spassky 1961, 11). This problem was mentioned by many authors of this period. For instance, Kotoshikhin noted that in the mid-seventeenth century: 'the state of Muscovy yields no gold or silver, though they write in *Chronicles* that the Russian land is fruitful in terms of gold and silver, but they cannot be discovered, and when found, the amounts are small' (Kotoshikhin [c. 1667] 1859, 81). This situation continued until gold, silver and copper prospecting was further initiated in Russia. Krizhanich noted the 'carelessness and negligence' of the Russian people in neglecting ore mining and the art of long-distance trade. The fear of losing an ore deposit or of provoking the tsar's wrath acted to prevent the development of mining. Therefore, Krizhanich believed it would be more reasonable to search for deposits in other countries, as was done by the Spanish, Germans and French. In addition, Krizhanich argued in favour of actively stimulating foreign merchants to bring silver, copper, tin and iron for trade (Krizhanich [c.1666] 1985, 51–56).

A separate problem regarding monetary circulation in Russia was the multiplicity of currencies that were used in trade. Money often lacked universality, since much depended on its final use, the territory of this use, and on the individual payer and the time of payment. For example, in his description of the state of Russia under Aleksey Mikhailovich, Kotoshikhin mentioned several different types of money, each with its own distinctive feature. Examples included: '*vorovskiye*' or counterfeit money; '*poshlinnye*' or money used for paying duties; special purpose money for distribution as charity during celebrations; *molebnye* for public prayer; *pogrebal'nye* for funerals; and *polonyanichnye* for paying the ransom of people held captive (Kotoshikhin [c. 1667] 1859, 152). Additional examples of this were: the stamping of gold coins, the use of fur and leather as units of account and special issues of counterfeit money.

Gold was practically absent from free circulation and the use of gold for the settlement of accounts between merchants was rare. In almost all cases, gold coins were used as an honorary decoration for a coat of arms on memorable occasions like royal weddings. For example, in 1654 it was decided to decorate each *kazak* from the army of Bogdan Khmelnitsky with a Muscovite gold coin. To this end, 75,000 to 100,000 pieces of gold were issued (Spassky 1961, 28–29). Even when gold coins had reached 10 per cent of all those stamped in the early nineteenth century, the majority were used mainly for court and military expenses, thereby remaining a resource reserved for special purposes.

Metallic currency was not the only means of payment and exchange. In Siberia furs were used for exchange and prices were sometimes charged in animal skins: Krizhanich mentioned a 'fur treasury'. The reforms of Peter I abolished the use of leather as a means of exchange and made payment with official money obligatory. In a Decree of 11 March 1700, it was said that in the Lower Volga area they had to clip silver coins due to the deficiency of small change and in Kaluga leather money was used in trade for the lack of silver (Sbornik 1887, 30). This phenomenon illustrated the deficiency of monetary units, which made the use of monetary substitutes attractive. At the same time, the growing universality of money was connected with a strengthening of the state and the introduction of national standards. In many cases, the archaic substitutes and the newly issued money represented two co-existing systems of circulation.

The profitability of coining money and the use of manual technology by the government until the eighteenth century created an atmosphere in which counterfeiting was highly prevalent. The techniques available were numerous. Some produced stamps, while others produced copper coins which were later coated with silver. Some even mixed tin or copper with silver at the mint. Coins imitating Russian coins were produced abroad as well. In the early eighteenth century counterfeit money was produced by the Danes, Swedes and perhaps also the English (Melnikova 2005, 203).

While mentioning the profitability of coining money, Kotoshikhin provided a lengthy discussion on the techniques of counterfeiting and measures for combating them. Common techniques were the stealing of stamps, silver and money as well as the mixing of copper, tin and lead with silver. Counterfeits involving weight reduction also occurred. The toughest police measures often did not work in discouraging counterfeiting. For example, mint workers were made to kiss the cross, were examined naked, were tortured if suspected and were punished by means of pouring molten tin down their throats and by severing their hands and ears. Some were even evicted from their houses and exiled to Siberia, but Kotoshikhin showed that in terms of results, these measures were ineffective (Kotoshikhin [c. 1667] 1859, 81).

Counterfeiting intensified with the issuing of copper money during the reform of Aleksey Mikhailovich. The minters were found building new stone and wooden houses for themselves, buying expensive dresses, foodstuffs and vessels of silver (Kotoshikhin [c. 1667] 1859, 82). Moreover counterfeit money was difficult to identify and there are reasons to believe that it was an integral part of exchange and had a parallel circulation. As a means of stopping the proliferation of fake coins, Krizhanich suggested the use of standards and the abandonment of revenues from the mint. A good law should approve all kinds of permitted money, and their weight, price and material should be recorded in order 'to be remembered forever'. Those violating this law should be executed (Krizhanich [c. 1666] 1985, 222–24).

Conclusion: Between Mercantilism and the Middle Ages

In the history of European economic thought, the sixteenth and seventeenth centuries were traditionally characterized as epochs of mercantilism. When it comes to characterizing this period in Russia, a comparison with the same epoch in Europe seems suggestive. However, giving an unambiguous definition to this system of thought or to this epoch is far from easy. It was only after Adam Smith that different authors identified mercantilists as a contrast to the classical school of political economy and the *laissez-faire* epoch. Eli Heckscher noted that:

> Mercantilism never existed in the sense that Colbert or Cromwell existed. It is only an instrumental concept which, if aptly chosen, should enable us to understand a particular historical period more clearly than we otherwise might. Thus everybody must be free to give the term mercantilism the meaning and particularly the scope that harmonize with the special tasks he assigns himself. To this degree there can be no question of the right or

> wrong use of the word, but only of its greater or less appropriateness (Heckscher [1931] 1935, vol.1, 19).

As an umbrella term, mercantilism can be understood as a special phase of economic policy that bordered the Middle Ages on the one side, and *laissez-faire* policy on the other. Mercantilism contained the destruction of institutions of the medieval economy. It was a doctrine centred on governmental interests, a general framework for striving for a stronger power-base through a system of protectionism and an active trade balance. However, for historians, it was problematic from the very beginning to accept the existence of a single doctrine. The differences faced by historians seem rather to refer mainly to methodology.

The importance given by Heckscher to the difference between mercantilism and the preceding epoch should be stressed. According to him, the difference lay 'in the domain of the ethical' (Heckscher [1931] 1935, vol. 2, 285). According to the medieval outlook, mercantilists set immoral aims and quite often chose immoral means. This observation puts Heckscher's book apart from other works on mercantilism. But elements of mercantilism in Russian economic thought can be traced quite clearly. Konstantin Bazilevich (1940) used archival materials to show the strengthening of protectionism from 1640 to 1667 via custom duties and tariffs and the limitations of the *Novotorgovyi ustav*. Kotilaine demonstrated both the success and the drawbacks of Russian mercantilism, particularly the underdevelopment of the merchant class, the lack of credit use and the attempts to 'expel' foreigners (Kotilaine 2004, 170–73).

In the view of this author, in order to understand economic thought in Muscovy, a comparison should be made not only with mercantilism, but with medieval economic thought as well. This is an approach that coincides with Heckscher's ideas and allows the possibility of differentiating subtle distinctions and identifying characteristic features. The social concepts and the religious and ethical aspects of Muscovite thought draw a perceptible boundary between mercantilism and the middle ages. It is quite right that Samuel Baron did not consider Yuri Krizhanich a mercantilist (Baron 1987, 80–85), because his understanding was built on religious and ethical notions. In this respect the title of one of his treatises, *On God's Providence*, was characteristic (Krizhanich, 1860). Thus the dispute over ecclesiastic landownership was impossible to understand without its religious component. Pososhkov turned out to be a pious man not only as a private person, but also as a developer of economic thought based on spiritual and religious foundations. There is no doubt that pragmatic calculations started to acquire more importance in trade at this time. But rather than in the works of the authors in question, it received a more extensive expression in the legal regulations passed at that time, especially during the reign of Aleksey Mikhailovich. In this respect Kotilaine noted that: 'It would not be an exaggeration to characterize the *Ulozhenie* as the single most important monument of Muscovite mercantilism' (Kotilaine 2004, 152).

With few exceptions, the features of the general Russian mentality of the period were also characteristic of Muscovite economic thought. Firstly, the majority of texts were addressed to the tsar and pursued governmental interests. Secondly, only by the beginning of the eighteenth century did texts appear in which the content did not appeal to religious foundations. Before this time, the majority of treatises belonged to the domain of applied ethics and thus the ideas they contained were similar in nature to medieval regulatory concepts. The similarity with mercantilism can be easily recognized in the idea of protectionism, the desire to protect commodity and financial markets, to increase the import of money and to export goods. However, with respect to how the value of money was determined (by the tsar's will or by metal content), it was difficult to uncover the common theoretical core of these conceptions.

In conclusion, with all its original elements, Muscovite economic thought still fitted into a shared European experience in the development of pre-economic thought at this time, fluctuating between mercantilism and medieval ideas. There was more mercantilism in practice, while the religious component dominated in the writings. Thus only having considered both of these two poles is it possible to understand the particularity and universality of economic thought concerning ownership, trade and money in Muscovy.

References

Baron, Samuel. (1987). 'Was Križanic a Mercantilist?', *History of Political Economy*, vol. 19 no 1: 67–86.

————. (1991). 'A.L. Ordin-Nashchokin and the Orel Affair', in *Explorations in Muscovite History*. 1–22.

Bazilevich, Konstantin V. (1940). 'Elementy merkantilizma v ekonomicheskoy politike Alekseya, Mikhailovicha', *Uchenye zapiski MGU*. Issue 41. *History*. vol. 1: 3–34.

Budovnits, I.U. (1947). *Russkaya publitsistika XVI veka*. AN SSSR: Moscow-Leningrad.

Chistyakova, E.V. (1950). Sotsial'no-ekonomicheskiye vzglyady A.L. Ordin-Nashchokina (XVII vek). *Trudy voronezhskogo gosudarstvennogo universiteta*. Vol. 20. Sbornik rabot po istorii. Voronezh: 3–57.

Chmeman, A. (1954). *Istoricheskii put' Pravoslaviia*. Chehova: New York.

Domostroi ([16 c.] 1994). *The Domostroi. The Rules for Russian Households in the Time of Ivan the Terrible*. C.J. Pouncy (ed and trs) Cornell University Press: Ithaca and London.

Fletcher, Giles ([1591] 1848). *Of the Russe Common Wealth*. Reprint. Moscow.

Heckscher, Eli F. ([1931] 1935). *Mercantilism*. Vols 1–2. London: George Allen & Unwin. Mendel Shapiro (tr).

Herberstein, von Sigmund. ([1557] 1968). *Notes upon Russia* (Rerum Moscoviticarum commentarii), R.H. Major (ed and trs) vols 1–2. Burt Franklin: New York.

Kliuchevsky, Vasili O. ([1907] 1994). *A Course in Russian History. The Seventeenth Century*. Alfred J. Rieber (ed), Natalie Duddington (trs).

Kotilaine, Jarmo T. (2004). 'Mercantilism in Pre-Petrine Russia' in *Modernizing Muscovy: Reform and Social Change in Seventeenth-century Russia*. J. Kotilaine and M. Poe (eds) Routledge Curzon: London and New York: 143–74.

Kotoshikhin, Grigorii. ([c. 1667] 1859). *O Rossii v zarstvovanie Alekseia Mikhailovicha*. St Petersburg.

Krizhanich, Iurii. ([c. 1666] 1985). *Russian Statecraft: the Politika of Iurii Krizhanich*. J. Letiche and B. Dmytryshyn (eds) Basil Blackwell: Oxford and New York.

————. (1860). *O providenii Gospodnem*. St Petersburg.

Kulisher, I.M. ([1925] 2004). *Istoriya russkogo narodnogo khozyaistva*. Izdatel'stvo: Nauka.

Leshkov, V. (1855). *Drevnyaya russkaya nauka o narodnom bogatstve i blagosostoyanii*. Moscow.

Melnikova, A.S. (2005). *Ocherki po istorii russkogo denezhnogo obrashcheniya XVI–XVII vekov*. Moscow.

Mordukhovich, L.M. (1962). *Sotsial'no-ekonomicheskiye vzglyady Yu. Krizhanicha*. Moscow.

Okenfuss, Max J. (1995). *The Rise and Fall of Latin Humanism in Early-Modern Russia. Pagan Authors, Ukranians, and the Resiliency of Muscovy.* E.J. Brill: Leiden, N.Y., Köln.

Pashkov, A.I. (1955). *Istoriya russkoi ekonomicheskoy mysli*. vol. I part I. IX–XVIII centuries. Moscow.

————. ([1955] 1964). *A History of Russian Economic Thought Ninth Through Eighteenth Centuries*. John M. Letiche (ed) Berkley and Los Angeles: University of California Press.

Patrikeyev, Vassian. (1859). *Razsuzhdeniya inoka Vassiana o neprilichii monastyriam vladet' otchinami*. Chteniya v Imperatorskom obshchestve istorii i drevnostei Rossiiskih pri Moskovskom universitete. Iyul'-sentyabr'. Kniga tret'ya: Moscow.

Pavlov, A. (1871). *Istoricheskii ocherk sekulyarizatsii tserkovnykh zemel' v Rossii*. Part 1. Popytki k obrashcheniyu v gosudarstvennuyu sobstvennost' pozemel'nykh vladenii russkoi tserkvi v XVI v. (1503–80). Odessa.

Pavlov-Silvansky, N.P. (1897). *Proyekty reform v zapiskah sovremennikov Petra Velikogo. Opyt izucheniya proyektov i neizdannye ikh teksty.* Kirshbauma: St Petersburg.

Philotheus ([16 c.] 2000). 'Poslaniya startsa Philotheya', in *Biblioteka literatury drevney Rusi*. vol. 9. Konets XV – pervaya polovina XVI veka. St. Petersburg: 290–306.

Pipes, Richard. (1999). *Property and Freedom*. Alfred A. Knopf: New York.

Pliguzov, A.I. (2002). *Polemika v russkoi tserkvi pervoy treti XVI stoletiya*. Indrik: Moscow.

Pososhkov, Ivan. ([1724] 1987). *The Book of Poverty and Wealth*. A.P. Vlasto and L.R. Lewitter (eds and trs). Stanford University Press: Stanford.

Rzhiga, V.F. (1908). *I.S. Peresvetov, publitsist XVI veka*. Moscow.

————. (1926). *Literaturnaya deyatel'nost' Ermolaya-Erazma*. Leningrad.

Shirokorad, Leonid D. (2008). 'Russian Economic Thought in the Age of the Enlightenment', in Vincent Barnett and Joachim Zweynert (eds), *Economics in Russia*. Ashgate. (Chapter 3 below.)

Sinitsyna, N.V. (1977). *Maxim Grek v Rossii*. Nauka.

Spassky, I.G. (1961). *Denezhnoe khoziaistvo russkogo gosudarstva v XV i XVII veke*. Leningrad.

Stremoukhov, Dm. ([1953] 2002). 'Moskva – Tretiy Rim: istochniki doktriny', in *Iz istorii russkoi kultury*. vol. II, Book 1. Kiyevskaya i Moskovskaya Rus'. Composed by A.F. Litvina, F.B. Uspensky. Moscow: Yazyki slavyanskoi kultury.

Svyatlovsky, V.V. ([1923] 2003). 'Istoriya ekonomicheskih idey v Rossii', in: *Istoriki ekonomicheskoi mysli v Rossii*, V.V. Svyatlovsky, M.I. Tugan-Baranovsky, V.Ya. Zheleznov; M.G. Pokidchenko, E.N. Kalmychkova (eds). Moscow: Nauka.

Sbornik (1887). *Sbornik ukazov po monetnomu i medalnomu delu v Rossii, pomejionnyh v polnom sobranii zakonov s 1649 po 1881 g*. Sost. M. Demmeni. St Petersburg. Vyp. 1.

Chapter 3

Russian Economic Thought in the Age of the Enlightenment

Leonid Shirokorad

The reforms of Peter the Great heralded Russia's entrance into the first stage of modernity, although during the entire eighteenth century the structure of Russian society remained close to that of the Middle Ages.[1] This contradiction between the new and the old consequently pervaded all spheres of society. An excessive separation of the economic, political and cultural development in Medieval Moscow and the insulation of Russia from all-European processes steadily edged the country to the periphery of the civilized world. However the threat of the loss of national independence, which became real in the Time of Troubles, made Russia consider the necessity of the modernization of all public structures. This could only occur in the form of borrowing European standards, as well as through the acceleration of economic development, the discarding of outdated traditions and the opening up of the country to the world.

The genius of Peter I was that he felt this historical necessity acutely, especially while travelling across Europe and he managed to mobilize all social resources to realize these progressive aims. Unfortunately, in many respects his perception of the European experience was superficial, due to the intellectual narrowness of the environment in which he had been formed. This was why he could not understand that further bonding peasants and developing industry on the basis of serfdom would eventually lead the Russian economy to a position of deadlock. Nevertheless he solved a number of complicated problems and accomplished many fundamental changes which became the cornerstone for strengthening the power of the Russian nation in the second half of the eighteenth century.

Ekaterina II – the sovereign with a European education and mentality – continued the reforms started by Peter I, but on a greater scale and with more reasoning. Like Peter, she was unable to fully implement all her political ideas, as she was constantly facing circumstantial resistance. But the entire eighteenth century in Russia passed under the determinant influence of the activity of these great reformers. One aspect of this activity was the encouragement of the development of scientific understanding. Both Peter I and Ekaterina II appreciated the achievements of the European Enlightenment and did much to cultivate these achievements in Russia. However, science frequently has its own internal logic of development. In initiating

1 This chapter was completed with support from the Russian Humanitarian Scientific Fund, 06-01-00289a.

the development of scientific patterns of thought, including those of economics, Peter I and especially Ekaterina II had let the rationalist genie out of the bottle, and this would bring Ekaterina II and her successors a great deal of trouble. This was one reason why the ultimate destiny of many economic thinkers in eighteenth century Russia was sometimes quite tragic.

In this chapter a comprehensive analysis of the development of economic thought in Russia in the eighteenth century will not be attempted. Instead an analysis of the ideas of only some of the leading thinkers in this field, such as Ivan Pososhkov, Vasily Tatishchev, Mikhail Lomonosov, Alexey Polenov and Alexander Radishchev, will be presented. There is a considerable existing literature on the views of Lomonosov and Tatishchev (Pavlova and Fedorov 1984; Lang 1959), therefore only a short account of their ideas will be given here. More attention is paid to authors that are less well known in the West, and to the debates on serfdom that were initiated by Ekaterina II in 1766 and which took place in the Free Economic Society.

I.T. Pososhkov

Peter the Great assimilated the rationalist ideas of seventeenth century European thinkers, which made up the basis of a theory of a regular ('police') state. Under Peter the state assumed an almost sacred value. It was this central tenet which became the official ideology of that time. The extensive transformative activity begun by Peter also demanded a scientific approach to solving the practical problems that were faced, including those focused on dealing with the economy. One of these problems was finding the material and financial means to implement the desired reforms. Many able-minded Russians, masters of their craft inspired by the struggle for a new Russia, offered the government various projects to increase public revenue:

> Their point of view, doctrine, and theories were revealed in Ivan T. Pososhkov's famous *On Poverty and Wealth*, the name of which itself allows us to know what was first and foremost in the minds of thoughtful Russian society aroused by the movement of this transformative era (Solovyev, [1872] 1984, 98–99).[2]

Ivan Tikhonovich Pososhkov was born in 1652 or 1653, his father being a peasant from Pokrovskoe, an aristocratic enclave located near Moscow. The serfs who resided in this area usually served various functions in the Sovereign's Court. Thus Pososhkov had in early childhood been trained in painting, engraving, sketching, armaments and especially in the crafts of joining, minting and distilling. These skills helped him achieve success in his entrepreneurial activities (Pavlov-Silvansky [1905] 1999, 604).

---

2 In as much as profound alterations in social development created large-scale tensions, especially amongst those of the lower social strata, Peter still had to contend with stubborn resistance: 'Peter's detractors weren't so much against his German improvements as they were against those sacrifices which the sovereign was demanding from the population for the fight against Sweden', complaining most of all that he had 'dragged all the boyars' children off to service', 'turned husbands into recruits, and orphaned their wives and children' (Pavlov-Silvansky 1897, 1).

The Book of Poverty and Wealth was completed in 1724, and in this text a wide spectrum of Russian society in the first quarter of the eighteenth century was colourfully represented. Thus the value of this book was partly its reflection of the widely dispersed social concepts and judgments of Peter's epoch. According to Pavel Milyukov: 'most of the opinions he [Pososhkov] stated were an echo of what was by and large said around him' (Quoted after Pavlov-Silvansky 1897, 3).

In particular, the entire system of state administration and the legal system, the officials' disregard for the law, and corruption among public servants was subject to severe criticism. Pososhkov was thus one of the first to pay attention to 'the still emerging but already extremely serious problem of the bureaucracy' (Gainutdinov 2003, 27). He wrote:

> In Western countries the well-being of men of diverse occupations, in particular that of the merchants, is carefully fostered and so the merchants in those parts are very rich. But our magistrates have no concern for persons at all and by their callousness impoverish the whole realm (Pososhkov 1987, 220).

In Pososhkov's view, it was necessary to draft a new legal code and to reform the entire court system of Russia. It was especially significant that Pososhkov spoke out in favour of the restriction of serfdom. He suggested the need to establish an exact level of required unpaid labour, to clearly separate the serf's land from that of their owner's, to reduce the tax burden of the peasantry and raise that of the nobility, and to introduce a compulsory system of basic education for the children of serfs.

Like many of Peter the Great's contemporaries, Pososhkov was an advocate of a strong state and a powerful government. He believed that it was the government that should organize merchant businesses, set the prices of goods, build factories, supply forced labour and even regulate the consumption of products (Kafengauz 1950, 100). Thus Pososhkov could be accused of underestimating the role of market forces and competition in economic development. For example, he stated that all sellers of a good should demand the same price for it as had been set by the authorities. He suggested that strict control of this system should be implemented to ensure compliance, including the punishment of offenders. Even some of Pososhkov's contemporaries understood the fallaciousness of this idea. In one of the surviving copies of *The Book of Poverty and Wealth* from the middle of the eighteenth century, next to the passage where Pososhkov commented on the necessity of implementing a single price, one may read the following remark: 'Old man, you can't put one price on a good, as it may have one name but its quality isn't the same. Even you're lying sometimes!' (Pososhkov 1951, 120 and 343–44).

Pososhkov's conception of money was linked to the general basis of his economic views. In so far as a tsar's power was unlimited:

> … it is not the silver that we honour nor the copper that we value; it is His Imperial Majesty's word that bestows honour and authority. So powerful is His Most Glorious Majesty's word among us that if he orders a copper coin of one *zolotnik* weight to be stamped and issued with the denomination of one ruble it would circulate for ever without fluctuation at the value of one ruble (Pososhkov 1987, 377).

One expert in monetary theories has linked Pososhkov's nominalism with the widely employed practice of the adulteration of coins employed during the reigns of Aleksei Mikhailovich and his son Peter: 'Pososhkov's views on this issue do not represent anything new in terms of corresponding comments on adulteration in Western Europe' (Eidelnant 1929, 261).

Pososhkov also distinguished between corporeal and immaterial wealth. 'The veritable Truth' he interpreted as immaterial wealth, without the 'planting' of which 'people could never be enriched' (Pososhkov 1987, 154–55). Thus the interweaving of economic ideas and Russian Orthodox ethics was a common thread throughout his work. Accordingly the real wealth of a state lay not in its financial health, but in the welfare of its people: 'For it is wrong that those who collect taxes for the Tsar should bring ruin on the people' (Pososhkov 1987, 350). It is important to note that a constant interest in the social aspects of economic problems was one of the peculiarities of much Russian thinking on economic affairs, and it was unsurprising that this found an expression in Pososhkov's book, as indicated in its title.

Pososhkov did not have a university education and he expressed a common point of view held by many Russians in his era. Without any influence of the emerging European science of economics, Pososhkov developed an explanation of some basic elements of the national economy on his own. He therefore deserves to be classified as the first Russian writer-economist. His arguments are often very simplistic, but this is also true for the first Western writers dealing with economic problems (Pavlov-Silvansky [1905] 1999, 617).

Pososhkov's life ended tragically. He was arrested by the secret police in August 1725 on serious political charges, although the surviving documents do not reveal the nature of these allegations. It is quite likely that the arrest was connected with his book, particularly with his accusing officials and the nobility of different kinds of malfeasance, and his insistence that national opinion should be considered when attempting to solve such issues. Of Pososhkov's economic suggestions, Kafengauz noted that they:

> … could turn out to be dangerous in that complex political climate. Pososhkov apprehended not without foundation that his enemies, 'would not allow me to live for a long time, but will take my life'. *The Book of Poverty and Wealth* brought its author to the dungeon of the Peter and Paul Fortress (Kafengauz 1950, 141).

Approximately six months after his arrest, Pososhkov died in prison.

V.N. Tatishchev

One of the most eminent state servants of the first half of the eighteenth century in Russia was Vasiliy Nikitich Tatishchev (1686–1750). At various periods of his life he directed mining concerns in the Urals and Siberia, was involved with a Monetary Commission and various expeditions, was the governor of Astrakhan and taught mining in Sweden. At the same time he was an outstanding scientist who made great contributions to several different disciplines. Tatishchev's main work was his *Russian History from Ancient Times*. It represented the first account of

Russian history written from the position of rationalist philosophy. His *Conversation of Two Friends on Science and Schools* became one of the most famous treatises on socio-political and philosophical issues in eighteenth century Russia. He also made significant contributions to geography and cartography and created the first encyclopaedic dictionary, *A Russian Historical, Geographical, and Political Lexicon* (Yukht 1994, 46).

Tatishchev was a typical representative of the Russian intelligentsia during the epoch of Peter the Great. According to a leading researcher of his work, he belonged to:

> … the generation of Russian people who were brought up … partially by self-education, partially carried away by the mighty stream of the reforms of Peter, who broadened their theoretical beliefs and practical habits, acquired many new needs, among which the strive for knowledge was not the last, and nevertheless they remained quite Russian … Tatishchev … was one of the greatest figures directing modern society to a realization of its shortcomings and mistakes and specified means and ways necessary to reach perfection (Popov 1887, 63–64).

Tatishchev's approach to the practical problems he dealt with was (for the time) quite scientific. He argued for the necessity of the prioritized development of processing industries (first of all metalworking), he opposed creating a raw materials orientation in the economy, and he supported the all-round development of small craft manufacture that could satisfy the home market, in order to strengthen the financial capacity of the people paying duties.

Being responsible for the management of mining plants in the Urals and later in Siberia, Tatishchev actively opposed the monopolies that were generated in this branch of the economy. He recognized that the treasury could not support all mines, therefore he believed that the majority of them, especially those that were unprofitable, should be privatized. Initially the state should support such private companies by granting loans and labour on preferential terms and by exempting them from taxes. Tatishchev considered that state-supported companies were pioneers that could help to establish an industry where private proprietors were unable to do so (Lesenko 1879, 41). In conditions of capital deficiency and a lack of qualified experts, Tatishchev advocated measures for the attraction of foreign capital. His requirement to give private companies the right to sell their products at market prices was also important.

The most serious obstacle for the development of industry in Russia in the eighteenth century was a shortage of labour. As most peasants were held on the land, only an insignificant part of the population lived in towns. In order to cope with the scarcity of labour, Peter I ordered homeless people to work in factories. Whole villages were also sold to the owners of enterprises that were executing state defence orders. Eventually in 1721, manufacturers and merchants were allowed to buy serfs, but all these measures still proved insufficient. Tatishchev felt the acuteness of the problem directly. In searching for new sources of labour he suggested using fugitive peasants and also exiled Old Believers. His suggestion to expand the practice of the application of civilian work was especially valuable.

One of the most acute problems that prevented the promotion of Russian goods not only on foreign markets, but also inside Russia, was their low quality. During the whole first half of the eighteenth century the government tried to change this situation. Not only administrative measures, but also economic ones, were applied, such as a reduction of duties on imported goods in 1731. This policy was opposed by many Russian manufacturers and merchants, who were often more interested in the creation of 'sweatshop' conditions for their businesses. In this regard Tatishchev recommended the introduction of single quality standards, especially for metallurgical and metal processing plants (Toropitsyn 2001, 203).

Tatishchev also centred his attention on many vital problems of fiscal policy. He recommended that the government should reconsider tax rates periodically, introduce a united tax system of direct taxes across the whole country, spend budgetary funds economically and carry out audits more often. Tatishchev was the first Russian economist who formulated requirements for an improved organization of public finances and he proposed the idea of changes in the economic position of tax bearers within fiscal policy (Troitsky 1966, 59–60; Toropitsyn 2001, 207). Much was also done by Tatishchev to organize a rational system of customs duty collection. Of special importance was his idea of the need for differentiated taxation of goods depending on their country of manufacture and the degree of Russia's interest in developing trade relations with the country in question (Toropitsyn 2001, 217–24).

In the eighteenth century the need to create credit institutions for the successful development of business in Russia became increasingly recognized. Tatishchev dealt with this question directly, suggesting that funds for a commercial bank could be formed out of the incomes of the nobility and the clergy. He emphasized the necessity of supplying bank credit to industry, although it has been suggested that, during the manufactory period and even in the initial stages of the development of industrial capitalism, commercial banks played an insignificant role in granting loans to industry, almost completely confining their operations to the granting of loans to merchants. Tatishchev's project thus had outstripped its time (Borovoy 1950, 100), and appeared in sharp contrast both with governmental practice, and with the claims of the nobility to create credit institutions (Toropitsyn 2001, 232).

As Bezobrazov remarked, Tatishchev represented a mixture of a person of science and a man of action:

> … he was quite a European judging by his education, and at the same time he was from head to foot a real Russian … He considered Russia an inseparable part of the whole European world, but still knew its special historical and national points … To be like this it was necessary to get quite a European education and study European science (Bezobrazov 1887, 98–99).

After Hugo Grotius, Samuel von Pufendorf and Christian von Wolff, Tatishchev considered natural law as an important source of legislation. Correct civil laws, he believed, were almost always drawn from natural law (Popov 1861, 512). As Bezobrazov outlined:

> Tatishchev often refers to natural law even in his orders and injunctions. But it is remarkable to note that, finding something useful for himself in theoretical compositions and foreign

> legislations, he was much less doctrinaire about abstract doctrines and foreign principles of life: he first of all searched for the deduction of legislative and administrative norms from developed Russian historical and vital relations in order to satisfy the practical needs of Russian life (Bezobrazov 1887, 93–94).

M.V. Lomonosov

The greatest Russian scientist in the eighteenth century was arguably Michael V. Lomonosov (1711–65). His work possessed extraordinary variety, contributing to the development of physics, chemistry, mineralogy, geology, geography, cartography, history, and Russian language and literature. He also left a bright imprint in the development of economics.

Lomonosov always progressed from practice to theory. First of all, he was interested in the actual problems of socio-economic development in Russia. Analyzing them he drew upon philosophical and economic theories widely distributed in the eighteenth century, mainly the theory of natural law and German cameralism. During his studies in Marburg in 1736–39, Lomonosov attended the lectures of Christian Wolff, the outstanding representative of the theory of natural law of his time. As Sukhoplyuev remarked, Lomonosov used the methodology of cameralism; in particular he aimed for a whole and complete description of particular phenomena and processes (Sukhoplyuev 1911, 184). From Wolff, Lomonosov also took the rationalistic method and a critical approach to the estimation of various features of social reality.

One of the most interesting works of Lomonosov in the field of economic policy was his letter to the Earl Ivan I. Shuvalov – a favourite of the Empress Elizabeth I. When Lomonosov returned from Germany, Shuvalov discovered his unusual abilities and provided him with patronage; Lomonosov expressed gratitude to his sponsor on various occasions. His well-known letter 'On the Multiplication and Preservation of the Russian People' was a birthday present to Shuvalov. This letter:

> … was not a private letter of one individual to another; it was a letter of a theorist who had received a West European education, had listened to lectures on philosophy of the most outstanding philosopher of first half of the 18th century and who had studied the views of Christian Wolff on domestic policy … (Sukhoplyuev 1911, 170).

Lomonosov devoted the letter to one of the sharpest political problems of the time, which was the centre of attention of both European and Russian statesmen. The letter gives clear evidence of how strongly he was influenced by the idea of natural law (Sukhoplyuev 1911, 179).

According to Wolff's doctrine, the main purpose of the state was to provide public welfare and a basic prerequisite of this was a sufficiently large population. This conclusion was especially important for Russia, which was scantily populated, a fact that hindered the effective use of natural resources. Additionally, the recklessness with which Peter's reforms were accomplished had led to a further decline in population. The arbitrariness of landlords, the weight of the tax burden, long military service and the prosecution of dissenters generated a mass exodus of peasants out of Russia, especially to Poland. According to one source the number of fugitives (mainly peasants) in the period 1719–27 reached 200,000 people (Sukhoplyuev 1911, 222).

In his letter Lomonosov developed a system of measures directed at increasing the birth rate, preserving the newborn and stimulating immigration. Considering the necessity of increasing the birth rate, he spoke out against the widespread custom of arranging forced marriages (Sukhoplyuev 1911, 192–93). Lomonosov even supported the right to contract a fourth and even a fifth marriage. In order to preserve the population, he suggested that the state should take care of illegitimate children, improve the level of medical care to the lower classes, and increase the understanding of childcare. According to Troitsky, Lomonosov's proposals contained a more democratic attitude than the writings of other ideologists of enlightened monarchy, who basically aspired to protect the interests of the nobility (Troitsky 1966, 90).

Especially striking was the difference between Lomonosov's and Pososhkov's treatment of the same issue. Comparing the reforms that they had advocated, Lomonosov's proposals did not aim primarily at increasing treasury funds, but instead focused on protecting the interests of the population. For example, in contrast to Pososhkov, Lomonosov was against the use of the death penalty (Sukhoplyuev 1911, 221).

The Free Economic Society

The second half of the eighteenth century in Russia was thoroughly permeated by an atmosphere of the reforms of Ekaterina II, who continued the reforms that had been initiated by Peter I. Even so the former monarch was much more cautious than the latter. She considered the opinions of the nobility, which was her basic social support, to a greater degree and her reforms were less impulsive and extemporaneous. The most important point was that she was aware of the economic theories of the physiocrats and, probably, also those of Adam Smith. It is not surprising therefore, that unlike Peter I she was a convinced supporter of free enterprise: 'There is nothing more dangerous … than to wish to fix the limits of everything' (Elen d'Ankoss 2006, 211)

In the eighteenth century the question of the abolishment of serfdom came onto the political agenda and for many decades it was to remain the most disputed question of Russian life. The late and incomplete solution adopted in the epoch of Alexander II predetermined many aspects of the economic and political development of Russia in the second half of the nineteenth century, and significantly contributed to the dynamics of revolutionary events in the first quarter of the twentieth century. The first Russian intellectual who raised the issue of the abolition of serfdom in public was V.V. Golytsin, who played a significant political role in the reign of Tsarina Sofia, and whom the historian V.I. Semevsky characterized as one of the few Russians of the time who had received a European education (Semevsky 1888, 1).

In the eighteenth century, serfdom in Russia was actually both amplified and extended. At the same time Pososhkov, Ekaterinian grandees Earl Peter I. Panin and Prince Dmitry A. Golitsyn, and one of leading figures of Masonry I.P. Elagin, wrote about the expediency of its restriction (but not about its abolition). Inspired by the ideals of an enlightened monarchy, Ekaterina II was also determined, especially at the initial stage of her reign, to restrict serfdom through legislation.[3] It was not by chance that in 1764 Ekaterina II authorized the publication (in German) of an article by Pastor Eisen von Schwarzenberg, who had come to Russia on the invitation of Peter III and had studied the situation of peasants in Liefland. It was the first article on serfdom published in St Petersburg (Eines Lieflaendischen Patrioten 1764, 491–527). The author showed that the position of the Lieflandian peasantry was even worse than that of the peasants in areas of the Empire, and suggested a number of measures to alleviate it. In particular, he drew attention to the positive experience of the Western European nations in the abolition of serfdom.

Realising the complexity of the issue and in view of the strong reaction of various interest groups, Ekaterina II decided to involve the recently formed Free Economic Society in finding a solution to this problem. The Imperial Free Economic Society for Encouragement of Agriculture and House-Building (FES) in Russia was founded in 1765 on Ekaterina II's initiative and was in existence up to 1919. It was the first scientific society in Russia and in 1909 it had 507 members. Scientists of different countries were corresponding members of it. The society published the 'Works of the Free Economic Society' in 281 volumes between 1765 and 1915; it also issued a number of journals and organized exhibitions, questionnaires and competitions on problems of political economy, agriculture and production techniques (Sokolov 1994, 449–50).

On Ekaterina's initiative the Free Economic Society asked in 1766: '… is it more useful for society that peasants have as property either land or only movable property, and how far should these rights on this or that property spread?' (Semevsky 1888, 48). In total the Free Economic Society received 162 answers to this question. In 2004 V. Somov discovered that one of the answers had been sent by one of the leading French physiocrats Mercier de la Rivière, although his composition was late and was rejected. Two compositions (in Latin and French) had been sent by Voltaire but were ignored, as they were too radical. Fifteen responses were ultimately selected for the competition. The winner was the doctor of law Bearde de L'Abbaye[4], who suggested a slow and evolutionary liberation of the peasants. He argued that: 'slaves should be prepared to accept liberty before they receive some property' (P.B. 1865a, 286). It was decided to publish three more compositions, including that of Galberstadt, canonic Wöllner who later became Prussian minister, and a Lieflandian Meck. All the German authors opposed serfdom and recognized its inefficiency, but at the same time they were anxious about the interests of landowners. Therefore

3 Vasily I. Sergeevich remarked that the first variant of the Empress's Decree on the Legislative Commission for Drawing Up a New Code 'said it straight about serf liberation' (Sergeevich 1878, 252). It was not accidental that 'the Code was published in Russia eight times in 30 years, but was banned in France' (*Political History: Russia–the USSR–the Russian Federation* 1996, vol. 1, 145).

4 As Johann Albrecht Eiler wrote to his Berlin colleague Samuel Forma, the results of this competition were known beforehand, as Bearde de L'Abbaye had fulfilled the requirement of powerful persons that would not allow too bold a piece of work to win (Somov 2004, 151–52 and 160).

they suggested that the land should not be transferred to the complete possession of peasants, but only given to them for perpetual use.

Semevsky claimed that the best essay had been delivered by Alexey J. Polenov, who for four years (1762–66) had studied at the faculties of law at Strasbourg and Göttingen universities. Polenov argued that private property was an incentive for efficient work and thus a necessary condition, both to supply industry with cheap raw materials and to supply the urban population with cheap food and consumer goods. This would increase the demand for labour and serve 'the destruction of the idea of an idle life in people's minds' (Polenov 1865, 290). The growth of the level of income among the population would improve the financial situation of the state and hence increase its power. Economic depression was 'not only harmful, but also dangerous', for it encouraged rebellion (Polenov 1865, 291–92).

In Polenov's opinion, the bondage of the peasants contradicted natural law. As it was the peasants who provided the whole ssociety with their means of existence, they represented a particular important estate that deserved the utmost attention. The situation of the peasants he described as tragic, as they had no legal protection and were constantly denigrated and sometimes even tortured (Polenov 1865, 298). Polenov consequently developed a programme of revival for the Russian peasantry. The basic elements of this were the introduction of basic education, healthcare and fire protection in the villages. In order to reconcile the interests of the peasants and the nobility, he suggested transferring the land not into the possession of peasants, but into constant and hereditary use. If the peasants regularly performed all duties, then the landowner could not confiscate their land. Only if this condition was violated could peasants be deprived of their land. Not being the full proprietor of the land, peasants had no right to sell it, or to divide it between their children (Polenov 1865, 307).

Although Polenov did not question the rights of the masters (and of the state) to keep a portion of the product of the peasant's work, at least their share would be guaranteed, so that the landowner had no opportunity to encroach on it. Polenov also suggested the idea of creating country courts to resolve disputes between peasants and also between peasants and landowners. But Polenov's severe criticism of the serf order reigning in Russia, as well as the measures that he proposed as reforms, frightened not only the Legislative Commission, which considered it so dangerous that dare not publish it, but also the Empress herself, who prevented Polenov's election to the Academy of Sciences (Semevsky 1888, 82). As a result, they remained unavailable not only for Russian society, but even for the majority of deputies of the Commission drawing up a new Code.

Polenov's work was finally published in Russia only 100 years after it had been written and after the abolition of serfdom. The commentary to this work declared:

> … it is remarkable that the author saw a century in advance the necessity and, even more, the impossibility of liberating peasants without providing them with land; with amazing clearness he specifies the harmful and fatal consequences to which such a great number of people who do not have any property can result… (Borzov 1865, 316).

The Pugachev rebellion was to make the correctness of Polenov's assessment painfully clear. In a number of cases the reforms suggested by Polenov were not even realised during the emancipation in the 1860s, as the peasants were not equipped with well-defined property rights, nor were any educational institutions established (Borzov 1865, 316–18).

Polenov was not the only Russian intellectual of his time to criticize serfdom. Nevertheless, his analysis stood out against the background, as it was more thorough, clearer in conception, and more comprehensive than most. All his efforts, however, had no practical results in his own era. As one Russian historian stated:

> … the activity of the Code Commission of 1767–1768 brought Ekaterina II to the conclusion of the impossibility of coordinating the interests of various estates and of mitigating the serf order, without the risk of losing the throne (Kamensky 1996, 128).[5]

A.N. Radishchev

The spirit of the enlightenment in eighteenth century Russia was most consistently represented by the works of Aleksander N. Radishchev. He was born in 1749 to a family of well-educated landowners in the Saratov province. From the middle of the 1750s, Radishchev was raised by his uncle who had close connections with Moscow University, and he was subsequently educated there, where his tutor was a fugitive counsellor of Rouen Parliament. It was he who acquainted Radishchev with the ideas of the Enlightenment for the first time (Lossky [1910] 1997, 382). In 1766, at the age of 17, Radishchev was sent to Leipzig University to study law. There he came under the influence of the ideas of G.W. Leibniz and the greatest French philosophers of the time, such as Claude A. Helvétius, Paul A. Holbach and Jean Jacques Rousseau.

In his principal work – *A Journey from Petersburg to Moscow* written in 1790 – Radishchev argued that the slave status of serfs and the lack of legal protection given to them would inevitably result in a new peasant uprising. Only the abolition of serfdom and the emancipation of the peasants, who had to become landowners, could prevent this danger. Radishchev also criticized the avarice of judges, the arbitrariness of officials and the degree of demoralization within ruling circles.

Radishchev's *Journey* was published only in a small print run by his own private printing house. In 1783 a decree of Ekaterina II had allowed the founding of private printing houses to publish books without requiring state permission, and in her well-known *Order* (1767), she emphasized that words would never be considered a

---

5 In the 1790s Ekaterina II recollected: 'Hardly have you dared to say that they (the serfs) are the same people as we are, and even when I say this myself, I risk that they will start throwing stones at me; I've suffered so much from this reckless society when in the Commission to draw up a new Code, they began to discuss some questions concerning this subject, and when ignorant noblemen … began to guess, that these questions can lead to some improvement in the present position of peasants … I think, there were not more than twenty persons who could treat this question humanely and as real people' (*Political History: Russia-USSR-the Russian Federation* 1996, vol. 1, 147–48).

crime. Therefore in printing the book, Radishchev did not consider the possibility of sanctions from the authorities, as writings containing liberal ideas (although not as radical as Radishchev's) had been published previously. Obviously, Radishchev had underestimated the impact of the French Revolution on Ekaterina's attitude towards the Enlightenment. During the last years of her reign, the Tsarina abolished most of the freedoms that she had previously granted and Radishchev became the first victim of her regressive course. Having acquainted herself with the *Journey*, the Tsarina accused him of the 'dispersion of French infection' and declared that he was a rebel worse than E. Pugachev. Radishchev was arrested and the subsequent investigation was supervised by the Empress herself. In 1790 he was sentenced to death through beheading, although this was soon commuted to exile to a remote area of Siberia.

The sharp response of Ekaterina II to the *Journey from Petersburg to Moscow* was due to the fact that the outbreak of a peasant uprising (1773–74), Radishchev's own book, and the French revolution of 1789–93, had frightened the ruling circles of the Russian Empire and initiated a period of reaction. At the beginning of the nineteenth century all private printing houses were closed, the level of censorship was increased and the import of foreign books was forbidden. A decree of 9 April 1798 had barred Russian citizens from studying at foreign universities 'owing to the harmful rules which have recently appeared there, and which inflame immature minds and instigate them to unrestrained and dissolute theorizing' (Kovalevsky 1915, 135).

Conclusion

On the whole it is possible to conclude that the reforms of Peter I and Ekaterina II gave a powerful impulse to the development of economic research in Russia. Its nature was often secular, and in a number of cases (the reform of serfdom as discussed in the Free Economic Society and in works by Radishchev; ideas for overcoming the demographic crisis as developed by Lomonosov) it was orientated towards the solution of practical political problems. However, in relation to the crisis of the feudal system, especially in connection with the French Revolution, the state increasingly prevented the free discussion of economic problems, if such discussions called into question the legitimacy of the class structure and the archaic system of political administration. In this connection the activity of the Free Economic Society in greater degree focused on studying concrete economic (mainly agricultural) questions that were divorced from political matters.

However, to analyze many concrete economic problems often demanded a full awareness not only of economic theory, but also of philosophy. In most cases such research was based on the theory of natural law and cameralism, Western theories that were widely developed during the Enlightenment. Many Russian scientists who received an academic education in the West, mainly in Germany, tried to apply the achievements of European science to their studies of the Russian economy. Only by this means, could the works mentioned in this chapter appear (the book by Pososhkov was an exception).

However, this was only a small part of the corpus of Russian economic literature of the eighteenth century. The reformist ideas of Feodor Saltykov, Ivan Filippov and V. Ershov have not been discussed, nor were the works of Peter Rychkov, Ivan Lepyokhin, Vasily Zuev and other fellows of the Petersburg Academy of Sciences. All this literature was of significant scientific value. In the works of the leading researchers of this time, purely theoretical problems were discussed, but always in the context of discussing concrete economic problems, not as independent subjects to analyse in themselves. Such an approach was typical for the majority of works of European economists of the eighteenth century. But in the field of pure theory (economic analysis according to the terminology of Joseph Schumpeter), Russian economic thought could not really compete with that of Western European until a long time later.

In the eighteenth century most Russian science was still syncretic, that is there was no precise isolation of the separate disciplines, including economics, which had not yet gained a firm hold as a subject in the system of university education. This occurred only at the beginning of the nineteenth century. At this time political economy and statistics and also financial law, were separated out as special disciplines. During the nineteenth century Russian economics began to achieve significant successes, and by the beginning of the twentieth century, the theoretical research of Russian economists had begun to draw the attention of many European economists. But this increased success would have been impossible without the earlier experiences that Russian economics had gained in the eighteenth century.

References

Anonymous (1764). 'Eines Lieflaendischen Patrioten Beschreibung der Leibeigenschaft, wie solche in Liefland ueber die Bauern eingefuehrt ist', *Sammlung Russischer Geschichte.* vol. IX, St Petersburg: 491–527.

Anonymous ([1904] 1999). 'Saltykova, (Saltychikha) Dar′ya Nikolayevna', in S. Platonov et al. (eds), *Russkii biograficheskii slovar′*. vol. Sabanyeev-Smyslov, Moscow: Aspekt Press: 69–70.

Bezobrazov, Vladimir (1887). 'Vasilii Nikitich Tatishchev', *Zapiski Imperatorskoi Akademii nauk,* vol. VL, appendix no 4. *Torzhestvennoye sobranie Imperatorskoi Akademii nauk 19 aprelya 1886 g. v. pamyat' dvukhsotlenei godovshchiny so dnya rozhdeniya V.N. Tatishcheva*: 65–101.

Borzov, Ya. (1865). 'Zametka k stat′e A.Ya. Polenova ob unichtozhenii krepostnogo sostoyanii krest′yan v Rossii v 1767 g', *Russkii Arkhiv*, vypusk 3: 316–18.

Borovoy, Saul (1950). 'Voprosy kreditirovaniya torgovli i promyshlennosti v Rossii XVIII veka', *Istoricheskiye zapiski*, vol. 33: 92–122.

d'Ankoss, Elen (2006). *Yekatarina II. Zolotoi vek istorii Rossii.* Moscow: ROSSPEN.

Dityatin, Ivan (1905). *Yekatarinskaya komissiya 1767 g. O sochinenii proyekta novogo Ulozheniya.* Rostov on Don: Paramona.

Eidel′nant, Alexandra. (1929). *Ocherki iz istorii denezhnoi teorii.* Moscow-Leningrad: Gosudarstvennoye izdatel′stvo.

Gainutdinov, Ravil (2003). 'Politiko-pravovye vzglyady I.T. Pososhkova (k voprosu ob osobennostyakh merkantilisticheskogo ucheniya v Rossii)', in Yu. Osipov et al. (eds), *Predtecha. 350 let so dnya rozhdeniya I.T. Pososhkova*. Moscow: TEIS: 15–43.

Kafengauz, Berngard (1950). *I.T. Pososhkov. Zhizn′ i deyatel′nost′*. Moscow-Leningrad: AN SSSR.

Kamensky, Alexander (1996). 'Yekatarina II', in V. Yanin (ed.), *Otechestvennaya istoriya. Istoriya Rossii s drevneishikh vremen do 1917 goda. Entsiklopediya*. vol. 2, Moscow: Bolshaya Rossiiskaya Entsiklopediya: 128–30.

Kovalevsky, Maksim (1915). 'Bor′ba nemetskogo vliyania s frantsuzskim v kontse XVIII i v pervoi polovine XIX stoletiya', *Vestnik Evropy*, October.

Lang, D.M. (1959). *The First Russian Radical: Alexander Radishchev, 1749–1802*. London: Allen and Unwin.

Lesenko, D. (1879). 'Mysli V.N. Tatishcheva o razvitii gornozavodskoi promyshlennosti, 1735–38', *Russkaya starina*, September: 35–42.

Lossky, A. (1997). 'Radishchev, Aeksander Nikolayevich', in B. Modzalevsky (ed.), *Russkii biograficheskii slovar′*. vol.Pritvits-Reis, Moscow: Aspekt Press: 382–88.

Milyukov, Pavel ([1891] 1905). *Gosudarstvennoye khozyaistvo Rossii v pervoi chetvertii XVIII stoletiya i reforma Petra Velikogo*. St Petersburg: Pirozhkova.

Pavlova, G.E. and Fedorov, A.S. (1984). *Mikhail Vasilievich Lomonosov. His Life and Work*. Moscow: Mir Publishers.

Pavlov-Silvansky, Nikolai (1897). *Proyekty reform v zapiskakh sovremennikov Petra Velikogo*. St Petersburg.

————. ([1905] 1999). 'Pososhkov, Ivan Tikhonovich', in N.P. Sobko and B.L. Modzalevskii (eds), *Russki biograficheskii slovar′*, vol. Plavil′shchikov-Primo, Moscow: Aspekt Press: 604–20.

P.B. (1865a). 'Ob unichtozhenii krepostnogo sostoyaniya krest′yan v Rossii', *Russkii Arkhiv*, vypusk 3: 285–86.

————. (1865b). 'Saltychikha', *Russkii Arkhiv*, vypusk 3: 247–48.

Polenov, Aleksei (1865). 'O krepostnom sostoyanii krest′yan v Rossii', *Russkii Arkhiv*, vypusk 3: 287–316.

Politicheskaya istoriya: Rossiya-SSSR-Rossiiskaya Fereratsiya. (1996). Moscow: Terra.

Popov, Nil (1861). *V.N. Tatishchev i ego vremya*. Moscow: Soldatenkova i Shchepkina.

————. (1887). 'Uchenye i literaturnye trudy V.N. Tatishcheva', *Zapiski Imperatorskoi Akademii nauk,* vol. LV, appendix no 4. *Torzhestvennoye sobranie Imperatorskoi Akademii nauk 19 aprelya 1886 g. v. pamyat' dvukhsotlenei godovshchiny so dnya rozhdeniya V.N. Tatishcheva*: 1–64.

Pososhkov, Ivan. (1951). *Kniga o skudosti i bogatstve i drugiye sochineniya*. Moscow: AN SSSR.

————. (1987). *The Book of Poverty and Wealth.* Stanford, California: Stanford University Press.

Semevsky, Vasilii (1888), *Krest′yanskii vopros v Rossii v XVIII i pervoi polovine XIX veka*. vol. 1, St Petersburg.

Sergeyevich, Vasilii. (1878). Otkuda neudachi Yekatarinskoi zakonodatel´noi komisii, *Vestnik Evropy*, no 1: 188–264.

Sokolov, N. (1994). 'Vol´noye ekonomicheskoye obshchestvo', in V. Yanin et al. (eds), *Otechestvennaya istoriya drevneishikh vremen do 1917 g. Entsiklopediya*, vol. 1, Moscow: Bol´shaya rossiiskaya entsiklopediya.

Solovyev, S.M. ([1872] 1984). *Publichnye chteniya o Petre Velikom*. Moscow.

Somov, V. (2004). 'Dva otveta Vol´tera na peterburgskom konkurse o krest´yanskoi sobstvennosti', in S. Karp (ed.), *Evropeiskoye prosveshcheniye i tsivilizatsiya Rossii*. Moscow: Nauka.

Sukhoplyuev, I. (1911). 'Vzglyady Lomonosova na politiku narodonaseleniya', in *Lomonosovskii sbornik*, St Petersburg: Imperatorskoi Akademii Nauk: 163–234.

Toropitsyn, Il´ya (2001). *V.N. Tatishchev i sotsial`no ekonomicheskoye razvitiye Rossii pervoi poloviny XVIII veka*. Astrakhan: Astrakhanskogo gosudarstvennogo pedagogicheskogo universiteta.

Troitsky, Sergei (1966). *Finansovaya politika russkogo absolyutizma v XVIII veke*. Moscow: Nauka.

Yukht, Alexander (1985). *Gosudarstvennaya deyatel´nost´ V.N. Tatishcheva v 20-kh nachale 30-kh godov XVIII veka*. Moscow: Nauka.

————. (1994). *Russkie den´gi ot Petra Velikogo do Aleksandra I*. Moscow: Finansy i Statistika.

Chapter 4

Russian Monetary Reformers: Speransky, Mordvinov and Bunge

Alla Sheptun

The nineteenth century in Russia was a period of transformation from a predominantly agricultural to a more industrialized economy. A conscious process of industrial development was started after Russia's defeat in the Crimean War (1853–56), when it became a primary concern for the tsarist government. Before this time, state industrial policy was haphazard and experimental, business institutions were poorly developed and the financial system was still primitive. According to one scholar: 'There was no industrial revolution in Russia during the early nineteenth century, a time when several nations in Western Europe were undergoing rapid economic growth' (Blackwell, 1970, 12).

Despite the fact that Russia was still an agrarian country in the first half of the nineteenth century, where serfdom and a feudal social structure were dominant, capitalist relations in trade and industry had started to develop. Consequently, the period before 1860 in Russia is known as a period of 'proto-industrialization', when the prerequisites for industrial development were being established: 'By 1804, manufacturing industry had nearly 2,402 major enterprises; these increased to 15,388 by 1860' (Russia, 2003, 417–18). New legislation in the 1830s on stock corporations paved the way for some growth in this form of business organization.

The question of encouraging the industrial development of Russia was debated within bureaucratic circles between supporters of free trade and protectionists. Many free traders argued that Russia could not at this time develop the capital necessary for a significant development of industry; the country had its own path of development and should remain an agricultural country. The protectionists argued that Russia would be able to generate sufficient capital for industrialization and recommended a policy of protective tariffs. Most of the proponents of industrialization have been viewed as political liberals because they advocated reforms usually identified with liberalism (Blackwell, 1968, 123–24). However the financial backwardness of Russia and especially the monetary instability associated with the ruble, placed some serious obstacles in the way of industrial development. Most of the small number of state banks confined their operations to providing credit for landlords, which often left trade and industry without finance. The necessity or otherwise of financial reforms was thus at the centre of the debate between government officials.

Russian monetary thought as a distinct entity began to develop initially within such reforming ideas, which appeared in different kinds of projects designed to improve the monetary system. In these projects, politicians of the nineteenth century such as Mikhail Speransky, Nikolai Mordvinov, Nikolai Bunge and others, tried to substantiate theoretically their proposals for the reorganization of monetary circulation and the expansion of credit and banking in Russia. They frequently based their ideas on the most advanced thinking of the West. While doing so they directed their theoretical efforts to the solution of concrete practical tasks connected with overcoming the economic backwardness of Russia, and thus most of their works addressed specific policy problems, as will be seen in what follows.

Speransky's Plan for Monetary Reform

Russia's financial situation during the first decade of the reign of Alexander I (1801–25) has usually been described as a period of monetary crisis, the origins of which went back to the reign of Catherine II (1762–96). In this period the issue of paper currency was, apart from foreign loans, the main source of treasury revenue – 'expedient, copied from Western Europe, and with equally unfortunate effects' (Raeff, 1957, 84). The state budget was thus in permanent deficit.

The first Russian paper money units – the assignats (or paper rubles) – were issued in 1769 as a short-term measure of war finance, but nevertheless they became regular policy. The Russian state continued to print assignats as new wars broke out, the amount of paper money in circulation eventually reaching 800 million rubles. The result of this policy was a continuous decline in their value, which by 1815 had fallen against silver by nearly four-fifths. As Marc Raeff noted, this policy was a result of a naïve conception of the role of the assignats that prevailed at the time. In order to avoid an economic collapse, the Russian government was forced to take radical measures. In 1806 the Emperor ordered the establishment of a special Commission for Financial Affairs, which was given the task of preparing a comprehensive plan for implementing a more sustainable monetary policy. In 1809 Mikhail Speransky was appointed to the Commission and under his energetic leadership new guidelines for financial policy were elaborated.

Mikhail Mikhailovich Speransky (1772–1839) was a political thinker, an economist, a statesman and also a Count (from 1839). He was the main architect of Russian liberal reforms during the reign of Alexander I, as he wrote the bulk of the proposals for improving the economic and political system that were developed at this time: 'The proposals and arguments for the reform of Russia's monetary and financial condition, which Speransky presented, marked a turning point in the history of Russian financial administration and thinking on economic matters …' (Raeff, 1957, 88). He is also considered to be the first Russian theorist of law.

Speransky collaborated with several outstanding political economists of liberal persuasion, such as Professor M.A. Balugiansky (1769–1847), the future rector of the University of St Petersburg, and Professor Ludwig von Jacob (1759–1827) from the University of Kharkov. Their combined efforts provided the theoretical framework for Speransky's Financial Plan ('Plan Finansov', 1810).[1] In this plan

1 First published in 1885 by A.N. Kulomzin (editor) in *Sbornik Imperatorskogo Russkogo Istoricheskogo obschestva*, vol. XLV, 1–72.

Speransky proposed a programme for a fundamental reorganization of the Russian financial system. He advocated two courses of action: policies of a long-term nature, to be supplemented by short-term measures, which must be taken immediately to prepare the way for an eventual solution of the monetary crisis.

Speransky's 'Plan Finansov' consisted of two basic parts and seven chapters, and had the following structure:

Part 1. Temporary financial arrangements for the year 1810.
Chapter 1. General principles
Chapter 2. On balancing state receipts and expenses for the year 1810

Part 2. Permanent financial arrangements for subsequent years.
Chapter 1. On expenses
Chapter 2. On revenues
Chapter 3. Theory of monetary and credit systems
Chapter 4. Reorganization of the monetary and credit systems
Chapter 5. On financial administration

Speransky proposed to work for the realization of three concrete goals: (1) the redemption of the assignats currently in circulation; (2) the establishment of a bank based on silver; (3) the introduction of a sound monetary system (Speransky, 1885, Plan Finansov, Sec 135, 55).

At the beginning of his long-term policy, he outlined that he wanted faith in the economy of the nation to be restored. To this end, the government should cease the issue of new assignats and all paper money in circulation should be recognized as 'a state debt on the security of national wealth' (Speransky, 1885, Plan Finansov, Sec. 38, 39, 11). This approach marked a new departure for the economic thinking of the Russian government. From the time of Catherine II, paper money was treated as 'real money' and accepted in the same manner as precious metals, since it was the common view that paper currency actually 'created money'. Instead Speransky pointed out that: 'Assignats are paper based on suppositions. Not having any intrinsic value, they are nothing else but hidden debts' (Speransky, 1885, Plan Finansov, 38). A clear recognition by government of the assignats as a debt, and the assumption of the obligation to redeem it, were very important steps in preparing the way for a stable financial system.

Speransky proposed to float a ten-year loan of 25 million rubles, the earned interest on which would serve to build up a redemption fund. In the event of failure it could be complemented by state lotteries (Speransky, 1885, Plan Finansov, Secs 143–47, 155–56, 158–60, 58–60). For the administration of the loan and redemption fund, Speransky suggested the creation of a special state bank, with its capital based on silver. The shareholders, proportionate to their participation, would manage the new institution. A portion of the bank's shares was to be held by the government, and the rest by private individuals. To forestall objections to his plan, Speransky cited the examples of the Bank of England and the Bank of France (Speransky, 1885, Plan Finansov, 64, footnote).

The next step to be taken was a reduction in the quantity of the assignats in circulation by stopping any further issues. To cover state expenditures and the cost of redeeming the assignats, new taxes were unavoidable and in this regard Speransky suggested the sale of state domains to those peasants who currently lived and worked on them. This would also increase the number of landowners and enable the levy of a general land tax as a first source of new revenue (Speransky, 1885, Plan Finansov, Sec 120–21, 26, Sec 166, 62.)

To achieve the goals of the long-term financial reforms, it was necessary to improve the system of financial administration. To this end, Speransky proposed to introduce a standard schedule of the state's receipts and expenditures. He divided all expenses into two groups: ordinary and extraordinary: 'In no case should new expenditures be incurred if no equivalent source of revenue has been found for them first' (Speransky, 1885, Plan Finansov, Sec 46, 13). For extraordinary expenses the government should have at its disposal, instead of currency reserves, the means of obtaining additional revenue. Such a suggestion, extending to public finance the principles of economic rationality that prevailed in private enterprises, was a new departure for the Russian Emperor and had never before been stated so clearly (Raeff, 1957, 93).

Speransky asserted that the only ideal type of money was silver and credit notes based on silver. These should be the standard of measure and accounting for all transactions, both private and public, instead of the fluctuating assignats and multiple additional currencies (Speransky, 1885, Plan Finansov, 44). Speransky consequently proposed the creation of private banks based on silver. To regulate the flow of credit, these banks would be allowed to purchase and sell precious metals. He outlined the following advantages that would follow the introduction of such banks:

1. The circulation of credit notes from private banks would reduce the domestic need for silver, thus quickening the rate of note circulation and as a result, the larger mass would balance the burden of foreign credit;
2. The circulation of these credit notes would also diminish the need for small change, releasing more copper for sale on the commodity markets (Speransky, 1885, Plan Finansov, 51).

Speransky believed that credit notes played a very important role in speeding up the rate of circulation of monetary capital. He wrote: 'In every state, and in particular in a state which has more capital in goods than in money, the task of true economy demands a quickening of the circulation of monetary capital, so that even small amounts when consolidated make possible the fastest and largest turnover; i.e. true economy demands that metal specie be represented by notes of credit' (Speransky, 1885, Plan Finansov, 31).

Speransky's Financial Plan was subsequently approved by the Emperor, after it had received a favourable recommendation from the Department of State Economy of the Council of State and a series of legislative measures were issued in 1810. The assignats were recognized as state debt and some other measures proposed by Speransky were adopted. However the implementation of the Financial Plan met some difficulties because of the confrontational policy of the Minister of Finance

D.A. Guriev, who directed the Ministry of Finance from 1810 to 1823. Hence, despite the Emperor's adoption of Speransky's proposals, most elements of the Financial Plan were not implemented. Speransky's lack of popularity among the landed nobility, whose interests had been challenged, led to his eventual dismissal from office in March 1812. While in exile Speransky was made governor of Penza (1816) and Siberia (1819). He returned to St Petersburg later in 1821 and was appointed a member of the State Council.

Speransky's plan, calling for the creation of a new silver ruble backed by metal deposits, eventually became a reality during the currency reform of 1839–43 that was initiated by Emperor Nicholas I (1825–55), and carried out by the Minister of Finance Egor F. Kankrin. After Kankrin's reform the 'credit ruble', freely convertible into silver, replaced ruble-assignats in the ratio of 1:3.5.

Speransky took an active part in discussion of the issues related to the preparation of this monetary reform. In the mid-1830s, he entered into official correspondence with the Minister of Finance (Kankrin) on the subject of monetary circulation. In his last essay entitled 'On monetary circulation', forwarded to Kankrin in January 1839 (less than a month before his death), Speransky presented his ideas in their most complete form. This essay was published in 1895 under the full title: 'Memorandum on monetary circulation by Count Speransky with comments by Count Kankrin'. The essay contained not only practical recommendations on replacing the assignats with credit notes, but it also discussed some theoretical aspects of monetary circulation.

Speransky wrote: 'The wealth of the state is created and increased by labour. Labour grows and expands by way of the free circulation of its products. Labour products circulate by way of exchange. This exchange is carried out in the form of barter, which occurs only infrequently, and mainly through money' (Speransky, 1895, 5). He noted that in no country could metallic money alone satisfy all demands of the private and public sectors, which was why the necessity had arisen of having auxiliary means of exchange, such as the assignats and credit notes. Speransky thus understood the importance of credit to the acceleration of monetary circulation and to providing the economy with monetary resources.

Speransky's ideas on monetary circulation were progressive for his time. They have received high appreciation from Mark Raeff, who wrote:

> For his time and place, Speransky's emphatic assertion that, in the absence of expanding productivity or national income, assignats were a state debt, a hidden domestic loan that had to be repaid, was quite 'revolutionary'. The only important economic thinker of the 18th century who had had a similar understanding of the nature of assignats had been Richard Cantillon ... Speransky shares with the latter the honour of defending a most sophisticated, modern, and accurate understanding of the principles which underlie the mechanism of credit and money circulation. It puts him above the popular economists of his time and brings him close to the important views expressed in England at about the same time by only a few specialists (Raeff, 1957, 99).

Mordvinov and Private Banking

In 1810, the Commission for Financial Affairs was placed under the direct supervision of the Department for State Economy of the newly organized Council of State. The head of the department was Admiral Nikolai Mordvinov, a close friend of Speransky's. He was one of the state officials who contributed most significantly to Russian economic thought and practice in this period.

Nikolai Semionovich Mordvinov (1754–1845), an outstanding Russian statesman, was the author of numerous proposals for improving different spheres of the economy such as manufacture, the monetary system and the state budget. He was one of the most prolific of the Russian political economists in this period.[2] From 1823–40, Mordvinov was President of the first Russian economic society, the Imperial Free Economic Society. He was highly educated and claimed command of six foreign languages. According to one scholar: 'Although Mordvinov has long been recognized in Russia as an important economic thinker, his relative obscurity abroad is unfortunate' (McCaffray, 2000, 573).

In January 1774, Mordvinov was sent to England for three years to improve his skills in navigation. There he was imbued with the spirit of English science and a respect for English institutions. During his stay, Adam Smith published his famous treatise *An Inquiry into the Nature and Causes of the Wealth of Nations* (1776), which influenced Mordvinov greatly, and made him a follower of Smith. This was apparent from in his later writings on financial matters (Ikonnikov, 1873, 4). Another English thinker to whom Mordvinov was a strong adherent was Jeremy Bentham. As a follower of Bentham, Mordvinov supported the idea of the importance of private property, which he considered a tremendous stimulus to the accumulation of wealth. For the well-being of the state, he believed it necessary to strengthen private property rights (Gnevushev, 1904, 56).

Mordvinov began to present his views on the management of finance as early as year one of Alexander I's rule. In 1801 he presented to Alexander a draft of a plan for a 'state bank for stimulating labour' to be backed by bullion, which would issue money and assist entrepreneurs ('Regulations for a Labour-Stimulating Bank', 1801). Being certain of the future implementation of this project, Mordvinov wrote a draft manifesto in the character of an appeal to Russian society. The project was based on the idea that money had no value other than its relationship to human labour and that only people's success in the production of goods to satisfy human needs was true wealth. He noted that many countries, without having sufficient gold and silver, abounded in the goods necessary for life and were therefore in reality quite rich (Mordvinov, 1945, 48).

A state bank for stimulating labour would, through the assistance of loans, inspire diligence in industry as a source of wealth, and thus contribute to the development of the country's productive forces. Besides issuing loans, this bank would provide technical counselling, support new initiatives and publish information on new inventions. It would also have its own printing shop, library and a vocational school.

2 Mordvinov's writings fill more than nine of the ten volumes of V.A. Bil'basov, *Arkhiv Grafov Mordvinovykh* (St Petersburg, 1901–1903).

In Mordvinov's opinion, a state bank for stimulating labour would help to provide a new economic rennaissance for the whole of Russia. From 1802 until 1837 he repeated his call for the creation of this type of bank, but the project was never fulfilled.[3]

As Head of the Department for State Economy in 1810–12, Mordvinov was a key political figure in the implementation of the monetary reforms outlined by Speransky in his Financial Plan. Mordvinov constantly criticized Minister of Finance Guriev for his unlimited issue of assignats to cover the budgetary deficit. He considered the assignats to be the worst feature of the Russian financial system and worked on plans to annul them, expressing this opinion in a paper entitled 'On the devastating consequences for the Treasury and private properties resulting from erroneous measures in the management of the State Treasury' of 1816. He saw that the excessive issue of assignats resulted in an equivalent reduction in everyone's income and, like Speransky, he viewed them as a concealed tax.

On several occasions, Mordvinov pointed to the necessity of protection and patronage for developing industry and trade in Russia. He proposed the introduction of tariffs to defend national industry against competition from more developed Western countries. He formulated his views on this matter in a work called 'Some considerations on the subject of manufactures in Russia and on the tariff' of 1815. The reason for the publication of this paper was connected to the appearance of Heinrich Storch's book *Cours d'economie politique ou exposition des principes qui determinent la prosperite des nations* (Vols 1–6, St Petersburg, 1815). In his paper Mordvinov entered into a debate with Storch about the correct path for Russia's economic development. According to Storch: 'for Russia's benefit it is necessary to give to the richest countries the rights of manufacturing and trading' (Mordvinov, 1945, 109). Mordvinov argued instead that the opinion that the Russian nation lacked the monetary capital necessary to establish factories was unfounded. Everything that was found in the country was built in a much shorter time than in other countries, and yet it required more capital. Mordvinov was sure that Russia would have enough capital available for building all the necessary factories 'as soon as all the obstacles, internal and external, are removed to allow the free movement of capital and its profitable use' (Mordvinov, 1945, 108–109).

Mordvinov's most significant idea was that Russia must follow in Great Britain's footsteps and become a manufacturing country, and that this should be the main priority of state economic policy. Thus to this end he favoured state intervention in national economic life. One commentator wrote that: 'The Russian liberalism of which Mordvinov was a prototype embraced individual economic liberty and property rights as well as energetic state support of the country's economic development ... his rejection of *laissez-faire* economics distinguishes Mordvinov from Smith' (McCaffray, 2000, 582). Another suggested that Mordvinov became both a follower and a critic of Smith (Blackwell, 1968, 133). Normano called Mordvinov the 'Alexander Hamilton of Russia' (Normano, 1945, 21–22).

3 Mordvinov's project for a state bank for stimulating labour was published later in the journal *Russkaia starina*, 1872, vol. 5 no 1, 43–61.

As Mordvinov saw it, the lack of sufficient capital in the country was one of the most serious problems hampering the development of Russian industry. He insisted that there was much private capital in Russia that still remained idle because of a lack of credit institutions. If followed, his recommendations could have relieved the situation by the establishment of more banks. He devoted a separate paper to this matter in which he emphasized the necessity of the widespread promotion of banking in Russia ('Thoughts on the benefits that may follow the establishment of private banks in the provinces').[4]

It should be noted that in fact, the history of organized banking in Russia began in the 1750s, when a small variety of government-operated banking institutions had been established. The main type consisted of banks that made loans to the land-owning nobility. In 1754 a Bank for the Nobility was established, which in 1786 was transformed into a Loan Bank. In 1754 a Bank for Merchants appeared in St Petersburg, which ceased to exist in 1782. In 1786 the Assignatsionni Bank was organized, while the State Commercial Bank was created in 1817.

Characteristically, Mordvinov began his work on private banks with a mention of the tremendous importance of money in the life of the state. He wrote: 'The description of everyday life through the centuries testifies to the fact that the welfare of the people was closely connected with the art of money management. Of all the powers of the state, money should be recognized as pre-eminent. It creates and multiplies abundance and wealth … Money nourishes labour, industry, and science …' (Mordvinov, 1945, 121).

Mordvinov noted that improvements in the monetary system should consist not in the multiplication of currency issued, but in the management of turnover required for commercial deals and for 'keeping people's profitable labour in full function' (Mordvinov, 1945, 126). He attached great importance to thrift and moderate expense. To inspire such thrift, it was necessary to open specialized savings institutions or 'public treasury vaults', which would always be open to accept and return deposits. With the existence of such institutions 'no part of the currency lies idle in trunks, but circulates actively and increases private and public profit' (Mordvinov, 1945, 126).

Mordvinov also paid attention to the fact that such institutions should be established in all the provinces, as he proposed to establish 52 banks instead of one Loan Bank. He wrote: 'One bank only in the country cannot manage the affairs of industry and commerce in the whole state and cannot provide monetary turnover with its due impetus' (Mordvinov, 1945, 127). He pointed out that: 'money in a big and populous city mostly feeds entertainment and luxury, and passes through a great number of hands … At the same time in small towns and big villages money goes directly into the hands of those engaged in useful and profitable work, and every ruble is applied to private and public improvement and enrichment. Money, divided

4 The very first publication of this work in the Russian language appeared in 1813, soon after the termination of the war with Napoleon. At that time 25 copies of the book were printed which were distributed among a narrow circle of Russian statesmen and some western European scholars. The book was then published in 1817 (2nd edn, with additions) and in 1829 (3rd edn) (Mordvinov, 1945, 253).

between all parts of the state in proportion to the needs and demands of each one, equally nourishes the whole body' (Mordvinov, 1945, 128).

Mordvinov suggested that it would be expedient to establish the proposed banks as private institutions. He held that it was not possible to rely solely on government finance and to seek funds 'only among its treasures'. Neither could government dispose of such sums that would be required for securing private and public welfare. Making general improvements in Russia thus depended on the efforts of private individuals, and in this regard he wrote that: 'every province should have its own special bank and every resident of the province should contribute to the growth of the capital of such a bank' (Mordvinov, 1945, 129).

This influx of free monetary capital into banks would, in Mordvinov's opinion, encourage the expansion of monetary turnover and accelerate the transition from a barter economy to a monetary one. Banks would assist in accumulating the monetary capital of each layer of society, such as the peasantry and craftsmen, as well as the 'ancestral capital' of the nobility. But, for the country's prosperity, it was not sufficient only to create capital, it was necessary to channel it correctly. To achieve this purpose, capital: 'should be distributed around the entire territory of the state … where its application may be most beneficial' (Mordvinov, 1945, 144). In addition, Mordvinov took banks to be social institutions, fulfilling not only monetary functions, but playing a very important role in educating the entire nation.

After the establishment of provincial banks a source of great income would be opened up: 'Considerable capital will come into circulation which until now has remained idle and doesn't do any good, either private or public. This capital, scattered and transient throughout the whole state, will be quite large after such consolidation' (Mordvinov, 1945, 150). Mordvinov believed in the creative power of capital and approached it as an important factor in the manufacture of wealth: 'All the estates, all the people's positions, their work, trades, commerce, will be made easier everywhere and will receive encouragement for beneficial and profitable exercises' (Mordvinov, 1945, 149). However, it should be noted that Mordvinov understood capital to be the result of saving, that is, as the sum of interest on bank deposits.

Mordvinov's proposal for the creation of private banks did not elicit a response among the provincial nobility and received no support from the Council of State. The number of the nobility involved in entrepreneurship was not great in Russia at this time, as economic development was being hindered by feudal relations. Although industry and commerce had a certain level of development, the country's economy was mainly agrarian. Under these conditions, banking could not develop to its full extent.

Mordvinov's work on banks provoked debate in the Russian literature of the time. One Russian journal, *Dukh Zhurnalov* (*Spirit of Journals*), published in 1818 a critical review, where an anonymous writer expressed his strong doubts over Mordvinov's project. He wrote that the project seduced the imagination: 'Fifty-two banks instead of one! Huge capital!' In his opinion, the error of the author of the project consisted in taking into account General Arithmetic instead of Political Arithmetic, which was not the same. The lack of available capital not only made the foundation of 52 provincial banks of little use, but also incurred additional maintenance costs that could be higher than profits received. However the author of the review did agree that the creation of private banks in some big cities would be useful and as trade and industry grew, they could be expanded into other cities.[5]

Mordvinov's work on private banks was translated into Italian and published in Milan in 1824. The review of the publisher from the Italian library, Melchiorre Gioja,[6] noted the novelty of the ideas it contained, in harmony with those that were later developed by French and German economists (Mordvinov, 1945, 184–90). As a general evaluation, Normano wrote on this subject: 'Mordvinov's propaganda for credit organization and his belief in its creative power anticipated the later theories of MacLeod' (Normano, 1945, 22).

Bunge on the Importance of Credit

In the middle of the nineteenth century, the Russian credit system was still represented by a number of government credit institutions. The capital accumulated in them was used for loans to the government to cover budgetary deficits and also for loans to the nobility, who used their estates as collateral. At this time in many European countries, there were already prominent business banks that financed industrial development, and the experience of these countries testified to the significant role of credit in economic progress. Many Western scholars proclaimed credit to be the single most important lever for the development of the national economy.

In Russia in the second half of the 1850s, the discussion of private banking was renewed. However, if at the beginning of the nineteenth century the interest in private banking was developed under the influence of English institutions, decades later a great impulse to the discussion was made by French socialist theories, particularly those of Henri de Saint-Simon. Russian economic literature extensively discussed the activities of the Paris joint-stock bank 'Crèdit Mobilier' (established in 1852), which became the practical implementation of Saint-Simonian 'credit dreams': 'Belief in credit and awareness of its importance had reached Russia … "Credit Mobilier" became a slogan of the epoch' (Levin, 1917, 76–79).

At this time, Russian liberal economists like I.K. Babst, V.P. Bezobrazov, N.Kh. Bunge, Y.A. Gagemeister and I.V. Vernadsky propagated the advantages of private credit (Levin, 1917, 79). Bunge and Bezobrazov were the first to develop the theory of credit in Russia. As Konstantin Hattenberger wrote in 1887: 'Credit hardly existed in Russia, and the nature of credit was not understood. The whole literature on the subject consisted of two translations of the well-known works of Coquelin and Courcelle-Seneuil. Bunge and Bezobrazov … were the first to treat the theory of credit in Russia' (H., 1887, 242–43).

Nikolai Khristyanovich Bunge (1823–95) was a well-known economist, professor and rector of Kiev University. He took part in the preparations for the Great Reforms of Alexander II (1855–81) and was a member of the commissions of 1859–60 for the abolition of serfdom and for the transformation of the credit system. At the beginning of the 1880s, Bunge was called upon to serve in the government,

5 *Dukh Zhurnalov,* 1818, vol. XXVII, 15–21.

6 Fascicolo CIII, luglio 1824 della Biblioteca Italiana da Melchiorre Gioja.

where he held the posts of deputy Minister of Finance (1880–81), then Minister of Finance (1881–86), and then Chairman of the Committee of Ministers (1887–95). As Minister of Finance, Bunge implemented a number of reforms aimed at modernizing the Russian economy, and he advocated measures to strengthen the Russian banking system. Bunge was the first university professor who was invited to hold the post of Minister of Finance. He was appreciated for his breadth of mind and for his awareness of the necessity of financial reform (Sudeikin, 1895, 2).

Bunge left a great number of published works on economic issues, including the subjects of money and banking. As early as his doctoral thesis on 'The Theory of Credit' (1852), Bunge wrote about the importance of credit for the rational use of capital, for the stimulation of the development of productive forces and for easing social controversies: 'Credit promotes the distribution of economic forces between different sectors of industry. Thanks to credit, idle free capital is channeled to where the demand for it is higher, to where it produces the maximum economic benefit' (Bunge, 1852, 141–42).

Bunge noted the important role of credit in the creation of new means of circulation, which not only helped to cut circulation costs, but also created a new basis for it (Bunge, 1852, 156). He wrote that credit-based means of circulation, such as deposit notes, bonds and especially bills, differed from other means of exchange in that they were created through circulation, and their value was purely representative (Bunge, 1852, 157). In his opinion, credit-based means of circulation had important advantages: (1) as they existed due to circulation their quantity was constant in accordance with real demand for the means of circulation; and (2) they existed until the credit deal which generated them was over, until the credit was realized (Bunge, 1852, 157).

Bunge was sure that credit would continue to develop and that exchange would be made by means of credit more often. He quoted Adam Smith, who compared money to a road that served to deliver products to the market, but did not produce anything itself (Bunge, 1852, 173–74). Bunge developed this comparison thus: 'Credit does not only lay out an air route, does not only eradicate the friction unavoidable with monetary turnover, but by taking specie out of circulation, it replaces heavy carts which carry products, i.e. coins, with Icarus's wings – paper credit notes' (Bunge, 1852, 177).

In this respect Bunge outlined three types of exchange: natural exchange, monetary exchange and credit exchange. He noted that credit transactions appeared with the expansion of the division of labour, being a necessary supplement to monetary circulation and a precondition for the further development of social economy (Bunge, 1852, 11–14). Here his thinking was similar to that of the German economist Bruno Hildebrand, who formulated the concept of a 'credit economy' as the most advanced form of economic life.

Bunge paid great attention to an analysis of different theories of credit, which he divided into three trends. The first theories of credit were formed by John Law and Isaac de Pinto under mercantilist influence. The second trend was represented by three groups of writers: (1) Richard Price and Mordvinov; (2) Smith and his followers; and (3) Storch and Coquelin. Their credit theories were developed according to the ideas of 'industrial freedom and private interest', but were not homogeneous.

Counter to these were the proponents of the school of industrial order, J.C.L de Sismondi and August Čieszkowsky, who comprised the third trend. Bunge noted that Čieszkowsky's system of credit had the same importance in the theory of credit as protectionism had for trade policy (Bunge, 1852, 181–82).

Bunge considered in detail the proposals of Mordvinov to enlarge the capital base of the country through the establishment of private banks, expressing a number of critical comments on this project. He wrote that, at a time when capital had achieved its leading place in economic theory and its profit potential was acknowledged, it seemed quite natural to think that capital grew as a result of the accumulation of compound interest. These ideas found their supporters in Richard Price and Mordvinov (Bunge, 1952, 209–10). Price wrote that: 'one penny, put out at our Saviour's birth to 5 per cent compound interest, would, before this time, have increased to a greater sum than would be contained in a hundred and fifty million Earths, all solid gold' (Price, 1774, 19). Bunge called Mordvinov a follower of Price, as his project for a new financial system was based on the idea of the accumulation of compound interest.

However Bunge stressed that capital was not formed by itself, through compound interest, but actually with the involvement of labour (Bunge, 1852, 212). In his opinion the ownership of capital simply for growth purposes led to limitations in its use. He called this approach 'utopian', as capital was being considered as something separate, independent of the force that really created it. Bunge underlined that: 'from the private, economic viewpoint, they should ... consider the increase of [capital] as the result of man's productive activity, and not as a result of compound interest accumulation' (Bunge, 1852, 214). Nevertheless, he appreciated Mordvinov's proposal for the establishment of private banks, as through them it was not the issue of funds, but accumulation of capital, which produced the enrichment of the state.

In a number of articles published at the end of the 1850s, Bunge called for the abandonment of the system of government credit. He believed that government banks would always remain bureaucratic institutions and would never be able to compete with the energy and expertise of private interest. In his paper 'The importance of industrial partnerships and the conditions for their dissemination' published in 1857–58, he called the joint-stock form of private property organization the most developed and efficient, while joint-stock societies themselves were 'a happy combination of individual and public activities' (Bunge, 1857, part 1, 16–17). He wrote that: 'the appearance of joint-stock bank partnerships would free our production from stagnation and ... would give profitable assignment to those funds for which our government can hardly find a placement' (Bunge, 1858, part 3, 40–41).

The need for a banking system designed to stimulate economic development was clearly formulated during the credit reform of 1859–60. The first Russian joint-stock bank was established in St Petersburg in 1864 and seven more such banks appeared during the next five years. A boom in the foundation of joint-stock companies occurred during the period from 1870–73, although it had some negative consequences. Thus, the Russian government had to take some restrictive measures and issued a law that prohibited the founding of new joint-stock banks. Bunge responded to this with an article in which he expressed his thoughts on the principles of banking policy.

Bunge agreed with the opinion that the principles of *laissez-faire* were not applicable to banking, which required instead a certain degree of regulation. He wrote that: 'Banking freedom is fruitful only where the majority of people are able to make an informed judgment on banking activity and … with a true appreciation of the consequences of their activity ... banks can easily be perverted into a means of speculation with people's savings. That is why the role of the state cannot be limited to a non-interference policy and why it is not possible to manage without banking regulations' (Bunge, 1874, 69).

However the juridical organization of the economy brought additional practical difficulties. Bunge admitted that: 'Law should correspond with the level of social and economic development of society' (Bunge, 1874, 70). The need for banking law in Russia appeared after the banking reform of 1859–60, when it was decided to allow the foundation of private banks – commercial, mortgage and land banks. The State Bank of the Russian Empire was created in 1860, becoming the central financial institution of the country. When Bunge had began his activities as Minister of Finance (1881–86) under Alexander III (1881–94), the development of the Russian banking system was one of his main concerns and a number of prominent transformations in the sphere of credit and banks were connected to his name.

Bunge attached great importance to an improvement in savings capacity, and the expansion of the savings bank network became a part of the restructuring of the entire credit system. In his university textbook *Politseiskoye Pravo* ('Police Law'), Bunge wrote that by keeping small savings, 'the savings banks acquire tremendous importance – they develop the spirit of foresight, prepare conditions for the emergence of public banks and very often serve as a transitional step to them' (Bunge, 1877, vol. 2, 221). Bunge deemed it desirable that savings banks should not only concentrate on savings, but should issue loans promoting the development of credit. In this respect he gave preference to rural savings and loan partnerships, which began to appear in 1865.

Bunge's most notable achievements as Minister of Finance were his contributions to the expansion of commercial credit and his reform of the banking system. During his administration he invested a great deal of effort in establishing new banks and reforming some others. He thought that a nation's rate of economic growth was related to the ability of the banking system to provide industrial and agricultural producers with available credit. By the end of the 1880s, the Russian Empire had a variety of credit institutions. These included the State Bank, joint-stock commercial banks, municipal banks, mutual credit associations, banks of private commercial credit, a number of small co-operative banks, state savings banks, government pawnshops and mortgage banks. In 1883 Bunge also organized the Peasants' Land Bank to enable peasants to purchase land.

Bunge can be seen as a 'managerial modernizer' who played a significant role in developing the Russian credit system, and in promoting liberal reforms in different spheres of the Russian economy. He initiated modern fiscal reforms in Russia, for example he introduced a five per cent income tax on stock and bonds, increased import duties in order to stimulate the domestic metal industry, and endeavoured to prepare the way for the return to specie payment. He also took the first steps in preparing the monetary reform carried out by Sergei Witte in 1895–97. He began the accumulation of a gold fund and advocated the legalization of private dealing in gold. Bunge also promoted labour legislation in Russia and introduced a system of factory inspection (Struve, [1930] 1957, 68). Bunge could thus be called the main architect of the liberal reforms of the last decades of the nineteenth century.

However, the period of liberal hopes turned out to be a short one, as Emperor Alexander III did not support the reform policy of his father, Alexander II. He declared a 'new course' and formed a government of conservative views. Despite Bunge being called to work for this government, he soon found himself a foreign body in its structure. Conservatives set about revising the laws introduced in the 1860s by the former government, and started a campaign against the party of liberal bureaucrats. By the middle of 1880, Bunge remained the only liberal minister among government officials. In December 1886 he had to resign, but from 1 January 1887, he was appointed Chairman of the Committee of Ministers. He was seen subsequently as a liberal minister who worked during Alexander III's rule, and who left a deep mark on government policy at the end of the century (Stepanov, 1998, 4). Mikhail Tugan-Baranovsky described Bunge as one of the two most truly remarkable men who occupied the post of Minister of Finance (Tugan-Baranovsky, 1915, 146).

Conclusion

Russian financial history has its own national peculiarity, which left a certain mark on the development of Russian monetary thought. As William Blackwell wrote: 'At the beginning of the nineteenth century, there was little evidence in Russia of the commercial and financial activities which are associated with a modern business economy and the growth of industry … Currency was unstable and scarce, particularly outside the main cities. Only a handful of small state banks and one stock company were in existence to facilitate borrowing and investment. The commercial and financial revolution which would hasten the transformation of this backward system into a more mature business economy had to await the emancipation of the serfs and the growth of banking and railroads which was to come in the late nineteenth century' (Blackwell, 1968, 72). The emancipation of the serfs in 1861 was the landmark separating capitalist from feudal Russia.

However, in the first 60 years of the nineteenth century, there were 'important modifications in the traditional pattern' which 'paved some of the way for the emergence of capitalism in Russia' (Blackwell, 1968, 72). These changes required an adequate monetary and credit system, which was a main concern of Russian government officials. Some of them had liberal views and advanced reforming ideas about the financial improvements to the state. These Russian monetary reformers – Speransky, Mordvinov and Bunge – had progressive views on money and banking, and expended great effort in the financial modernization of the country. They were enlightened thinkers in imperial Russia and promoters of the financial innovations of their time. At the same time they were sure of their belief in the leading role of the state in the national economy.

Holding prominent posts in government, the Russian reformers acted primarily in the interest of the government, whilst being aware of the necessity of achieving a balance between private and public interests. They attached great importance to the promotion of industry and commerce as the chief spheres of activity for private initiative. They considered the well-being of the state to be directly dependent on the well-being of private persons and saw private property as a tremendous impetus to the creation of wealth. Their views reflect definite stages in the development of liberal ideas in the sphere of economic thought. The liberal thinking of that epoch was stimulated by Adam Smith's political economy and by the philosophy of the French and German Enlightenment.

Developing different issues of financial policy, Russian monetary reformers urged the necessity of adjusting monetary circulation, the expansion of credit and the development of private banks. Some of their proposals remained only as liberal dreams, but they still left a mark in the history of Russian economic thought. They contributed to the formation of a so-called 'bureaucratic direction in Russian economic science'.[7] At the very beginning of Russian industrialization, their projects promoted awareness by the imperial government of the important role of monetary institutions in the economic development of the nation.

References

Barnett, Vincent (2005) *A History of Russian Economic Thought*. London: Routledge.

Blackwell, William L. (1968) *The Beginnings of Russian Industrialization 1800–1860*. Princeton, New Jersey.

———. (1970) *The Industrialization of Russia: An Historical Perspective*. New York.

Bliumin, I.G. (1940) *Ocherki ekonomicheskoi mysli v Rossii v pervoi polovine XIX veka*. Moscow-Leningrad.

Borovoi, S.Ia. (1958) *Kredit i banki v Rossii*. Moscow.

Bunge, N. Kh. (1852) *Teoriya kredita*. Kiev.

———. (1857–58) *Znachenie promyshlennykh tovarischestv i uslovia ih rasprostranenia*. St Petersburg, part 1 (1857), part 2, 3 (1858).

———. (1874) 'Bankovskiye zakony i bankovskaya politika', *Sbornik gosudarstvennykh znaniy*, tom 1, St Petersburg.

———. (1877) *Politseiskoye Pravo*, vol. 2. Kiev.

'Bunge Nikolay Khristyanovich', (1988) in *The New Encyclopaedia Britannica*. vol. 2. Micropaedia, Encyclopedia Britannica Inc.

Gnevushev, A.M. (1904) *Politiko-ekonomicheskie vzgliady grafa N.S. Mordvinova*. Kiev.

H., (1887) 'Economic Thought in Russia', *Quarterly Journal of Economics,* vol. 2, no 1, (October).

Ikonnikov, V.S. (1873) *Graf N.S. Mordvinov.* St Petersburg.

7 Exposition of the main characteristics of the bureaucratic direction in Russian economic science as a particular view was the main task of Chris Monday in his PhD dissertation *Economic outlook of the Russian bureaucratic elite during the epoch of the Emperor Nicholai I* (Monday, 2004).

Korf, M.A. (1861) *Zhizn grafa Speranskogo*. vol. 1, St Petersburg.

Levin, I.I. (1917) *Aktsionernye kommercheskie banki v Rossii*. Petrograd.

McCaffray, Susan R. (2000) 'What Should Russia Be? Patriotism and Political Economy in the Thought of N.S. Mordvinov', *Slavic Review*, vol. 59, no 3 (Autumn).

Miakotin, V. (1963 [1934]) 'Speransky, Mikhail Mikhailovich', *Encyclopaedia of the Social Sciences*, Editor-in-Chief Edwin R.A. Seligman, New York, vol. 14.

Monday, Chris (2004) '*Ekonomicheskoye vozzrenie biurokraticheskoy eliti Rossiiskoi imperii Nikolaevskoi epokhi (na primere Kankrina)*'. PhD thesis, St Petersburg.

Mordvinov, N.S. (1945) *Izbrannye proizvedeniia*, Moscow.

Morozov, F. (1945) 'N.S. Mordvinov kak economist: Kratkie biograficheskie svedenia', in Mordvinov, N.S. *Izbrannye proizvedeniia*, Moscow.

Normano, J.F. (1945) *The Spirit of Russian Economics*, John Day, New York.

Pesda, John Lawrence (1971) '*N.K. Bunge and Russian Economic Development*', PhD. Diss., Kent State University.

Price, Richard. (1774) *An Appeal to the Public on the Subject of the National Debt*, 2nd edn, London.

Raeff, Marc (1957) *Michael Speransky. Statesman of Imperial Russia,* The Hague: Martinus Nijhoff.

'Russia', (2003) in *The Oxford Encyclopedia of Economic History,* Editor in Chief Joel Mokyr, vol. 4, Oxford.

Russian Economists (*XIX – nachalo XX veka*) (1998) L.A. Zubchenko and L.I. Zaitseva (eds), Moscow: IE RAN.

Snow, George E. (1981) *The Years 1881–1894 in Russia: A Memorandum Found in the Papers of N.Kh.Bunge*. A Translation and Commentary. – The American Philosophical Society. Philadelphia.

Speransky, Mikhail (1885) 'Plan Finansov', *Sbornik IRIO*, vol. XLV.

———. (1895) *Zapiska o monetnom obrashchenii grafa Speranskogo s zamechaniyami grafa Kankrina*, St Petersburg.

'Speransky, Mikhail Mikhailovich' (1988) in *The New Encyclopaedia Britannica*. vol. 11. Micropaedia, Encyclopedia Britannica Inc.

Stepanov, V.D. (1998) *N. Kh. Bunge: Sudba reformatora*. Moscow.

Struve P. ([1930] 1957) 'Bunge, Nikolay Christianovich', in *Encyclopaedia of the Social Sciences*, vol. 3 Editor-in-Chief Edwin R.A. Seligman, New York.

Sudeikin, V.T. (1895) *Zamechatelnaya epokha v istorii russkih finansov*. St Petersburg.

Tugan-Baranovsky, M.I. (1915) 'Vitte i Bunge kak ministry finansov', *Severniye zapiski*, no 3, March.

Chapter 5

Between Reason and Historicity: Russian Academic Economics, 1800–1861

Joachim Zweynert

Economics has (especially by its critics) often been called a child of the 'Age of Reason'. Being inseparably connected with Enlightenment philosophy, the teachings of both the physiocrats and the classical economists aimed at detecting a 'natural' order according to a human nature that was taken as more or less unchangeable. As many authors have rightly argued, it is inaccurate to accuse Adam Smith of being ignorant of history. However, both in the *Theory of Moral Sentiments* ([1759] 1976) and in the *Wealth of Nations* ([1776] 1976), he took as his starting-point the reality of the economically and politically most advanced country of the time, without paying much attention to the issue of whether the 'system of natural liberty' could be applied to other countries and times as well.

The way in which Smith's – and later Ricardo's – ideas were received in continental Europe provides evidence of the historicity of economic thought (Nau and Schefold (eds), 2002). In the individual countries, different versions of classical doctrine emerged, each reflecting on the one hand this society's stage of economic development and its economic problems, and on the other hand its prevailing intellectual traditions.[1] Russia was and was not an exception to this rule. It was not an exception, because the development of Russian academic economics was part of European discourse while reflecting the intellectual and socio-economic peculiarities of the country. It was an exception, because at the time when political economy became fashionable all over Europe, higher education was still in its very beginnings in Russia.[2]

Almost everywhere in continental Europe, classical political economy was an imported science. But the degree of intellectual independence was decisively lower in Russia than in France, Italy, the Netherlands or Germany. In contrast to these countries, classical economics was not imported into Russia directly from Great Britain, but intermediately through German scholars.[3] When the German version of

---

1 For an overview on these different versions see Karl Pribram, 1983, 190–208.

2 On Russian education policy in the first quarter of the 19th century see Borozdin, 1912, 349–79; on its impact on economic research see Shirokorad, 2005, 29–38.

3 This intermediation took place both in the forms of German professors teaching in Russia (in economics Christian von Schlözer, Ludwig Heinrich von Jakob, and Karl Hermann) and Russian students studying at German universities with Göttingen in the first decades of the 19th century playing the dominant role. The University of Göttingen at this time was

classical economics spread to Russia, it was modified – by the Germans who taught in Russia and also the first Russian classical economists – in a way that reflected the intellectual climate and conditions of the country. Nevertheless, the emerging Russian version of classical economics shared a basic feature with the German one, namely an idealist orientation and an awareness of the relativity of economic doctrines – and this awareness certainly reflected the economic backwardness of Germany and Russia compared to Great Britain.

As a further manifestation of a still low degree of intellectual independence, up to about 1890 it can be observed how Russian intellectuals in different periods followed the models of different Western countries. The author of one of the earliest histories of Russian economic thought, Vladimir V. Svyatlovsky, even organized his book into periods of British, French and German dominance (Svyatlovsky, 1923).[4] Although such a periodization is much too schematic, at least it can be clearly observed how in the 1830s and 1840s the German influence lost its dominance to the French. With this change of orientation there emerged a tension between idealist social philosophy that formed the basis of the German version of classical political economy, and the rationalist methods of reasoning that were characteristic of the teachings of the French liberal and socialist thinkers.

This tension was reinforced when in the 1850s, the ideas of Friedrich List and the older German historical school made their way to Russia.[5] They were not only taken up by academic economists, but also by conservative romantics using the idea of historical relativity against both liberals and socialists. The debate between socialists and Slavophiles brought many Russian liberal academic economists into a difficult situation. Although the majority of them were well aware of the problem of historical specificity (Hodgson, 2001), in order to defend their liberal conviction against the Slavophile challenge, they often defended the general validity of economic laws, and by doing so often got entangled in methodological contradictions. This way, the conflict between reason and historicity became a typical feature of Russian academic thought in the first half of the 'long' nineteenth century, that is, until the emancipation of the serfs in 1861.

Two 'German-Russian' Classics

In the first quarter of the nineteenth century, two authors competed for the title of the 'first' Russian economist: Christian von Schlözer (1774–1831) and Heinrich von Storch (1766–1835). As their names revealed, both were German or of German

---

strongly under British intellectual influence and thus also the centre of Smithianism at the European continent (Normano, 1945, 20).

4 The earliest larger work on the history of Russian economic thought was Helmut Winther's *Die wissenschaftliche Bearbeitung der Staatswirthschaftskunst nach dem literaturgeschichtlichen Entwicklunsgange der Staatswirtschafts-Systeme und des Finanzwesens* (1836), which was published as book IV of the 'Scientific Notes edited by the Imperial University of Kazan'.

5 On the reception of the ideas of the historical school in Russia from the last third of the 19th century onwards see Barnett, 2004, 231–53.

descent. Born in Göttingen as the son of a well-known Western expert on Russian history – August von Schlözer (1735–1809) – Christian von Schlözer went to Moscow in 1796, where he first worked as a private tutor. In 1800 he became professor of law at the University of Dorpat, in 1801 he became professor of law at Moscow University and in 1804 was appointed to the newly established Chair of Political Economy in Moscow, a position he kept until he returned to Germany in 1826 (Maikov, 1911). Schlözer's main economic work, *Foundations of Governmental Economics or the Science of National Wealth*, had been issued by the Ministry of Enlightenment for use in grammar schools. From 1804–1807 it was published in Russian, German and French. Divided into a theoretical and a political volume, with the latter making up roughly two thirds of the total, the *Foundations* represented an attempt to provide a basic outline of the 'state of the art' in political economy, and to apply it to Russian conditions.

The first volume provided a basic outline of German contemporary classical political economy that still contained traces of cameralist teachings. Schlözer frequently referred to the omnipotence and the interests of the ruler, organically defined society 'as a single great whole' (Schlözer, 1805–1807, vol. 1, 3), and in the theory of value emphasized the relevance of subjective 'value in use' without developing a consistent theory of value and prices on this basis (Schlözer, 1805–1807, vol. 1, 40–49).[6] However, Schlözer stressed that he had not mechanically copied other authors' ideas. Indeed, with his theory of 'personal capital', he delivered a pioneering contribution to the theory of human capital that Storch later developed, and which in the 1840s and 1850s became a central element in Russian classical economics.[7] Certainly, Smith and Say – the latter was not quoted in the *Foundations* – had already seen a parallel between the accumulation of material capital and the acquisition of knowledge. But Schlözer went further than his precursors by regarding untrained labour as an exception rather than the rule, and also by interpreting it as the lending of personal capital when an artist was hired (Schlözer, 1805–1807, vol. 1, 75).

In the second volume of the book, Schlözer more strongly diverged from the classical canon than in the first. This was not only due to the fact that he – like most German classicals – had been brought up in the cameralist tradition. It was also a reflection of the difficulties caused by the application of classical ideas to backward countries facing the challenge of catching up.[8] Addressing this problem, Smith's German recipients tended to argue at a much lower level of abstraction than their British colleagues.[9] Russia was significantly more backward in comparison to Great Britain than Germany was. This was one of the reasons why Schlözer focused even

---

6 On subjectivist value theory in German classical economics see Priddat, 1997.

7 As another article has been dedicated to the theory of internal goods, the details of this topic will not be discussed here, see Zweynert, 2004, 525–44.

8 On the role of this problem for both the development of German and Russian economic thought see Barnett, 2004, 234.

9 Georg Sartorius (1796) referred extensively to statistical and historical material in his textbook. In the second edition of this work (Sartorius, 1806), he expressly criticized Smith's attempt to formulate economic laws independent of time and space.

more strongly than his German colleagues on the problem of economic development, an idea he introduced by quoting the famous Russian historian Nikolai M. Karamzin (1766–1826): 'The symbol of Russia is a splendid youth bursting with energy and life and who loves action whose motto is: effort and hope!' (Schlözer, 1805–1807, vol. 1, xi). Like many other classical economists, Schlözer developed a stages theory of economic development. What distinguished him from other classicals was that he connected it with a marked relativism regarding economic policy:

> They [the laws of classical political economy] can never be applied unrestrictedly. Their application depends to a great extent on time and conditions. A law that may have been very suitable for a country twenty years ago is not necessarily still appropriate today (Schlözer, 1805–1807, vol. 2, 57).

The question of how the policy recommendations of classical political economy had to be modified when applied to a less developed country was a central theme in the *Foundations*. For example, when discussing monetary policy, Schlözer first argued that monetary expansion generally only had a short-term effect, if any at all (Schlözer, 1805–1807, vol. 1, 108–109). However, he then allowed for 'time and specific conditions' and even the 'character of the people' (Schlözer, 1805–1807, vol. 1, 115), and reached the variant conclusion that 'in a still strongly progressing society', monetary expansion might contribute to capital accumulation without causing significant inflationary pressures (Schlözer, 1805–1807, vol. 1, 142).

A similar historical relativism can be detected in the works of Heinrich von Storch. Born in Riga, between 1783 and 1787 Storch studied in Germany before moving to St Petersburg, where from 1788 he taught fine arts at the Cadet College (Somov, 1911; Shtorkh, 1881). In 1796 he was appointed a member of the Russian Academy of Sciences, and later he became its president (1828–30) and vice president (1830–35). Until the end of the eighteenth century Storch worked in the fields of history and statistics. Only after he had been appointed tutor of political economy to the Grand Dukes in 1799, did his scientific interests shift increasingly to economic questions. In 1815 Storch published his *Cours d'economie politique* in six volumes.[10] In parts of the work he copied verbatim from other authors, namely Say and Garnier, and this was the main reason why his originality was long underrated.

In fact, Storch delivered some highly original theoretical contributions, such as a formulation of the theorem of comparative costs, a definition of land rent as a residual quantity, and an analysis of overshooting exchange rates (Bernholz, 1982; Rentrup, 1989; Schefold, 1997; Schumann, 1992). His most original and – at least in Russia – most influential contribution was his theory of internal goods (Schumann, 1999, 11–23). The main idea was that the accumulation of immaterial goods such as health, skills, knowledge, morals and religion were just as important to determining the wealth of nations as material capital was. To contemporary observers, it was obvious that Russia's developmental problems were not only due to a lack of material capital, but also to immaterial factors. According to Storch, 'economics is the science

10 Poor command of French forces reference to the slightly shortened German translation by Karl Heinrich Rau, *Handbuch der National-Wirthschaftslehre* (3 vols, Hamburg 1819–20).

of those laws of nature which determine the nations' welfare, i.e. their wealth and education' (Storch, [1815] 1819–20, vol. 1, 9), and this broad understanding of economic problems became typical of Russian economics in the first half of the nineteenth century.

Like Schlözer and other German classicals, Storch warned against too abstract a vision of political economy, favouring instead an approach that was:

> based not on dry calculations ... but on the study of man and humanity. One must have a knowledge of the condition of human society in different times and places, consult the historians and travellers, see with one's own eyes not just laws and institutions, but also analyse their execution and performance, look at everything related to the running of a household ... check the general traits by observing the particular and without letup bring science closer to daily life (Storch, [1815] 1819–20, vol. 1, 16–17).

In view of this statement in favour of inductivism, it comes as no surprise that Storch, like Schlözer, connected his stages theory of economic development with a relativist position in which policy recommendations had to take into account the specific conditions of time and place (Storch, [1815] 1819–20, vol. 2, 222). Storch was especially interested in the link between economic development and the accumulation and distribution of internal goods. Interestingly, there was a trace of romanticism in his thinking when he argued that the emergence of a craft sector produced an increasingly unequal distribution of knowledge (Storch, [1815] 1819–20, vol, 2, 408–09; McGrew, 1976, 57). From this he concluded, as had Schlözer before him, that Russia should remain an agrarian country for as long a possible. Both Schlözer and Storch were critical of serfdom, and Storch's blunt formulations on this issue[11] may well have been the main reason why an unfinished Russian translation of the *Cours* was published only in 1881.

The thesis that Schlözer and Storch, with their focus on development and awareness of relativity, could be regarded as precursors of the historical school was first formulated by Wilhelm Roscher (1817–1894), one of the founders of the older German historical school, in the sixth chapter of his *Geschichte der National-Oekonomik in Deutschland.* He saw them as members of a 'German-Russian school', a group of Germans who lived and taught in Russia in the early nineteenth century and who became more and more critical of classical economics. In their search for an alternative methodology they anticipated certain aspects of the historical approach. Although there was never anything like a 'German-Russian school',[12] there was at least some truth in Roscher's thesis that Schlözer and Storch anticipated some elements of historicism. However, there was never a clear break between the German version of classical economics and 'old' historicism, as even the German classicals preferred a lower degree of abstraction and paid attention to historical specificity (Streissler, 2001). Nevertheless, in their emphasis on processes and their relativist approach, Schlözer and Storch both came closer to historicism than their German

---

11 'The whip has never so much power over the slave as the prospect of improving his situation over the free man' (Storch, [1815] 1819–20, vol. 2, 290).

12 For a critique of Roscher's thesis of a 'German–Russian school' see Seraphim, 1924, 319–33; Zweynert, 2002, 92–108.

colleagues, and there are reasons to believe that their modifications of classical teachings were a result of their attempt to understand the problems of a backward country.

The First Russian Textbook on Political Economy

After the uprising of the Decembrists in 1825, from the rulers' perspective political economy became a suspicious science and was almost banished from the curriculum of Moscow University (Karatayev, 1956, 52).[13] This was one of the reasons why, after the publication of Storch's *Cours*, it took no less than 32 years before a new textbook on political economy was published, under the title *Sketch on National Wealth or on the Foundations of Political Economy* (3 vols, 1847). Its author, Alexander Butovsky (1817–90), was a young clerk in the Ministry of Finance (Anonymous, 1912).

The *Sketch* was a clear reflection of the official conservative political mood under the reign of Nikolai I (1825–55). In contrast to Schlözer and Storch, Butovsky defended serfdom with the argument that serfs were often better off than small farmers (Butovsky, 1847, vol. 1, 177–78). Also, he held that financial discipline was usually higher in monarchies than in republics (Ibid, vol. 3, 94–95) and explicitly approved the restriction of university autonomy (Ibid, 498–99). Yet the reign of Nikolai I was not only marked by official conservatism, as it also saw the emergence of a left-orientated intelligentsia that was inspired by the ideas of French socialists (Normano, 1945, 41–51). As a counter-movement to the Westernizers, in the 1840s there emerged a group of romanticists or Slavophiles, who where strongly influenced by German idealist philosophy (Walicki, [1975] 1989).

To Butovsky, two points were of essential importance to the methodology of the social sciences. Firstly, he regarded development as 'the main law of mankind' (Butovsky, 1847, vol. 1, 185). Secondly, society was to him more than 'a simple congregation like a flock of animals', and thus the embeddedness of an individual into society was 'a basic fact' of all moral sciences (Butovsky, 1847, ix–x). As the conditions of time and place could lead to 'deep differences in the economic situation not only of different countries, but also of the same country in different periods of its existence' (Butovsky, 1847, xxxi), Butovsky favoured a relatively low level of abstraction:

> The national laws cannot be viewed abstractly: they express not only the will of the legislator, but also the force of circumstances and the level of the people's sophistication. They [the national laws] only improve if they, if one may say so, manure the moral foundations in which they are expected to take root. Any change that does not find nourishment in this soil is useless or harmful. Just as there are no jumps in nature, there are none in man's development either; there cannot be (Butovsky, 1847, 324–25).

---

13 The Decembrists were a group of officers who after the death of Alexander I in December 1825 tried to enforce a constitution and the abolition of serfdom (Lincoln, 1978; Nechkina, 1978), and whose ideas had been partly inspired by Adam Smith (Semevsky, 1909, 219).

This passage might have been written by Wilhelm Roscher,[14] and Butovsky emphasized his historical relativism when he wrote that 'much of what is bad and unbearable for a country under the given circumstances, might be excellent for another country' (Butovsky, 1847, 185). Like Schlözer and Storch, Butovsky saw subjective value in use as an important determinant of value and prices, and dedicated almost one fifth of the first volume (Chapter 8) of his book to the theory of internal goods, which he adopted from the French liberal economist Charles Dunoyer (1786–1862).

Regarding the relationship between reason and historicity, the decisive point was that despite all of his idealist-relativist methodology in his critique of the socialists who he regarded as 'half-educated' and whose interest in political economy he claimed to be 'superficial' (Butovsky, 1847, 13), Butovsky again and again referred to a 'natural order' that was valid at all times and places. This idea was born of the philosophy of rationalism and contrasted sharply with the idealist understanding of society that had been introduced into Russian economics by Storch and Schlözer. Since the latter was present in Butovsky's organic perception of society as well as in his historical relativism, it can be said that he indicated for the first time a contradiction that can be considered symptomatic of Russian academic economics in the first half of the nineteenth century.

The Peak of the Conflict Between Reason and Historicity

In the 1850s, this conflict was increased by two factors: the fierce debates regarding the abolition of serfdom, and the spread of the ideas of the older German historical school. In 1856, Alexander II had declared that the emancipation of serfs was a political goal. In the five years between this announcement and the actual liberation of the serfs in 1861, liberal economists, socialists and Slavophiles debated heatedly about the details of the reform (Zweynert, 2002, 206–10). The main issue was whether the *obshchina*, the Russian rural commune based on collective cultivation and a periodical redistribution of land, should be maintained (Grant, 1976). The debate began between the liberal economists and the Slavophiles, and only later did the socialists enter the discussion and join the Slavophiles in their critique of an order based on individual property. They based their critique on the same logic employed by the liberals but reached the opposite conclusion, namely that individual property contradicted the demands of reason (Shtein, 1948).

The liberal classical economics in the 1850s found a particularly spirited champion in Ivan V. Vernadsky (1821–81), who between 1850–57 held the chair of political economy at Moscow University, before he became editor of the weekly *Ekonomist* and 'clerk for special tasks' in the Ministry of the Interior. Strongly influenced by Frederic Bastiat (1801–1850) and Charles Dunoyer, Vernadsky saw the main task of political economy as 'detecting the natural laws of production' that were universally valid (Vernadsky, 1856, 136). In view of his unshakable belief in the natural order, he recommended the immediate abolition of the rural commune,

14 Butovsky was not familiar with Roscher's early writings.

because he believed that collective cultivation hindered the emergence of a rational agriculture (Vernadsky, 1857).

In contrast, the Slavophiles wanted to prevent Russia from following the 'rationalist' developmental path of Western Europe. Having been challenged in their convictions by some learned economists, the second generation of the movement tried to introduce economic arguments into their defence of the *obshchina* (Dmitriev, 1941, 85–97). In the teachings of Friedrich List (1789–1846), the Slavophile Yurii F. Samarin (1819–1876) found strong support for the thesis that there was no 'ideal' economic order, but that social institutions should be judged in view of the specific conditions of a country. He and others criticized their liberal opponents not only for arguing in excessively abstract terms, but also for being unfamiliar with Russian rural reality:[15]

> We can say only one thing to our opponents: put aside Say's 'Catéchisme Economique' for at least one week and go out into the countryside. There you will see what you take to be unnatural and impossible – the Russian *obshchina* – try it! (Samarin, 1858, 300)

The spread of the ideas of the older historical school in Russia that was closely connected with the work of Ivan K. Babst (1824–81)[16] coincided exactly with this debate, and must be understood in this context.

Born into a family of German ancestry, Babst studied history at Moscow University under the supervision of the influential 'Western-minded' liberal historian Timofei N. Granovsky (1813–1855). Unable to find a position as a historian, in 1851 he became lecturer in political economy at the University of Kazan. A speech 'On some Conditions Favouring the Enlargement of National Capital', which he delivered at Kazan University in 1856, proved to be decisive for his career. He used an enhanced level of freedom of speech to make a passionate statement in favour of economic and political modernization: 'The effects of plagues, epidemics and famines', so runs the most famous sentence in the address, 'can not be as fatal for the national wealth as a despotic and arbitrary government' (Babst, 1856a, 26). This sensational speech suddenly made Babst a figure of public life.[17] A year later he harvested the fruits of his courage when he was appointed to the prestigious chair of political economy at Moscow University, after Vernadsky had vacated the post.

With his historical academic education, Babst was in a way predestined to become a popularizer of the ideas of the older German historical school. In 1856, he published 'The Historical Method in Political Economy', a review of the *Foundations of National Economy* by Wilhelm Roscher, the author whose methodological views Babst had adopted so completely (Babst, 1856b). Like Roscher, Babst was prone to methodological compromises. On the one hand, he regarded self-interest as

15 Most of the Slavophiles themselves were landowners and therefore very well informed about the workings of Russian agrarian life.

16 On Babst's role in the development of Russian historicism in economics see Barnett, 2004, 238–39.

17 For example, Nikolai G. Chernyshevsky, the spokesman of the pre-Marxian socialists of the 1850s, wrote in a review of Babst's speech: 'His name became so dear to all of us as those of our historians, belletrists, poets, journalists' (Chernyshevsky, [1858] 1974, 471).

the motivating drive of human action and acknowledged the existence of general economic laws (Babst, 1872, 8). At the same time, he thought these laws to be so strongly modified by climate, national character and historical fate that they always had to be qualified with regard to these factors (Babst, 1872, 159).

Regardless of this contradiction, in questions of economic policy Babst was a convinced liberal and 'Westernizer' who spoke out in favour of freedom for commercial activities. Simultaneously he emphasized that it was impossible to construct anything like an ideal economic order independent from the concrete conditions of economic life. For example, in his review of Roscher's *Foundations* he wrote about 'ideal' orders:

> Each of them can claim to be valid for a people at a particular time; the mistake is to claim that such ideas are unconditionally valid for all and everybody. For the person at the peak of his powers both the apron strings to which the child is tied and the stick that supports the old man are a hindrance: here sense becomes stupidity and a benefit a drawback (Babst, 1856a, 104).

When the Slavophiles exploited exactly this argument in order to reject the liberal Westernizers' call for the abolition of the *obshchina*, and for an economic policy oriented towards the recommendations of contemporary classical political economy, Babst answered this challenge with a remarkable revision of his own methodological position:

> In Russia one often hears the opinion that political economy does not apply to us, that its laws have not been written for us, that our conditions and needs are totally different. My God, must a separate economic theory be created for each country then? … Science fulfils its function only if the laws that it expresses are general, reasonable, absolute and derived from actual economic activity so that economic activity in each place is inevitably subject to them … while any deviation from them inevitably causes economic damage (Babst, 1857, 113).

Even if Babst in the same article rebuked the classical economists for arguing on too high a level of abstraction, and warned of an 'overestimation of one's capabilities, one-sidedness and a claim to absoluteness' (Babst, 1857, 115), this could only superficially cover the deep conflict between his belief in the superiority of a liberal economic policy, and his methodological conviction that the conditions of time and space were of crucial importance for economic performance and structure.

Mixing it all up

According to a famous dictum of a German opponent of historicism, the teachings of the older historical school were no more than 'a historical dressing over a classical dish' (Wilbrandt, 1926). Although this was an exaggeration, it certainly contained an element of truth, as Roscher, Hildebrand and Knies did not see themselves as strict opponents of the classical doctrine, but rather they tried to supplement it with a historical dimension. Therefore, it is not surprising that Russian economists, who at this time were still mainly occupied with absorbing Western ideas, undertook the attempt to integrate historicist ideas into the classical canon.

Such attempts found their clearest manifestations in the *Foundations of Political Economy* (2 vols, 1859–62) by Ivan Ya. Gorlov (1814–90), who had studied in Moscow and after a brief stay in Kazan became professor of political economy at the University of St Petersburg (Anonymous, 1913). The aim of his textbook, which for many years was mandatory reading for Russian students of political economy, was not to make an original contribution to knowledge, but to show how existing theory could be applied to Russian reality. In this way, Gorlov wanted to refute the Slavophile reasoning that 'Western' theories were not applicable to Russian society (Gorlov, 1859–62, vol. 2, i–ii). However, his book was not only directed against the Slavophiles. Gorlov also dedicated large parts of it to a critique of socialists, and he repeatedly reminded them that the existing order was nothing else but an expression of the Holy Creation (Gorlov, 1859–62, vol. 1, ii).

Gorlov based his arguments on the views of many West European authorities, with J.S. Mill, Karl Heinrich Rau, Charles Dunoyer and Wilhelm Roscher being the most frequently quoted authors. In view of these divergent influences, it is little wonder that Gorlov's *Foundations* were marked by deep contradictions. In the methodological introduction to the book, Gorlov did not only emphasize the relevance of the ancillary sciences of history and statistics. In keeping with the historical school he even argued that the comparative analysis of different nations at different times had to precede the development of a theory (Gorlov, 1859–62, vol. 1, 30).

Despite this commitment to inductivism, in the main part of the book he argued in a purely deductivist fashion and paid little if not no attention to the historical embeddedness of the economy. Gorlov was clearly less interested in theoretical questions than his Russian classical precursors. The detailed theoretical analysis of value as was typical of previous textbooks, he argued, had only resulted in 'metaphysical refinements', without really contributing to a better understanding of economic reality (Gorlov, 1859–62, vol. 1, 417). What Gorlov regarded to be the main task of political economy emanated from the fact that his critique of Slavophile and socialist ideas demanded more space than his elaboration of theoretical issues. In trying to find a compromise between liberalism, socialism and the romanticists' challenge, he proved unable to define his own position clearly.

Apart from cryptic statements such as that *laissez faire* was a 'great' but not an 'exclusive' principle (Gorlov, 1859–62, vol. 1, ii), this was most obvious in his discussion of the *obshchina*. He fully agreed with the Slavophiles that:

> only the historical method can produce a reasonable solution to economic questions; hence, one should not embark on the investigation of such an important institution such as the redistribution of land by the mir and the communal ownership of land without sufficient knowledge of the facts (Gorlov, 1859–62, vol. 1, 248).

But when he took up the basic argument of Western-minded liberals that collective cultivation was inefficient because it undermined the drive for profit, he did so without any reference to historical facts. As a compromise he proposed the idea that in order to prevent the proletarianization of the rural population, a certain percentage of the soil could remain in the hands of the *obshchina*.[18] Like Storch, Gorlov was sceptical about the welfare effects of technical progress, and agreed with the Slavophiles that farmers' handicraft production deserved support in its struggle against the growth of factories. Just how sceptical he was about the Western path of social development, also became apparent from the fact that this 'bourgeois vulgar economist' was the first Russian author to refer to Friedrich Engels' *The Condition of the Working Class in England* (Gorlov, 1859–62, vol. 1, 353). This fact was not mentioned in Soviet literature on the history of economic thought.

From Classicism to Historicism (but not from Reason to Historicity)

This chapter will end with an economist who continuously struggled with the conflict between reason and historicity, and who (at least at first glance) turned from being an adherent of classical political economy into a historicist – Nikolai Kh. Bunge. In his last work, published in the year of his death, Bunge remembered how:

> in the course of many years I was influenced by some of the leading teachings on political economy, how my enthusiasm diminished and how I convinced myself ... that knowledge is not the result of belief in dogmas and theories, but of the careful analysis of phenomena! (Bunge, 1895, 1)

Born in 1823 in Kiev into a family of Swedish descent, Bunge became friends with Ivan Vernadsky, whose chair of political economy at the University of Kiev he occupied in 1850 when Vernadsky left for Moscow (Struve, 1930). After participating actively in the economic debates of the 1850s, in 1859 he became rector of Kiev University. This position, together with other public activities, absorbed most of his time, and he only started publishing again in the 1870s, issuing a large number of works including his influential textbook *Foundations of Political Economy* (1870). In 1880 he was appointed deputy and one year later Minister of Finance, and in 1887 he became Chairman of the Council of Ministers, a post he held until his death in 1895. In this year he also published his last work, the *Sketch of Politico-Economic Literature*, which consisted of revised versions of his earlier writings.

Both Bunge's theoretical views and his views on economic policy underwent a significant transformation between his two main periods of publication (1852–60 and 1868–95). In the 1850s, Bunge could in theoretical terms be regarded as a classical author. In political terms and alongside Vernadsky and Babst, he defended liberal ideas against Slavophile and socialist ones. In contrast, in the 1870s Bunge became an adherent of the younger German historical school both in theoretical and policy issues. However, the break was not as sharp as it first appeared, as there

---

18 This idea had been first formulated by Pavel I. Pestel' (1793–1826), the leader of the 'southern' more radical subgroup of the Decembrists, who was sentenced to death after the uprising. Since his main work, *Russkaya Pravda* (*Russian Law*), intended as a constitution for the intermediate government after the putsch, was not published until after 1905, it is rather unlikely that Gorlov was familiar with its contents.

were some common elements linking the two periods. From the beginning, Bunge was mainly occupied with two questions, the relationship between inductive and deductive methodology and that between economic theory and policy. As early as in his second dissertation *The Theory of Capital* (1852), he demanded a 'vivid and tangible' economics that should not consist only of 'abstract formulas' (Bunge, 1852, vii–viii).

Such demands had previously been formulated by most classical Russian economists. But when Bunge called for attention to be paid to past and future developments, and for the formulation of developmental laws, it became obvious that even in his early works he was influenced by the ideas of the older historical school. However, in his 'Letter on the Study of Political Economy' published in 1857, Bunge defended the classical claim of the general validity of economic laws even against his own arguments from the methodological introduction of *The Theory of Capital*. Towards the end of his first publication period, Bunge found a preliminary solution to the conflict between his methodological and political preferences in the works of Henry Charles Carey (1793–1879). Carey, to whose 'first system'[19] Bunge had in 1860 dedicated a small book, had managed to combine a pronounced inductivist methodology with an enthusiastic outline of the advantages of a *laissez-faire* economy.

However, Bunge's belief in *The Harmony of Economic Relations* (the title under which he published his summary of Carey's ideas) was only an intermediate stage in his development. Eight years later, in an article on J.S. Mill, he connected his critique of deductive economics with that of the notion of *laissez-faire*. Consequently, he now regarded increased state regulation of the economy as a 'natural' result of cultural and economic development. Referring to the famous *Methodenstreit* between Schmoller and Menger, in his *Sketch on Political Economy* he simply remarked that Schmoller had presented 'a proper view on these issues' (Bunge, 1895, 195). It is important to see, however, that Bunge agreed with Schmoller regarding the importance of inductivism, but not – or at least to a much smaller degree – regarding the relativity of economic knowledge. In the methodological introduction of his last work he still rejected the idea 'that all our knowledge is relative and is only valid for certain periods under concrete conditions' – despite his general sympathy for historicist economics. In his view, every science had 'unshakeable theorems', and thus the historical approach bore the risk of 'unlimited opportunism' (Bunge, 1895, 180–81).

Conclusion

As had been the case in France, in Russia the development of theoretical economics was impeded by the fact that since the 1840s, academic economists were again and again drawn into ideological debates with opponents of the exchange economy and private property. In view of the fierce critique of the market from both the socialists

---

19 In his early works Carey was an adherent of *laissez-faire*, later he became a spokesman of government regulation and protectionism (Pribram, 1983, 207–8). Bunge has the young Carey in mind when he spoke of his 'first system'.

and the Slavophiles, many Russian economists saw their main task as 'enlightening' society about the basic advantages of the market, instead of developing the analytical tools of economic theory. This also found expression in the fact that all economists elaborated upon here – with the exception of Schlözer and Storch – did not only publish scientific works, but also participated in public debates.

However, there is an important difference compared to the French case. The French liberal economists, who defended the liberal order against the socialist challenge, were (as rationalists) convinced of the general superiority of an order based on the principles outlined regarding exchange and private property. In contrast, in Russia, economics had been imported via Germany, and this meant that even many classical economists were aware of the problem that an 'ideal' order could only be developed taking into account the historical conditions of a concrete society. On the one hand, this somewhat weakened their belief in the liberal order. On the other, the idealist understanding of society and the argument about relativity might have provided a good line of reasoning against the socialists' belief that a society could be completely transformed according to the demands of reason. However, precisely this argument was used by the Slavophiles against the liberals. Hence, authors like Bunge and Babst saw the only possible way of defending the market in referring to arguments that an exchange economy *in general* was the superior order, an argument actually contradicting their own methodological convictions.

Russian economics in the first half of the nineteenth century has sometimes been regarded as not being worth any detailed study, as at this time Russian economists were mainly occupied with acquiring Western knowledge. This was certainly true to a large extent, but it is interesting to see how different influences interacted in the genesis of economic thought in a 'backward' country, and from this case study, much is to be learnt about knowledge transfer into developing countries in general. Also, the conflict between reason and historicity was important for the further evolution of Russian economic thought in at least two respects.

First, the need to defend the significance of 'economic laws' against the Slavophile dogma that Western ideas could not be applied to Russia, reduced the attractiveness of the work of the younger historical school. In fact, many Russian economists were excited about the social engagement of the Schmoller school, but in methodological terms they remained sceptical about a far-reaching denial of general laws. Without being able to prove this thesis conclusively, even at the turn from the nineteenth to the twentieth century, in their methodology many Russian historicist economists remained closer to Roscher than to Schmoller. And this was by no means due to any form of 'backwardness', but rather to their agreement with the notion that too absolute a version of relativism was not desirable.

Secondly, and perhaps more importantly, the conflict between reason and historicity partly explains why the teachings of Karl Marx found such a fertile breeding ground in Russia. Marx's philosophy of history delivered a solution to the conflict between reason and historicity that attracted not only socialist thinkers but also academic economists, such as one of the first scientific interpreters of Marx internationally, Nikolai Ivanovich Ziber. However, this is a different story that occurred in the second half of the century and hence cannot be covered here.

References

Anonymous (1912). Butovsky, Aleksandr Ivanovich. Brokgaus/Efron, vol. 9. St Petersberg: 84–85

——— (1913). Gorlov, Ivan Yakovlevich. In *Novyi entsiklopedicheskii slovar' Brokgauza i Efrona*, vol. 13. St Petersburg: Brokgauz-Efron: 211.

Babst, Ivan K. (1856a). *O nekotorykh usloviyakh, sposobstvuyushchikh umnozheniyu narodnogo kapitala*. Kazan: Tipografiya Kazan'skogo universiteta.

———, (1856b). Istoricheskii metod v politicheskoi ekonomii. *Russkii vestnik*, no 5: 94–141.

———, (1857). Teoriya i praktika. *Ekonomicheskii ukazatel'*, no 5: 108–15.

———, (1872). *Izlozhenie nachal narodnogo chozyaistva*. Moscow: Tipografiya Gracheva.

Barnett, Vincent (2004). Historical political economy in Russia, 1870–1913. *European Journal of the History of Economic Thought*, vol. 11 no 2: 231–53.

Bernholz, Peter (1982). *Flexible Exchange Rates in Historical Perspective*. Princeton, N.J.: Department of Economics, Princeton University.

Borozdin, I.N. (1912). Universitety v Rossii v pervoi polovine 19. veka, in E.V. Anichkov, (ed.), *Istoriya Rossii v 19. veke*, Moscow: Granat, vol. 2: 349–79.

Bunge, Nikolai Kh. (1852). *Teoriia kredita*. Kiev: Universitetskaya tipografiya.

———, (1860). *Garmoniya khozyaistvennykh otnoshenii. Pervaya politiko-ekonomicheskaya sistema Keri*. St Petersburg: D.E. Kozhanchikov.

———, (1868). Dzhon Styuart Mill kak ekonomist. *Zhurnal Ministerstva narodnogo prosveshcheniya*, vol. 140, no 10: 1–100.

———, (1870). *Osnovaniya politicheskoi ekonomii*. Kiev: Universitetskaya tipografiya.

———, (1895). *Ocherki politiko-ekonomicheskoi literatury*. St Petersburg: Tipografiya V. Kirshbauma.

Butovsky, Alexander I. (1847). *Opyt o narodnom bogatstve ili o nachalakh politicheskoi ekonomii*. 3 vols St Petersburg: Tipografiya vtorogo otdeleniya sobstvennoi E.I.V. Kantselyarii.

Chernyshevsky, Nikolai G. ([1858] 1974). O nekotorykh usloviyakh, sposobstvuyushchikh umnozheniyu narodnogo kapitala. In *Polnoe sobranie sochinenii*, vol. 4. Moscow: Pravda: 470–501.

Dmitriev, S. (1941). Slavyanofily i slavyanofil'stvo. *Istorik-marksist*, no 1: 85–97.

Gorlov, Ivan Ya. (1859–62). *Nachala politicheskoi ekonomii*, 2 vols St Petersburg: Tipografiya Kulisha.

Grant, Steven A. (1976), Obshchina and mir. *Slavic Review*, vol. 35, no 4: 636–51.

Hodgson, Geoffrey M. (2001). *How Economics Forgot History. The Problem of Historical Specificity in Social Science*. London: Routledge.

Karataev, Nikolai K. (1956). *Ekonomicheskiye nauki v Moskovskom universitete (1755–1955)*. Moscow: Moskovskogo universiteta.

Lincoln, W. Bruce (1978). Decembrists. In *The Modern Encyclopedia of Russian and Soviet History*, vol. 8. Gulf Breeze: Academic International Press: 229–37.

McGrew, Roderick E. (1976). Dilemmas of Development: Baron Heinrich Friedrich Storch (1766–1835) on the Growth of Imperial Russia. *Jahrbücher für Geschichte Osteuropas*, N.F., vol. 24: 31–71.

Maikov, P. (1911). Shletser, Khristian-Avgust. In *Russkii Biograficheskii Slovar'*, vol. Shebanov-Shyuts. St Petersburg: Tipografiya Glavnago Upravleniya Udelov: 345–47.

Nau, Heino H. and Schefold, Bertram (eds) (2002). *The Historicity of Economics. Continuities and Discontinuities of Historical Thought in 19th and 20th Century Economics*. Berlin: Springer.

Nechkina, M.V. (1978). Decembrists' Uprising. In *The Modern Encyclopedia of Russian and Soviet History*, vol. 8. Gulf Breeze: International Academic Press: 237–47.

Normano, Jack F. (1945). *The Spirit of Russian Economics*. New York: John Day.

Pestel', Pavel I. (1906). *Russkaya pravda. Nakaz Vremennomu Verchovnomu pravleniyu*. St Petersburg: Kul'tura.

Pribram, Karl (1983). *A History of Economic Reasoning*. Baltimore: John Hopkins University Press.

Priddat, Birger P. (ed.) (1997). *Wert, Meinung und Bedeutung. Die Tradition der subjektiven Wertlehre in der deutschen Nationalökonomie vor Menger*. Marburg: Metropolis.

Rentrup, Konrad (1989). *Heinrich von Storch, das Handbuch der Nationalwirthschaftslehre und die Konzeption der inneren Güter*. Heidelberg: Physica-Verlag.

Roscher, Wilhelm ([1874] 1924). *Geschichte der National-Ökonomik in Deutschland*. München and Leipzig: Duncker and Humblot.

Samarin, Yurii F. (1858). Retsenziya na 'Pozemel'naya sobstvennost' i obshchinnoye vladenie', soch. S. Ivanova, Russkii vestnik 16, 1858. *Sel'skoe blagoustroistvo*, no 12: 271–328.

Sartorius, Georg (1796). *Handbuch der Staatswirthschaft zum Gebrauche bey akademischen Vorlesungen, nach Adam Smith's Grundsätzen*. Berlin: Unger.

————, (1806). *Handbuch der Staatswirthschaft nach Adam Smith's Grundsätzen*. Göttingen.

Schefold, Bertram (1997). Einleitung. In B. Schefold (ed.): *Heinrich Friedrich Storch. Cours d'économie politique* [Reprint], 6 vols Hildesheim et al.: Olms-Weidmann, vol. 1: I–LXV.

Schlözer, Christian (1805–1807). *Anfangsgründe der Staatswirthschaft oder die Lehre vom Nationalreichthume*, 2 vols Riga: Hartmann.

Schumann, Jochen (1992). Heinrich von Storch: Ein russischer Klassiker deutscher Herkunft. In H. Rieter (ed.), *Studien zur Entwicklung der ökonomischen Theorie XII: Osteuropäische Dogmengeschichte*. Schriften des Vereins für Socialpolitik 115, XII. Berlin: Duncker and Humblot: 33–63.

————, (1999). Heinrich von Storch's Theory of Inner Goods as Determinants of a Nation's Civilization. *Argumenta Oeconomica*, 7 1999: 11–23.

Semevesky, Vassilii I. (1909). *Politicheskiya i obshchestvenniya idei Dekabristov*. St Petersburg: Tipografiya Trudovoi Arteli.

Seraphim, Hans-Jürgen (1924). Die deutsch-russische Schule. Eine kritische Studie, *Jahrbücher für Nationalökonomie und Statistik*, vol. 122: 319–33.

Shirokorad, Leonid D. (2005). Deutsche Einflüsse auf die russische Wirtschaftswissenschaft im Kontext der russischen Bildungspolitik im 18. und frühen 19. Jahrhundert, in H. Rieter et al. (eds), *Deutsche und russische Ökonomen im Dialog. Wissenstransfer in historischer Perspektive*. Marburg: Metropolis: 11–46.

Shtein, Viktor M. (1948). Ocherki razvitiya russkoi obshchestvenno-ekonomicheskoi mysli XIX–XX vekov, Leningrad: Izdat. Leningradskogo Gosudarstvennogo Ordena Lenina Univ.

Smith, Adam ([1776] 1976). *The Theory of Moral Sentiments*. Glasgow Edition, Oxford: Oxford University Press.

————,([1776] 1976). *An Inquiry into the Nature and Causes of the Wealth of Nations* Glasgow Edition, Oxford: Oxford University Press

Somov, A. (1911). Storkh, Andrei Karlovich (Heinrich Storch). In *Russkii biograficheskii slovar'*, vol. Shebanov–Shyuts. St Petersburg: Imperatorskogo Russkogo istoricheskogo obshchestva: 428–43.

Storch, Heinrich (1815). *Cours d'économie politique ou exposition des principes impériales qui déterminent la prospérité des nations. Ouvrage qui a servi à l'instruction de Leurs Altesses, les Grand-Ducs Nicolas et Michel*. St Petersburg: Pluchart.

————, (1819–20). *Handbuch der National-Wirthschaftslehre*, slightly shortened translation by Karl Heinrich Rau. 3 vols, Hamburg: Perthers and Besser.

Shtorkh, Nikolai A. (1881). Biograficheskii ocherk uchenoi i sluzhebnoi deyatel'nosti Andreya Karlovicha Shtorkha. In G. Shtorkh, *Kurs politicheskoi ekonomii ili izlozhenie nachal, obuslovlivayushchikh narodnoye blagodenstviye*, translated and edited by I.V. Vernadsky. St Petersburg: Slavyanskaya pechatnya I.V. Vernadskogo, i–xvi.

Streissler, Erich W. (2001). Rau, Hermann and Roscher: Contributions of German Economics around the Middle of the Nineteenth Century. *The European Journal of the History of Economic Thought*, vol. 8, no 3: 311–31.

Struve, Petr B. (1930). Bunge, Nikolay Khristianovich. In *Encyclopedia of the Social Sciences*, vol. 3. New York: Macmillan: 67–68.

Svyatlovsky, Vladimir V. (1923). *Istoriya ekonomicheskikh idei v Rossii*. Petrograd: Nachatki znanii.

Vernadsky, Ivan V. (1856). Predmet politicheskoi ekonomii. *Zhurnal Ministerstva narodnogo prosveshcheniya*, vol. XC: 127–44.

————, (1857). O pozemel'noi sobstvennosti. *Ekonomicheskii ukazatel'*, no 22: 506–10, no 25: 583–86, no 29: 677–85.

Walicki, Andrzej ([1975] 1989). *The Slavophile Controversy. History of a Conservative Utopia in Nineteenth-Century Russian Thought*.

Wilbrandt, Robert (1926). Das Ende der historisch-ethischen Schule. *Weltwirtschaftliches Archiv*, vol. 24, no 2: 97–118 and 332–33.

Zweynert, Joachim (2004): The Theory of Internal Goods in Nineteenth-Century Russian Classical Economic Thought. *European Journal of the History of Economic Thought*, vol. 11, no 4: 525–44.

———, (2002). *Eine Geschichte des ökonomischen Denkens in Russland. 1805–1905*. Marburg: Metropolis.

Chapter 6

Searching for an Ethical Basis of Political Economy: Bulgakov and Tugan-Baranovsky

Natalia Makasheva

The subject matter and method of political economy, and the issue of its interrelation with ethics, attracted the attention of many economists in Russia and the West at the turn of the twentieth century. Each national intellectual tradition as a whole, as well as the individual economist's world-view, had an important impact on the treatment of the problem that was attempted. In this chapter, the approach to this concern is investigated through the views and convictions of two outstanding representatives of Russian economic thought, who worked at a time known in Russian history as the Silver Age.[1]

The intellectual and personal fates of Mikhail Ivanovich Tugan-Baranovsky (1865–1919) and Sergei Nikolaevich Bulgakov (1871–1944) had much in common, yet they also greatly differed from each other. Their similarity was rooted in their belonging to a generation of Russian intellectuals who were lucky (or doomed) to live in one of the most dramatic eras in Russian history. Both were born soon after Alexander II launched his sweeping reforms. Both embarked on an academic career and started public activity at the end of the nineteenth century, and the peak of their creativity coincided with two wars, the Russo-Japanese and the First World War, as well as two Russian revolutions, those of 1905 and 1917.

They came from mutually contrasting social strata. Tugan-Baranovsky was born into a nobleman's family, while Bulgakov's father was a lowly priest. Both excelled in their education. Tugan-Baranovsky received degrees in law and natural sciences from Kharkov University, and Master and Doctorate degrees from Moscow University, while Bulgakov graduated from the law department of Moscow University, and later received Master and Doctorate degrees. Both scholars taught throughout much of their life, Tugan-Baranovsky at the University and Polytechnic

1 The Silver Age is a term traditionally applied by historians of Russian culture to the period from the 1890s to the end of the Russian Civil War. Primarily it was applied to poetry and to literature to mark an exceptionally creative period. It was also a great period of ferment in Russian intellectual life in general, when different currents and schools, including mysticism, decadence, neo-Kantianism, Marxism and others gained popularity among the Russian intelligencia. Primarily an age of culture, this period was marked by progress in many other fields from medicine to political economy.

Institute of St Petersburg, and Bulgakov at the Kiev Polytechnic Institute and the Moscow Commercial Institute. Following his ordination in 1918, Bulgakov taught at the Simferopol University and later at the Orthodox Theological Institute of St Serge in Paris.

Both scholars were actively involved in Russian political and social life. At the end of the 1890s, Tugan-Baranovsky edited the Social Democratic magazines *Novoye slovo* (*The new word*) and *Nachalo (The beginning)*, and he sided with the Constitutional Democratic Party during the 1905 Revolution. After the October Revolution, he had a portfolio in the Central Rada (the Ukrainian government), and stood at the cradle of the Ukrainian Academy of Sciences and the Ukrainian cooperative movement. Bulgakov edited the magazines *Novy put'* (*The new path*) and *Voprosy zhizni* (*Questions of life*) in tandem with Nikolai Berdiaev. The Religious Philosophical Society in Memory of Vladimir Soloviev was established on his initiative in 1905. Bulgakov took part in the establishment of the Christian Political Union, and was elected to the State Duma as an independent Christian Democrat in 1907 (Barnett, 2005, 47–58; Nove, [1987] 2004; Zander, 1948, vol. 1).

These two representatives of the Russian intelligentsia had an extremely wide range of academic interests, including economics, philosophy, ethics and politics. Bulgakov also took an interest in theology. Both were deeply concerned with the capitalist and socialist prospects of Russian development, and with the role of the intelligentsia in public life. They both studied the history of economic and social thought and discussed the future of political economy, and in this regard their views went through various dramatic changes.

As with many other Russian intellectuals, Tugan-Baranovsky and Bulgakov were initially enthusiastic about Marxism, this being, in Berdyaev's words, 'the process of westernization of the Russian intelligentsia' (Berdyaev, [1949] 1990, 118). Very popular among Russian intellectuals, Marxism was far from being homogeneous. Some of its adherents who appreciated Marx's sociology and criticisms of capitalism, considered his materialistic philosophy too primitive to be a sound foundation for Marxism as a world outlook. Moreover, the objectivism of Marx's socio-economic doctrine could hardly be accepted by those inspired by the ideal of universal happiness. Bulgakov and Tugan-Baranovsky were among those who grew out of their youthful Marxism fairly quickly.

As with many other Russian intellectuals, Tugan-Baranovsky and Bulgakov regarded the 1905 Revolution as a crucial event. It made them finally divorce themselves from Marxism, and shift from materialism to idealism, which found reflection in their ideas on the fundamentals of political economy. Thus, as Bulgakov analyzed the role of the ideal in economic life, which he started in 1903 in the essay 'On the Economic Ideal' (Bulgakov, 1903), he began to regard the goals of political economy from a Christian point of view. In his 1906 *Sketch on Political Economy*, he put forward an outline of a new political economy and also criticized the political economy dominating in the West (Bulgakov, 1906). In the same year, Tugan-Baranovsky published an essay, 'How the Socialist Ideal Materialises' (Tugan-Baranovsky, 1906a), and also a book, *Contemporary Socialism in Its Historical Development* (Tugan-Baranovsky, 1906b). His sensational essay, 'The Ethical

World-View of Dostoyevsky', better known as 'Three Great Ethical Problems', appeared in 1908 (Tugan-Baranovsky, 1908b).

Both scholars were actively involved in debates on the Russian intelligentsia connected with the publication of the collection *Vekhi* (*Landmarks*) in 1909, opposing each other in this instance. Bulgakov criticized the Russian intelligentsia in his article 'Heroism and Asceticism: Reflections on the Religious Nature of the Russian Intelligentsia', mainly for its messianic faith in its own righteousness, for its materialism, for a dependence on outward circumstances, and for its thirst for great actions at the expense of the individual, which it held in contempt. This attitude would bring tragic fruit in the Russian situation (Bulgakov, [1909] 1990). Tugan-Baranovsky, on the contrary, championed the intelligentsia, pointing out its major role in Russian cultural progress (Tugan-Baranovsky, [1910] 1996).

Western economists know Tugan-Baranovsky mainly from his analyses of trade cycles in *Industrial Crises in Contemporary England, Their Causes and Immediate Influence on National Life* (1894), a historical work on *The Russian Factory*, and certain others that were translated into European languages (for example, Tugan-Baranovsky, 1970; Tugan-Baranovsky, 1913; Tugan-Baranovsky, [1910] 1966). His ideas on monetary theory, namely, his conjunctural theory of money, are far less understood. Even lesser known are his works on the philosophical and methodological problems of economic science, despite the appearance of a few very recent publications devoted to the whole body of his ideas and on methodology in particular (Barnett, 2000, 2004). As for Bulgakov, in the West he is known mainly as one of the Silver Age religious thinkers, a theologian and a philosopher, one of the spiritual leaders of Russian émigrés in France, and an ecumenical activist.

Not only Soviet but also Western historians traditionally attribute both thinkers to the so-called Legal Marxist category, and their preference for legal political activities over underground organization is highlighted.[2] The Soviet period saw only critical references to them, labelling them apostates from the 'correct' version of Marxism (Karyakin, 1960; Zverev and Klushin, 1970). The brand of Legal Marxism was certainly political, and is more likely to mislead than to adequately describe their views.

The theme of this paper was chosen in relation to reviving debates about the nature of economic research and its connection with practice, the criteria of truth and the role of ethical and political factors in scientific progress, debates that are currently led by methodologists and historians of economic thought. This theme is of interest not only from the viewpoint of the history of Russian economics, but also as an attempt to reconcile political economy and ethical philosophy.

2 The term 'Legal Marxism', invented by V.I. Lenin, was applied to the movement within Russian Marxism that was a 'reflection of Marxism in bourgeois literature'. Lenin referred to Legal Marxists when criticizing Russian populists. He opposed his own point of view (revolutionary Marxism) on prospects of the economic and political development of Russia to liberal and democratic views of some Russian Marxists, Tugan-Baranovsky, Bulgakov and Berdyaev being the most famous. In contrast to Lenin they appealed not to the proletarian revolution and 'proletarian socialism', but to an evolutionary transition, 'bourgeois liberalism' and democratic socialism.

Methodological Discussions in Late Nineteenth-Century Russia

Contemporary historians of economic thought usually describe the concluding decades of the nineteenth century mainly as the time of the marginal revolution, when the foundations of neoclassical economics were taking shape. At the same time, this was a period of importance for economic methodology, when the triadic structure of political economy (its positive and normative parts, and art) was precisely fixed (Keynes, 1891). In accordance with that structure, whatever had a bearing on ethics ought to be placed outside of economic science. The abstract deductive method was regarded as the most appropriate method for positive economic science. Indicatively, Léon Walras proposed as early as 1874 an analogous structure of economic science, to demonstrate the capabilities and the limits of its positive (theoretical) component (Walras, [1874–1877] 1988, 25–34).

Such methodological debates on economic science did not proceed in a vacuum. The issue of ethics in economics displayed a link with the latter's stance on social problems, which concerned the representatives of all trends of social thinking from Social Democrats to Catholics. This was when the Catholic Church was actively elaborating the fundamentals of its social doctrine, and when Social Democrats were drafting their programmes (Nitsch, 1990). This was why Bulgakov's attempt to find a basis in Orthodoxy for analyzing socio-economic problems appeared part and parcel of the general social thinking of the time, just as Tugan-Baranovsky's attempt to graft Kantian ethics onto political economy was.

In connection with the problem of ethics, the long discussions that the Social Democrats had on the moral grounds of socialism should be mentioned. Such debates started as early as in the mid-1870s, with the publication of Eugen Dühring's works (Dühring, 1871) and criticism by Frederick Engels. The approaching bicentenary of Kant's birth gave these debates a new lease of life in the beginning of the twentieth century. As is known, the Marxian theory of social development included two basic theses. The first was that socialism was the logical result of economic and social development. The second was that moral rules were generated by historical and social circumstances. There was no such thing as a universal moral code, as morals only expressed class interests (Engels, [1878] 1947). Social Democrats, who were later branded as revisionists, strongly criticized this view at the turn of the twentieth century. They turned away from the logic of historical objectivism to recognize the importance of subjective factors (for example Eduard Bernstein), opting for an ethical not a class-based political economy, and for an alliance between socialist theory and Kantian ethics.

Russia witnessed a major interest in methodological discussions in the 1890s and 1900s. In this regard many Russian economists sided with a principle that divided political economy into theory and practice, although they were not as prepared as their Western colleagues to strictly demarcate these two parts of political economy. This was true even for economists engaged in pure theory – not because they regarded political economy as a science that 'comprises several research disciplines largely differing in terms of methodology' but because many of them did not think that the theoretical part could be value-free (Tugan-Baranovsky, 1908a, 18). That was the specificity of Russian economic thinking, which:

> … had not yet become a fully autonomous discipline that was in accordance with the nature of Russian social thinking in general. The latter apprehends all theoretical teachings mainly from a practical perspective and in connection with problems of applied ethics and social programmes, the doctrines being transformed into social trends (Bulgakov, 1904, no 10, 261).

Using Thomas Kuhn's terminology one historian said that Russian economic science had not yet reached complete maturity, or that it was still in its pre-paradigm stage, but another saw this trait as a universal characteristic feature of Russian political economy in general (Makasheva, 2006).

Even Tugan-Baranovsky, one of the most pro-Western Russian economists of the time, was not so decisive as compared to J.N. Keynes when demarcating the theoretical and practical parts of political economy. Although Tugan's and Keynes's views on 'the application of ethical consideration to practical economics' might be seen as very similar (Barnett, 2004, 87), Tugan could hardly be seen as advocating the idea of a value-free economic science. Moreover, he asserted that political economy was not independent of normative presuppositions that had their roots in class interests. He claimed that class interests cast a shadow on basic theoretical concepts and he gave the concept of wages as an example. He wrote that from the capitalist point of view, wages were part of expenditure, but from the point of view of the working class, wages were income (Tugan-Baranovsky, 1908a, 7–8; 1915, 29–31). Yet Tugan considered the class-based approach as self-contradictory and ultimately rejected it, instead favouring an ethical ground for the political economy of the socialist future.

In the last decades of the nineteenth century and the beginning of the twentieth century, Russian economists took the greatest interest in their country's socio-economic prospects, including the socialist option, which was discussed both within a framework dominated by Marxism, and within a socio-historical discourse. As Marxian development theory claimed, the development of capitalism inevitably produced forces that lead to its own destruction and transformation into socialism. These were: a growing capital concentration and production centralization; an increase in the number of hired workers and a growing reserve labour army; the impoverishment of the working class; and crises of overproduction that would grow ever worse. Critical analyses of these theses became certain economists' starting point for diverging from the economic component of Marxism, but also from historical materialism as a whole. Such was the evolution of Tugan-Baranovsky and Bulgakov.

Tugan-Baranovsky: From a Critic of Marx to Marginalist Socialism

Tugan-Baranovsky placed in doubt nearly every fundamental postulate of Marxist economic theory. His theory of cycles and crises demonstrated the possibility of harmonizing total production with total consumption under capitalism. His analysis of reality revealed workers' rising living standards, and his analysis of statistical data showed that Marx's proposition on production concentration as a general principle was wrong at least for agriculture (Tugan-Baranovsky, 1894; Bulgakov, 1900). Last but not least, an analysis of Marx's reproduction schemes led Tugan-Baranovsky to conclude that the thesis of the falling rate of profit as a result of the growth in the organic composition of capital had no convincing substantiation (Tugan-Baranovsky, 1899).

He finally came to the conclusion that it was impossible to prove that capitalism had to end due to objective economic and social processes (Tugan-Baranovsky, 1915, 584–85). Hence the new socialist system must naturally and inevitably grow from the womb of the old system (Tugan-Baranovsky, 1996, 248), but in contrast to orthodox Marxists, Tugan-Baranovsky believed the downfall of capitalism was a consequence of the contradiction 'between its basic economic principle and the basic ethical norm of our time' (Tugan-Baranovsky, 1904, 205). This was what led him to turn to the social ideal as the guiding principle in economic restructuring, and to strive for the transcendental ethical principle as a ground for the political economy of socialism.

As with many Social Democrats in the West, Kantianism was a component part of the world-outlook of many Russian intellectuals. A focus of much attention was the categorical imperative in its formulation: 'we should never act in such a way that we treat humanity, whether in ourselves or in others, simply as a means, but always as an end in itself' (Kant, [1785] 1912, 55). This formula stated the unique value of the human personality, and Tugan-Baranovsky claimed that it was a universal principle of supreme value. In 'Three Great Ethical Problems', he discussed some consequences of this principle through the prism of ethical questions that Dostoevsky raised in his novels.

Tugan-Baranovsky regarded this as the only possible ethical principle in the contemporary world, and as a principle compulsory 'for all persons of normal moral consciousness'. Unlike Marxian class morality, the universal nature of the ethical ideal allowed it to form the ethical basis of political economy as the *general* science of economy. As Tugan-Baranovsky saw it, the recognition of this ideal in a particular society guaranteed both the objectivity of political economy based on it, and the unity of both its parts, the practical and the theoretical. This attitude was what determined his stance on pivotal methodological issues.

Tugan-Baranovsky did not deny the division of political economy into theory and practice. Moreover, he regarded abstract deduction as the basic method of the theoretical part. However, that part was not immune from the influence of morality. The major methodological problem was not to design a value-free political economy, but to find an ethical principle to become the foundation for the political economy of socialism. He viewed the principle of the supreme value of the human personality as the only appropriate one. His next task was to embody this principle in a theory of value.

As Tugan-Baranovsky saw it, the specific value theory that corresponded to this principle was a synthetic theory of value, which combined a labour theory of value (explaining objective factors) and a marginal utility theory (dealing with subjective factors).[3] The objective factor was the input of human labour made to acquire a

3 Tugan-Baranovsky was not the only Russian economist who attempted to reconcile the marginal utility theory with the labour theory of value. V.K. Dmitriev also tackled the

certain commodity, or the labour costs. Tugan-Baranovsky assumed that the value of a commodity was equal to its marginal utility, the latter depending on its volume, which, in its turn, depended on the labour input made to acquire a certain volume of commodity. To explain the ethical component of his viewpoint, Tugan-Baranovsky asked the following:

> Not only individuals but also means of production take part in the production process. Why, then, do we regard the entire product as made by human labour alone? Why do we recognise only human labour as the active producer? And why, on the other hand, do we equalise in that respect all kinds of labour, making no difference between them? Why do we see all kinds of human labour as mutually comparable, and why do we unite them all in one lump – the one general category of social labour? ... Doubtless, that is because we proceed from the guiding ethical idea of political economy, which we take for granted – the supreme value, and so the equipollence of the human personality (Tugan-Baranovsky, 1915, 64).

On the other hand, only individuals determined the subjective utility of a particular commodity, the amount of utility depending on the amount of the commodity, which, in turn, depended on the volume of labour expended to reproduce commodities. The possibility of combining the two aspects of value (subjective and objective) was thus determined (Tugan-Baranovsky, 1890, 217–18).

Based on Tugan-Baranovsky's arguments, his pupil Nikolai Stolyarov formulated a theorem postulating quantitative correlations of labour inputs and utilities in the instance of an optimal allocation of resources: 'When the basic economic principle – the desire to obtain maximum utility with the smallest possible input – guides production, the relation between the marginal utilities of freely reproduced products and their labour costs are equal' (Stolyarov, 1902, 4). He offered an algebraic proof of this statement in 1902 and solved a standard problem of social welfare function maximization within a given labour constraint. His short work was one of the first mathematical essays attempting a formal approach to the social welfare function.

Tugan-Baranovsky attempted to implement the idea of a merger of the marginal utility theory and the labour theory of value in the context of an outline of a socialist economy. In his work of 1918, *Socialism as a Positive Doctrine*, he argued that a planning body should guarantee such allocation of resources that would lead to maximizing the social utility function. For this, planners should comply with the conditions of his theorem. As he saw it, direct (in hours) accounting of labour inputs was possible, though not easy, under socialism and was a way to avoid regarding the labour force as a commodity, that is, to follow the Kantian principle. According to Tugan-Baranovsky, the state should reveal individual preferences using a price mechanism similar to the Walrasian auctioneer. Such a method would make Walrasian prices genuine prices in the socialist economy, while the medium of account (numéraire) would reflect the essence of money under socialism as 'a mere symbol with no value at all' (Tugan-Baranovsky, [1918] 1996, 401).

---

problem. For him, however, it was a technicality related to price level determination rather than a philosophical or an ethical issue (Dmitriev, [1904] 2001).

The utopianism of such a model of socialist economy is more evident today. However, unlike the Russian Marxists who attempted to implement the socialist project in Russia, and unlike the Western theoreticians of market socialism who attempted to demonstrate that effective resource allocation in a planned economy was possible, Tugan-Baranovsky analyzed the problem in a broad ethical and historical context. He wrote that socialism was possible only in a mature society, with its developed sense of duty and social solidarity, and high level of education. Otherwise, 'instead of a realm of freedom and general affluence, socialism will be doomed to become the realm of slavery and overall poverty' (Tugan-Baranovsky, [1918] 1996, 426). Furthermore, he was aware of the connection of socialism with spiritual culture and personal freedom. Apprehensive of the dictates of the state, he preferred a cooperative socialist model to a bureaucratic one.

And contrary to present-day conceptions of equality as a socialist ideal, Tugan-Baranovsky regarded the freedom of the individual as paramount, although the struggle for equality was justified when the minority trampled on the interests of the majority. Socialism would bring equality, but equality in itself was not a 'positive benefit', rather it was merely a stage on the way to implementing the social ideal: 'not social equality but social freedom is the social ideal' (Tugan-Baranovsky, [1918] 1996, 365).

Socialism as a Positive Doctrine was Tugan-Baranovsky's last major work. It summed up many years of socialist theorizing and striving to find a compromise between the economic and ethical aspects of human life. It is remarkable that the author finished it less than a month after the October Revolution in 1917. It crowned not only his numerous years of economic research, but also a long tradition in which socialism was, above all, a moral ideal.

Bulgakov: Against Economism and towards Christianity

It has become conventional to discern three periods in Bulgakov's intellectual evolution: Marxist (before 1905), idealist (1905–1917) and religious (1917–1944). Researchers often rely on this accepted chronology. Here an attempt will be made to follow another approach, and to formulate his position on issues of interest proceeding from his works on the economy, mainly his principal work on economic philosophy, which was *Philosophy of Economy* of 1912.

Bulgakov's world-view was, on the whole, religious. There was no contradiction with his enthusiasm for Marxism, not merely because his 'Marxist period' was very short, but also due to the specifics of Marxism itself. Marxism possessed the features of an atheistic religion. The theory of economic evolution that it offered had a pronounced social slant, despite its aspiration to be objective. Marxism might be seen as a protest against the individualistic ethics which ignored economy as the manifestation of 'humanity as a whole, as an organism'. Not the individual person, but the community was considered the subject of history, and the latter idea was attractive to people brought up in the Christian spirit. Bulgakov was one of those people. 'But the tragedy was inevitable as Marxism defined this common subject as a special group within the world: the working class or the social state' (Hallensleben, 1995, 68). Thus, Bulgakov inevitably diverged from Marxism.

Initially, just as with Tugan-Baranovsky, Bulgakov's divorce from Marxism started with theoretical issues. Very soon, however, they began to involve more profound problems of his underlying world-view. In his first work written in regard to discussions on capitalist prospects in Russia, *Capitalism and Agriculture* (Bulgakov, 1900), Bulgakov criticized the Marxist thesis of the inevitability of the concentration of production that would lead to the social control of the means of production. After that, he put into doubt the principles underlying the Marxian forecasts of socio-economic development. Moreover, he expanded his criticism to non-Marxist political economy. He believed that conventional political economy and so-called scientific socialism had common roots in an economic philosophy that Vladimir Soloviev had termed 'economism', considering the growth of material wealth as the main determinant of economic development and social life. Conventional political economy saw social life in the light of material wealth production, and the human being as striving only for material interests.

As he followed Soloviev in his criticism of economism, Bulgakov was anxious to counter it with a 'religious-ethical world-view', or the philosophy of economy.[4] He understood the latter as a general economic world-view, which represented 'a particular system of evaluations, norms and ideals as applied to economic life' (Bulgakov, 1918, 4). This was a profoundly Christian system of standards. Bulgakov regarded the philosophy of economy as an alternative to the philosophy of science, the fundamentals of which, being the brainchild of Auguste Comte, led to an instrumental conception of truth. For Bulgakov, the problem of overcoming the fragmentation of academic knowledge was linked to the problem of humanity as maker of academic knowledge (Bulgakov, 1990 [1912], 128–44). Unlike Tugan-Baranovsky, Bulgakov did not seek to reconcile the labour theory of value with marginal utility theory, as he believed that both theories shared a common philosophical basis: economism.

The philosophy of economy regarded the following issues as pivotal: the essence of economy and economic activity; the connection between the material and the spiritual worlds; and the individual in those two worlds. Bulgakov attempted to solve these issues by turning to the doctrine of Sophia as the Wisdom of God. Apart from Bulgakov, Vladimir Soloviev, Pavel Florensky, Evgeni Trubetskoi, Nikolai Berdiaev and other religious thinkers elaborated on Sophianist ontology. Two layers are usually discerned in Bulgakov's Sophiology: a purely theological and a philosophical one,

4 The Russian language has two terms, *khozyaistvo* and *ekonomika,* synonymic but not identical. The former, close to the German *Wirtschaft*, denotes a system or activities to guarantee the existence of a person, a nation or a community, hence the phrases *narodnoye khozyaistvo* (national economy), *mirovoye khozyaistvo* (global economy), or *domashneye khozyaistvo* (household economy or daily chores). The word *ekonomika* does not have such an extensive semantic range, and applies to a system of commodity production and distribution resting on labour division and human contacts either through the market, as in *rynochnaya* (market) and *kapitalisticheskaya* (capitalist) *ekonomika* (economy), or through a plan, *sotsialisticheskaya* (socialist) *ekonomika.* Here Bulgakov was using the word *khozyaistvo,* the title of this work in Russian being 'Filosofiya khozyaistva'.

the latter being a preset programme of economic activity, which the human race as a transcendental subject was destined to implement.

Within his philosophy of economy, Bulgakov took up a large number of ethical and philosophical problems closely linked to economic thinking in the broad sense of the term. Moral justification of wealth was paramount, a problem that had many dimensions, the historical being one of them. Christian ethics had always striven to find a compromise between asceticism and the cult of material wealth (Bulgakov, 1918, 158). The Reformation had forced mediaeval morality to come to terms with the economic drive. A spiritual link between economic and religious progress was duly proclaimed. However, as Bulgakov saw it, the process of the moral justification of the striving for wealth had led to the domination of the economic aspect. As it was legitimized, economic science was divested of morality in its quest for objectivity, ultimately producing the universal model of *homo œconomicus*.

As he criticized economism and conventional political economy, Bulgakov had a different mission: to determine the meaning of material wealth as a condition for the spiritual progress of humanity and, consequently, to reformulate the foundations of political economy. He desired to connect this new basis with Christian ideals and to determine the trend of economic and social policies. Bulgakov regarded the accumulation of wealth as a 'negative condition of spiritual life' (Bulgakov, 1906, 7), that is, as a necessary prerequisite for reducing the dependence of humanity on nature. As he saw it, to free people from external conditions was an indispensable prerequisite for the manifestation of the human spirit and of free choice. There was no free choice in cases of involuntary poverty imposed by events beyond individual control. Hence the rights of freedom could not be implemented unless involuntary poverty was eliminated. 'That is why the struggle against poverty is the struggle for the rights of the human spirit' (Bulgakov, 1903, 116).

Bulgakov suggested a more extensive treatment of the category of wealth than a mere sum of material benefits that a person owned. First of all he saw wealth as a phenomenon related not only to an individual, but to society as a whole. Bulgakov regarded wealth as a condition of the material existence of a particular community, and the extent of its power over nature (Bulgakov, 1906, 8). That was where the possibility of reconciling the striving for personal wealth with social wealth might be found. He also defined an increase in wealth not as an increase in the amount of material benefits, but as a growth of material wealth that did not increase inequality, a stance that has something in common with John Rawls's ideas on the criterion of social welfare (Rawls, 1972).

Certain other Russian economists have also pointed out the importance of moral standards to successful economic development. It will suffice to mention Ivan Yanzhul's *On the Economic Importance of Honesty*. In this work Yanzhul argued that a tolerance of theft and deception leads, in present-day terms, to an increase in transaction costs, and thus to a decrease in economic effectiveness, and even to the impediment of innovation (Yanzhul, [1906] 2005, 402–20).

Last but not least was another basic premise of the philosophy of economy, the thesis of the integrity of economy. Bulgakov wrote that although economic activity was empirically expressed as a myriad of separate acts:

> … if we look at it dynamically, over time, we see that it is actually a unified and connected activity whose subject is not the individual but the genus. We would miss the essential content of economy (or of science) if we failed to perceive the whole that exceeds the limits of these particular economic (cognitive) acts. An atomistic approach, which proceeds by division, would in this case prevent us from making the appropriate analysis, for *economy* as a whole is not only logical but also empirically prior to separate economic acts. The economic system must already be in existence in order for these separate acts to be possible, and not the other way around: they are not simply fractions but part of an organic whole that is larger than the simple sum of its parts and that alone can endow them with meaning (Bulgakov, [1912] 2000, 123–24).

With some daring, one can interpret this stance as a step to what is known nowadays as the institutionalist approach to understanding the economy. In general the philosophy of economy determined a specific angle from which socio-economic policies and their connection with political economy were viewed. Bulgakov was especially active in discussing these problems in 1904–1907, when his political activity reached its peak. Though *Philosophy of Economy* was written sometime later, the practical conclusions drawn from it would not run counter to what he outlined about politics at this time, at least to the extent that such conclusions can be made.

Although Bulgakov's attitude to socialism was complicated and not always consistent, the idea of socialism as a social ideal retained its attraction even when the destructive fruits of a revolution under socialist mottos became evident. Bulgakov refused to denounce the idea of socialism when he taught at the Simferopol University in the early 1920s, when an anti-Bolshevik White government was ruling the Crimea. His last work, *The Orthodox Church*, confirmed his loyalty to 'socialism in a general sense, that is, as the negation of the system of exploitation, of speculation, of cupidity' (Bulgakov, 1988 [1935], 173).

While recognizing a wide range of political opinions, Bulgakov saw the practical task of political economy as the determination of ways of increasing wealth as a prerequisite for personal and spiritual progress. What he termed as 'idealism' was a social and economic policy guided by that goal. In the context of practical politics, idealism naturally presupposed greater state intervention. Along with many people of socialist convictions, Bulgakov expected such intervention to overcome economic chaos, to redistribute income and to implement progressive social programmes.

Private property was one of the crucial political issues of the day, one in which the goals of practical policy intertwined with social, ethical, philosophical and religious ideas. Bulgakov's stance contrasted with that of the Marxists, the *Narodniks* (Populists) and that of liberal economists. Essentially, his approach diminished the importance of the problem of the form of ownership, to regard it in the context of a guaranteed increase of wealth as conditioning the spiritual progress of society. He wrote: 'Private property is a historical institution whose form, as well as social importance, are constantly changing; it has no enduring intrinsic value' (Bulgakov, [1935] 1988, 175). Accordingly, Bulgakov wanted to subordinate the property form question to the above-mentioned goal of politics, rather than to adjust the latter to the property form, a reflection of an approach that he described as relativism of methods with the goal remaining unchanged.

This was a principle that guided Bulgakov as he was making his choice between capitalism and socialism. He came to the conclusion that: 'the best form of economy – whatever its name, and however it combines capitalism and socialism – is that which, in any given circumstances, best assures personal liberty, protecting it from natural and social slavery' (Bulgakov, 1988 [1935], 175).

Conclusion

The end of the nineteenth century and the beginning of the twentieth was a time when, under positivist influence, economists attempted to give a precise definition to their subject matter, and to affirm at the methodological level the division between positive and normative knowledge. An interest in social problems in society as a whole, many rising social movements and a growing awareness by the ruling elite of its responsibility to the community also prompted a practical orientation of political economy, while its theoretical part was being strengthened. This contradiction was solved through the personal stances of certain outstanding British economists such as Alfred Marshall.

The positivist trend was less pronounced in Russian economics due to its specific evolution and the specificities of Russian social thinking as a whole. Furthermore, at the time under consideration, economists viewed many problems through the prism of national socio-economic development, and so a social ideal was always present in the background of their works. Russian economists rarely sought to concentrate only on pure theory. Even when they did, they were not ready to acknowledge a full separation of economic theory from ethics. On the contrary, many of them regarded ethics as the basis of economic discourse.

The example of two outstanding Russian thinkers, Tugan-Baranovsky and Bulgakov, showed the two directions that the quest took. One, idealistic, was rooted in Kantian doctrine. The other, religious, stemmed from Christian Orthodoxy and from the doctrine of Sophia. As both sought a compromise between ethics and political economy, Tugan-Baranovsky arrived at a political economy of socialism, while Bulgakov came to the idea of the world being a household, which he understood in a specific religious sense. The practical political aspect of his doctrine can be described as Christian socialism.

Now that socialist doctrine has lost its historical argument with liberal ideas, the two scholars' quest may appear something of a deviation from the mainstream of 'correct' economic science. But, even a hundred years later, the achievements of pure theory do not fully satisfy all economists, and do not prevent some of them from seeking a fulcrum not in formal logic and empirical knowledge, but elsewhere. We cannot say for sure whether Tugan-Baranovsky's and Bulgakov's experiences were lessons not to follow, or a prophecy never fully appreciated.

References

Barnett, Vincent. (2000). 'Tugan-Baranovskii's Vision of an International Socialist Economy', *European Journal of the History of Economic Thought,* Spring 2000: 115–35.

————. (2004). 'Tugan-Baranovsky, The Methodology of Political Economy, and the "Russian Historical School"', *History of Political Economy*, vol. 36 no 1: 79–101.

————. (2005). *A History of Russian Economic Thought.* London, New York: Routledge.

Berdyaev, N.A. [1949] (1990). *Samopoznanie.* Moscow: Mezhdunarodnye otnosheniya.

Bulgakov, S.N. (1900). *Kapitalism i zemledelie.* 2 vols, St Petersburg.

————. (1903). 'Ob economicheskom ideale', *Nauchnoe slovo*, no 5: 102–25.

————. (1904). 'Bez plana: 'Idealism' i obshchestvennye programmy', *Novyi put',* no 10: 260–77, no 11: 342–60, no 12: 302–21.

————. (1906). *Kratkii ocherk politicheskoi ekonomii: Osnovnye cherty sovremennogo khozyaistvennogo stroya*. Moscow: Religiozno-obshchestvennaya biblioteka.

————. (1918). *Ocherki po istorii economicheskikh uchenii*. Moscow.

————.[1964] (1991). *Pravoslavie. Ocherki ucheniya pravoslavnoi tserkvi*, Moscow: Terra.

————.[1935] (1988). *The Orthodox Church,* Crestwood: St. Vladimir Seminary Press.

————.[1909] (1990). 'Geroizm i podvizhnichestvo', in *Vekhi. Sbornik statei o russkoi intelligentsii.* Moscow: Novosti.

————.[1912] (1990). *Filosofiya khozyaistva*. Moscow: Nauka.

————.[1912] (2000). *Philosophy of Economy: The World as Household.* New Haven: Yale University Press.

Dmitriev, V.K. [1904] (2001). *Economicheskie ocherki.* Moscow: State University Higher School of Economics.

Dühring, Eugen. (1871). *Kritische Geschichte der Nationalökonomie und des Socialismus*. Berlin.

Engels, Friedrich. [1878] (1947). *Anti-Dühring: Herr Eugen Dühring's Revolution in Science*. Moscow: Progress Publisher.

Forlender, Karl. (1909*). Kant i Marks*. St Petersburg.

Hallensleben, Barbara. (1995). 'Who is the Subject of History?', in J. Diskin and N. Makasheva (eds), *S.N. Bulgakov (1871–1944): Economics and Culture*. Moscow: Russian Academy of Sciences. Institute for Social and Economic Problems of Population.

Graves, Charles. (1995). 'The Sophiology of father Sergius Bulgakov', in J. Diskin and N. Makasheva (eds), *S.N. Bulgakov (1871–1944): Economics and Culture.* Moscow: Russian Academy of Sciences. Institute for Social and Economic Problems of Population.

Kant, Immanuel. [1785] (1912). *Osnovopolozheniya k metafizike nravov.* Moscow.

Karyakin, Yurii. (1960). 'Bulgakov', in *Filosofskaya entsiklopedia*, 5 vols Moscow: Sovetskaya entsiklopedia, vol. 1.

Kant i socialism. Obzor noveishikh teoreticheskikh techenii v marksizme. (1906). Moscow.

Keynes, John N. (1891). *The Scope and Method of Political Economy*. London: Macmillan.

Kondratiev, N.D. (1998). *The Works of Nikolai D. Kondratiev*. N. Makasheva, W. Samuels, V. Barnett (eds). 4 vols, London: Pickering and Chatto.

Makasheva, Natalia. (2006). 'Economicheskaya nauka v Rossii v period transformatsii (konets 1980'kh – 1990-e gg.): Revolutsiya i rost nauchnogo znaniya', in Ya. Kuzminov (ed). *Istoki*. Moscow: State University Higher School of Economics.

Nitsch, Tomas. (1990). 'Social Economics: The First 200 Years', in M. Lutz (ed.), *Social Economics: Retrospective and Perspective*. Boston, MA: Kluwer.

Nove, Alec. [1987] (2004). 'Tugan-Baranovsky, Mikhail Ivanovich', in J. Eatwell, M. Milgate, and P. Newman (eds). *The New Palgrave. A Dictionary on Economics*. 4 vols, New York, Basingstoke: Palgrave, vol. 4.

Rawls, John. (1972). *A Theory of Justice*. Oxford: Clarendon

Stolyarov, N.A. (1902). *Analiticheskoe dokazatelstvo predlozhennoi M. Tugan-Baranovskim politiko-analiticheskoi formuly*. Kiev.

Schumpeter, Joseph. [1912] (1961). *The Theory of Economic Development*. New York: Oxford University Press.

Tugan-Baranovsky, M.I. (1890). 'Uchenie o predelnoi poleznosti khozyaistvennych blag, kak prichina ich stoimosti', *Yuridicheskii vestnik*, vol. 6 no 1: 192–230.

———. (1894). *Promyshlennye krizisy v sovremennoi Anglii i ich vliyanie na narodnuyu zhizn*. St Petersburg.

———. (1899). 'Osnovnaya oshibka abstraktnoi teorii kapitalisma Marksa', *Nauchnoe obozrenie*, no 5: 973–85.

———. (1904). 'Krushenie kapitalisticheskogo stroya kak nauchnaya problema', *Novyi put'*, no 10: 166–206.

———. (1906a). 'Kak osushchestvlayetsay sotsialisticheskii ideal', *Mir Bozhii*, no 5:166–89.

———. (1906b). *Sobremennyi sotsialism v svoem istoricheskom razvitii*. St Petersburg.

———. (1908a). 'Metodologiya politicheskoi ekonomii', *Obrazovanie,* no 12: 1–19.

———. (1908b). 'Nravstvennoe mirivozzrenie Dostoevskogo', *Voprosy obshchestvovedeniya*, no 1: 243–59.

———. (1909). 'Predislovie', in Forlander, K. *Kant i Marks*, St Petersburg.

———. (1913). *Les crises industrial en Angleterre*. Paris: M. Giard et Brière.

———. (1915). *Osnovy politicheskoi economii,* 3rd ed. Petrograd.

———.[1910] (1966). *Modern Socialism in its Historical Development*. New York: Russel and Russel.

———. (1970). *The Russian Factory in the 19th Century*, Homewood, Ill.: Richard D. Irwin Inc.

———.[1910] (1996). 'Russkaya intelligentsiya i sotsialism', in Tugan-Baranovsky, M.I., *K luchshemu budushchemu. Sbornik sotsialno-filosofskikh proizvedenii,* Moscow: ROSSPEN.

———.[1912] (1996). 'Tri belikich eticheskikh problemy', in Tugan-Baranovsky, M.I., *K luchshemu budushchemu. Sbornik sotsialno-filosofskikh proizvedenii.* Moscow: ROSSPEN.

———.[1918] (1996). 'Sotsializm kak polozhitel'noe uchenie', in Tugan-Baranovsky, M.I., *K luchshemu budushchemu. Sbornik sotsialno-filosofskikh proizvedenii.* Moscow: ROSSPEN.

———. (1996). *K luchshemu budushchemu. Sbornik sotsialno-filosofskikh proizvedenii.* Moscow: ROSSPEN.

———.[1898] (1997). *Russkaya fabrika v proshlom i nastoyashchem: Istoricheskoe razvitie russkoi fabriki v XIX veke*. Moscow: Nauka.

Walras, Léon [1874–77] (1988). *Eléments d'économie politique pure ou théorie de la richesse sociale* (Auguste et Léon Walras œuvres économiques completes. Vol. VIII). Paris: Economica.

Yanzhul, I.I. [1906] (2005). 'Ekonomicheskoe znachenie chestnosti', in Yanzhul, I.I. *Izbrannye trudy*. Moscow: Nauka.

Zander, Lev. (1948). *Bog i mir. Mirovozzrenie o. Sergiya Bulgakova.* 2 vols, Paris: YMCA Press.

Zverev, Vladimir, and Klushin, Vladimir. (1970). 'Tugan-Baranovsky', in *Filosofskaya entsiklopedia.* 5 vols, Moscow: Sovetskaya entsiklopedia, vol. 5.

Chapter 7

The Enigma of A.V. Chayanov

William Coleman and Anna Taitslin

A.V. Chayanov is a remarkable figure in the history of economics. His mix of contrasting talents is so rare that it is hard to find another economist, inside or outside of Russia, to compare him with. This singularity makes him more difficult to 'locate', and that difficulty has doubtless contributed to him being misunderstood and misrepresented in the profuse literature on him. A little demythologization is therefore in order. Nevertheless, in undertaking to clear away the maze of puzzles and apparent contradictions that surround him, the historian of ideas should allow that, in some significant measure, they might have been produced by a disjointedness in Chayanov's intellectual constitution. At least a part of the puzzle might also lay in the complexities and contradictions of the Russian intellectual scene of the time. We begin by attempting to place him correctly in that scene.

Was Chayanov a Neo-*Narodnik*?

One of the aspects of Chayanov in which the literature gives contrary answers is whether or not he should be placed within the *Narodnik* (agrarian populist) stream of thought. In Soviet historiography at least three positions may be distinguished. In the late 1920s, during the campaign against him in the Soviet press, he was labeled as a 'neo-*Narodnik*' (Kantor, 1927, 28–40). Similarly members of the so-called 'Organization-Production School' (OPS), of which Chayanov was a member alongside with N.P. Makarov and A.A. Rybnikov, were defined as *Narodniks* and neo-*Narodniks*. However, towards the 1980s a different interpretation of the OPS (in respect to their position in the League of Agrarian Reforms in 1917) emerged, that they were 'bourgeois' economists close to the *Kadets* (Spirina, 1987, 90). In the very late 1980s, following the rehabilitation of Chayanov, he was treated by Soviet authors not as a *Narodnik*, but as a thinker developing under many influences, not entirely without parallels to Marx (Chayanov, 1989, 32).

In the West, T. Shanin could be seen as close to subscribing to the post-rehabilitation position (Shanin, 1986, 18). To Shanin's mind, the term 'neo-*Nardonik*' was just a convenient label to apply to someone who was neither a Marxist nor a 'bourgeois economist'. In truth, said Shanin, Chayanov took his cues from Marxists and liberals, as well as from genuine *Narodniks*. Not unlike Kerblay, he contended that Chayanov's ideals were borrowed from Kropotkin, as well as from anthroposophy. They were ideals, in other words, of 'the cosmopolitan Russian intelligentsia rather than expression of the peasant tradition'. Rather paradoxically to

Kerblay, Chayanov's vision of peasant life was also very conservative and appeared to reflect 'bourgeois' ideals (Chayanov, 1966, xlvi).

In comparison, in the most recent Russian textbook on the history of economic thought, the view of the OPS (of which Chayanov was a member) as neo-*Narodniks* was described as 'not without foundation' (Avtonomov, 2006, 444). Also recently Shuichi Kojima noted the *Narodnik* influence on Chayanov as well as his non-capitalist ideology (Kojima, 2004, 14–15).[1] In this chapter we will attempt to provide some additional arguments to the thesis that Chayanov's vision of peasant economy was rooted in the *Narodnik* ideal of peasant socialism.

The *Narodniks* – An Overview

Narodnik ideology took peasant collectivism as a vehicle for non-capitalist development in Russia. Above all, the *Narodniks* of the 1860s (from *Zemlia i Volia*) saw the Russian peasant commune as a buffer against market forces preventing the pauperization of its weakest members.[2] According to the 1879 program of the new (terrorist) *Narodnik* group *Narodnaia Volia*, 'all the land should be transferred to the hands of working people and was to be considered people's property ... Every region should give the land for use in communes or to individuals, but only to those who were toiling on it' (Ginev, 1977, 46, n. 138).

However, an important innovation in *Narodnik* ideology took place at the end of 1890s, partly in reaction to Lenin's book *The Development of Capitalism in Russia*. Lenin attacked the *Narodnik* assumption of the non-existence of capitalist development in peasant agriculture. To Lenin, there was an inevitable process of class differentiation in the countryside, with the emergence of a minority of peasant capitalists (*kulaks*) and the eventual proletarianization of the rest.[3] In reply, the *Narodiniks* of the 1890s emphasized the inherent advantages of peasant agriculture, pointing out that the peasant, being both a worker and an owner, had the advantage of being the sole receiver of all agricultural income. So peasants could compete with capitalist agriculture through increased intensification of their own labour, and also by decreased consumption (Ginev, 1977, 25).

---

1 Kojima's correct observation of Chayanov's non-capitalist or even anti-capitalist orientation led him to conclude that Chayanov was closer to the basic ideas of the Bolsheviks than Kondratiev (Kojima, 2004). In our view, Chayanov was closer to the basic ideas of the Bolsheviks only so far as he, as a *Narodnik*, adhered to the shared 'socialist' ideal of non-capitalist development. In a sense, it was Kondratiev who was closer to Lenin's position, as far as he accepted the inevitability of capitalist development in the countryside.

2 The commune's critics argued that it promoted irresponsibility, discouraged agricultural improvement, and limited the civil rights open to peasants. Nevertheless, the commune survived not only the 1861 abolition of serfdom, but also Stolypin's reforms. The peasant communes were direct beneficiaries of the February Revolution; and, from 1917 to the collectivization of 1929, the communes were in control of Russian agricultural land.

3 To Lenin, in contrast to the *Narodniks*, the system of economic relations in the commune was a petty-bourgeois one (Lenin, 1956, 172–73). The Russian rural proletarian was, to Lenin, the class of allotment-holding wage-labourers (ibid, 178).

Thus the principle difference between the Marxist and *Narodnik* positions was set, with Marxists insisting on the inevitable development of capitalism in the countryside, and the *Narodniks* postulating the inherent advantages of unique peasant agriculture. The particularity of the modernist *Narodnik* view was that peasant agriculture was seen as a non-capitalist family economy, employing the labour of its members to provide for the household's consumption. Thus, Chayanov's conception of peasant family agriculture could be traced back to the modernized *Narodnik* views of the 1890s.

The theoreticians of the *Narodnik* journal *Russkoe Bogatstvo*, such as A.V. Peshekhonov, attempted a partial revision of the hard-core *Narodnik* pro-commune ideology. The commune, in Peshekhonov's view, contained an uneasy mix of a territorial administration function and an economic union function. To the moderate *Narodniks*, the future of collectivism lay in a growing cooperative movement, rather than in the old commune (Ginev, 1977, 68). The moderates moved away from the old *Narodnik* vision of the Russian peasant commune as a 'ready-made' institution of peasant communism, focusing instead on family economy as the basis for peasant agriculture.

The core of moderate *Narodniks* formed the Popular Socialist party (*Narodnye Sotsialisty*) in 1906. Two years earlier, the 'traditional' *Narodniks* had formed the Social–Revolutionary party (the S-Rs). The S-R minimum program (1906) advocated the socialization of the land – making the land free to everybody, and thus ultimately making it to belong to no one (Kostrikin, 1975, 87). Land titles were to be transferred to local communes, or unions of local land users (Ginev, 1977, 69). The land was to be distributed to households according to a so-called 'working norm' (Ginev, 1977, 175). The more controversial S-R maximum program called for the ultimate collectivization of agriculture and the socialization of industry (Radkey, 1958, 41). Even so the S-Rs opposed the state centralized management of economy. In contrast to most Marxists, the *Narodiniks* believed in the priority of consumption (and distribution) over production. To the S-R leader V.M. Chernov, socialism in an economic sense was nothing else than a colossal consumption organization (Spirina, 1987, 153–54).

The Popular Socialists (the P-S) supported the nationalization of land through confiscation (with the possibility of compensation) as an orderly process, in contrast to the S-R idea of the 'socialization' of the land, which would encourage uncontrolled local expropriations of land (Ginev, 1977, 70). The P-S planned to create a state land fund, composed of state, church and 'surplus' private land, with the remaining land being held in 'toiling' ownership (Kostrikin, 1975, 83–84).

Chayanov, together with A.N. Chelintsev, N.P. Makarov, A.A. Rybnikov, was a member of the OPS, which emerged in 1911 from various interests concerned with the spread of agronomic knowledge. The agronomists continued the old *Narodnik* tradition of 'going to the people' to enlighten peasants. The OPS aimed at conducting scientific research into the organization plans of peasant family economy, with the emphasis on the peasant as a master tradesman. Understanding an organization plan meant uncovering the structure of family peasant economy, the proportion of agricultural and non-agricultural income, the family budget, the turnover of money and products, the distribution of labour costs in time and among different activities, and the influence of local and general economic conditions (Chayanov, 1989, 33–34).

The main premises of the OPS could be traced in the moderate *Narodnik* paradigm of the 1890s regarding the non-capitalist development of peasant family agriculture, although members of the OPS took part in the organization of cooperative and agronomic movements, rather than in *Narodnik* party activity. Chayanov thus described himself as 'non-party socialist'.

Chayanov's Discussion of Agrarian Reforms in 1917

Early in 1917 the February Revolution transformed the abstract discussions on the agrarian question into practical ones. Most debates were about the equal right of all to the land and the possibility of compensation for expropriation. The S-Rs rejected the idea of compensation, in contrast to the P-S (Ginev, 1977, 173).[4] The most intensive theoretical discussions about the direction of agrarian reforms in Russia were conducted in the League for Agrarian Reform, established in April 1917 on Chayanov's initiative (Chayanov, 1917, 4). The League's platform proclaimed the general principles of reform as follows:

1. The self-employed co-operative peasant farm should form the foundation of the agrarian system in Russia and that the country's land should be handed over to it.
2. This transfer should take place on the basis of a state plan for land reorganization, drawn up with due regard for the special features of the economy of different regions (Chayanov, 1917, 5–7).

In his 1917 pamphlet *Chto takoye agrarnyi vopros? (What is the agrarian question?)*, Chayanov argued that a peasant farm, using the labour of the head of the household and his family, had an innate advantage over capitalist farming using hired labour. In his view the aim of peasant enterprise was to supply the means of existence for the family, through the use of the available means of production and the family workforce. The aim of capitalist enterprise was to maximize profit on capital. So while capitalist enterprises aimed at maximizing 'net' profit, labour enterprises aimed at increasing 'gross' profit. To Chayanov, the use of family enterprises would lead to the maximization of national income, with the most labour allocated to land use (Chayanov, 1917, 27–28).

Chayanov reviewed the various contrasting proposals for land reform of the S-Rs, the P-S, Mensheviks, the supporters of a single land tax and the OPS as follows. Land reform could be accomplished through socialization, as the abolition of all ownership ('it belongs equally to everybody, like the light and the air' – so there would be no land tax and no hired labour), with all land coming under the control

4 In the course of 1917, the S-Rs were moving away from an insistence on exclusively communal land distribution, towards an acceptance of peasant farming alongside communal agriculture, even hesitating to call for the expropriation of land in excess of the so-called 'working norm' (Ginev, 1977, 173).

of land communes. Alternatively, land could be nationalized, where it would be transferred into the ownership and control of the state. The state would then receive all land rent as the main source of state finances, as well as the right of disposition of the land in the public interest. A municipal form of nationalization would occur if local self-government institutions were in control of land distribution (Chayanov, 1917, 42–47).

Otherwise, land reform could turn on the introduction of a 'single tax on land' (following the idea of Henry George), in order to collect a rent for the benefit of the people. Finally, there was the idea of a system of state regulation of agriculture. The right of private property in the land would be preserved, but the sale of land to any private party would be prohibited. Land could only be sold or bought by the state, and the state could also expropriate land (Chayanov, 1917, 44–46).

Chayanov argued that the system of state regulation of agriculture, with its progressive land taxation, abolition of free transactions in land and the right of state expropriation, would provide the state with the necessary means for land reform. It might even make possible the move to nationalization or municipalization in one or two decades. He proposed to finance the compensation for expropriation through government debt, which would be repaid over 50–100 years (Chayanov, 1917, 55–61). Chayanov and other members of the OPS thus differed from the S-Rs and the P-S in their pragmatic approach to the socialization of land. But in his support of the eventual distribution of land (through taxation) to working peasant enterprises, and even in his advocacy of compensation (like the P-S), Chayanov was well within the moderate *Narodnik* paradigm.

Chayanov's Vision of Peasant Family Economy

To Chayanov, peasant family income, which could not be divided into wages and profit as in capitalist enterprises, depended on the number of workers in the family, their productivity and degree of self-exploitation (working time), as well as on market conditions, distance from the market, quality of land and the availability of means of production (Chayanov, 1989, 119). Any (marginal) addition to family labour income could be seen from two contrasting points of view: increases in the fulfillment of family consumption needs and increases in the intensiveness of labour necessary for additional income, so that the subjective evaluation of the increase in self-exploitation was balanced by the subjective evaluation of increased consumption. Thus, depending on the size of the family in respect to the size of allotment, the family would vary its degree of self-exploitation in order to achieve the necessary level of consumption, even without any change in market conditions (Chayanov, 1989, 120).

Chayanov further developed his views on peasant economy by attempting to analyze the isolated state (Chayanov, 1921). With an obvious debt to the ideas of Johann Heinrich von Thunen, Chayanov explored the relationship between population growth and intensification of land cultivation. His conclusion was that in the non-capitalist labour economy, population growth would lead to intensification of agriculture and to an increase in the agricultural population in comparison to the urban. In the case of capitalist agriculture, in his model, intensification of agriculture would be below the degree of intensification in labour economy (the same applied to national income).

Chayanov employed the findings of the *Zemstvo* (local government) statisticians, such as N.N. Chernenkov, that in conditions of communal agriculture, the distribution of allotments depended upon the size of the family (Chayanov, 1989, 154). Thus Chayanov envisioned a specific cause of differentiation in peasant economy in respect to land cultivation and livestock holdings, dependent on the demographic size of the family (the relationship of the numbers of all members to the number of workers) (Chayanov, 1989, 95–108).

Chayanov's other interest was in developing peasant cooperation on the basis of family enterprises, in progression from consumption cooperation to agricultural cooperation, for the supply of agricultural means of production, production credit and the sale of agricultural products (Chayanov, 1925). This vision of agriculture, based on family peasant economy socialized through co-operation, came closest to realization during the New Economic Policy (NEP) (1921–29). After War Communism (1918–20), Lenin decided to retreat on the economic front and allow small-scale private production. This meant aborting any attempt at forced agricultural collectivization, focusing instead on the development of voluntary co-operation, effectively adopting an ideology of co-operation such as that presented by Chayanov.[5]

At the close of NEP, Chayanov came under increasing pressure from Marxist theoreticians, who revived Lenin's thesis about the peasant economy's inherent tendency to capitalist development. To Marxists such as L.N. Kritsman, there was a process of differentiation onto capitalist (own means of production and hired labour), independent (labour family economy) and proletarian peasant economies (Kritsman, 1926). In reply Chayanov pointed out that (aside from capitalist peasant enterprise and proletarian peasant economy), there were also semi-capitalist and semi-labour enterprises (Chayanov, 1989, 426–27). Thus only the fully capitalist peasant enterprise could be identified as *kulak* (rich peasant).

The Marxist vision of a polarized differentiation in the countryside was eventually the victorious one, as forced collectivization meant the end of family peasant agriculture. The fate of Chayanov's vision reflected the struggle (and the eventual defeat) of the *Narodnik* vision of a decentralized peasant agriculture socialized through cooperation, as an alternative to Marxist agricultural collectivization.

Chayanov's *Peasant Utopia*

Further enlightenment on Chayanov's neo-*Narodnik* positions may be obtained from his utopian fancy published pseudonymously in 1920, entitled *Journey of my Brother Alexei into the Land of Peasant Utopia*. This text, nevertheless, offers puzzles as well as answers. *Journey* tells of a 'Russian Peasant Republic' flourishing in the year

5 In preparation for writing his article 'On Co-operation', Lenin had studied Chayanov's works on cooperation and he had seven of Chayanov's works in his library in the Kremlin.

1984. More boldly than most utopians, Chayanov provided a fantasy narrative of the steps by which the utopia was created.

In Chayanov's telling, the total nationalization of agriculture that Soviet power attempted ultimately failed, as the peasantry would not accept collectivization. From 1932 a peasant majority dominated the Congress of Soviets and the Central Committee, leading to the evolution of the regime towards a peasant-based one. In 1934, after a failed revolt by the intelligentsia and metal workers, the first purely peasant government was formed. It obtained a decree for the liquidation of cities at the Congress of Soviets. By 1984, streets of the old urban type remained only in the very centre of Moscow. Otherwise the city was one giant park, interspersed with architectural groupings resembling small townships. All around Moscow the countryside contained almost continuous agricultural settlements, broken by public forests, cooperative pastures and large national parks. Where farmsteads prevailed a family allotment was about 3–4 hectares, and peasant houses stood close to each other, separated only by orchards.

The reader is struck by the audacity and the novelty of Chayanov's demographic vision: Russia's cities were to be dynamited. This radicalness was sustained by an abiding affection for the past. 'We had no need of any *new* principles' explained Minin, the utopian ideologist (Chayanov, 1977, 88). Instead, the population relived the past. Women wore crinoline, the militia dressed in the 'picturesque costume' of the days of Tsar Alexei Mikhailovich (1645–76), and their cuisine was from 1818. Evidently, Chayanov has mastered the paradox of *how to be really new by being really old,* a paradox also brought off by some artistic movements (for example the pre-Raphaelites). Art was central to the utopia, as artistic motivation was the basis of action. 'We are artists' declared Minin at the climax of one of his orations. But in keeping with the utopian attachment to 'centuries-old' traditions, their artistic allegiance was to the past: woman devoted themselves to 'ancient Russian embroidery'; peasant carpenters made cabinets in the style of André-Charles Boulle (1642–1732); galleries gave prominence to paintings by Rubens, Velasquez and other old masters. This was the artistic renaissance that Chayanov conjured up at the peak of the Russian *avant-garde*.

There are other paradoxes in *Journey*, but Chayanov did not ride these so easily. The *Journey* opened with the intention of providing a 'liberal utopia'. 'It has always been the weakness of liberal doctrine that it was incapable of creating ideologies and had no utopia' (Chayanov, 1977, 74). The Peasant Republic was Chayanov's retort to the multitude of socialist utopias of Bellamy, Morris, Moore, Blatchford and Fourier. It was in keeping with this intention that Minin declared: 'we have stripped the state of virtually all political and economic functions' (Chayanov, 1977, 98). It was also in keeping with this intention that the bountiful state of the Peasant Republic was contrasted with a famished Germany, where all agriculture was under state control.

Peasant socialism amounted to the use of large cooperative enterprises in branches of agricultural production, wherever large-scale units had an advantage. Cooperative units controlled wholesale and retail trade, and even thrived in manufacturing industry. Private enterprise survived only where collective enterprises were unimportant, and where organizational geniuses were able to overcome draconian taxation through technological advances. The state was relieved from almost all its social and economic functions by the various associations, cooperatives, congresses, leagues, academies and clubs. The state itself owned only forestry, oil and coal production. Industry would be co-operative in a manner reminiscent of the Yugoslav model. Chayanov's industry would be economically and financially independent (as the capital of enterprises would be the collective property of its members). Chayanov even allowed for small-scale private enterprises that were regulated by discriminatory taxation.

Yet it is doubtful if the Russian Peasant Republic can really be described as liberal. Markets and competition were never mentioned. Conscription for two years and educational travel were both obligatory. Even more incongruously, this 'liberal utopia' contained 'large and powerful organizations' that had millions of people under observation (Chayanov, 1977, 100) for the purpose of 'artificially selecting talented individuals'. We learn that both political rights and duties were just a means to an end, and that there was little conscious political decision-making by the population. Instead a manipulative elite managed all events.

The very publication of *Journey* raised some puzzles that can probably never be answered. The political authorities were unlikely to be charmed by Chaynov's tale of the destruction of Soviet power by a peasant revolt that ushered in bliss. Neither would they be soothed to read that Marxism was 'born in the dungeons of the German capitalist factories' (Chayanov, 1977, 88) and that 'hirelings themselves, the workers, in constructing their ideology, made servitude an article of faith'. Beyond that, several details can only be described as provocative. The principal Bolshevik protagonist was diagnosed as suffering from 'persecution mania' and mental degeneration. The memoires of Ekaterina Kuskova – a vocal anti-Bolshevik, angrily denounced by Lenin, and condemned to be shot – are recorded as entering their 38th edition in the peasant utopia.

It is not surprising that Chayanov anticipated a hostile reception. By January 1923, Chayanov was 'terrified' (in his own words) that his identity as the author of the (pseudonymous) *Journey* would be inadvertently revealed, and implored an editor that he be allowed to censor a forthcoming review of *Journey* that might give him away. He prayed: 'Dear God put in the corrections' (Chayanov, 1999, 79). Nevertheless, *Journey* was published by a state press agency. We might contrast this with the treatment of Zamyatin's *My* (*We*), that was circulating in 1920–21, but was refused publication, subject to violent attack, and finally in 1922 formally banned. There was nothing as *blatantly* provoking in *We* as some of the contents of *Journey*. It was true that Zamyatin, as Chairman of the Leningrad branch of the Union of Writers, was a much bigger fish than Chayanov. It was also true that in being published, *Journey* was saddled with a highly negative introduction. Nevertheless, what purpose of the authorities was served by the publication of *Journey*?

Whatever the answer, *Journey* seems to have been forgotten, apart from by its author's persecutors in the 1930s. Perhaps *Journey* is best known today on account of the coincidence that Chayanov's future utopia was set in the same year as George Orwell's dystopia, *1984*. It was a coincidence that tempts the hunt for any other parallels among the many differences between Orwell and Chayanov. There are some generic similarities. In using this date, both chose to set their works in the near future, thereby avoiding the biological fantasies of Aldous Huxley or the engineering fantasies of Zamyatin. At the same time, the near future permitted both to supply a plausible 'historical' narrative of how their contemporary world transformed into the world of 1984. In Orwell this was a straight repeat of Russian events in the 30 years after 1917. Chayanov's own narrative has been noted. Both also shared the same vision of a world segmented into empires. In the aftermath of communism, Orwell's world was divided into three empires: Oceania, East Asia and Eurasia. Chayanov's world was divided into five empires: American-Australian, Anglo-French, German, Russian and Sino-Japan.

These parallels need not signify much. The conference between Stalin, Roosevelt and Churchill at Tehran in 1943 had encouraged Orwell to think in terms of a world partitioned into empires. The impact of the coincidence in dates is reduced by the fact that *Nineteen Eighty-Four* was originally entitled *The Last Man in Europe*. It is further reduced by the fact that in the earliest manuscript, Orwell set the book in the year 1980. It was shifted to 1982, before settling on 1984. It has also been noted that Orwell's first wife composed in the 1930s a poem entitled 'End of the Century 1984'. Finally, in keeping with the Orwellian suppression of fact, Winston Smith was not even sure the year *was* 1984.

It seems that Chayanov saw nothing incongruous about the jarring elements in his mental constitution. He expressly described *Journey* as 'a scientific work' (Chayanov, 1999, 22). He was interested in anthroposophy, the 'spiritual science' founded by Rudolph Steiner, author of *Occult Science: An Outline*, who championed a union of science and spirit. In the 1920s this took a more practical turn that included biodynamic farming. Steiner's mixture of the rational and the occult, and of the modern and the traditional, had considerable resonance in the interwar period, including among some would-be ideologists of National Socialism. Perhaps predictably, understanding Chayanov on this score is made no easier by the fact that in his Peasant Republic, anthroposophists were subject to arrest.

Jevons and *The Theory of Peasant Economy*

One of Chayanov's most famous works in economic theory was undoubtedly his *Theory of Peasant Economy* of 1925. The analytical core of this book was, it will be argued here, taken from one of the more prosaic of scientific economists, W.S. Jevons.

Chayanov's model of farm enterprise in *The Theory of Peasant Economy* assumes a one-period, utility maximizing, price-taking enterprise, where labour was the one variable input, and utility was increased by consumption but reduced by labour. Although the farm's choice variable was labour, as labour can be mapped into output for given technology and price, the farm's optimization problem can be presented in terms of an optimal choice of income, as shown in Figure 7.1.

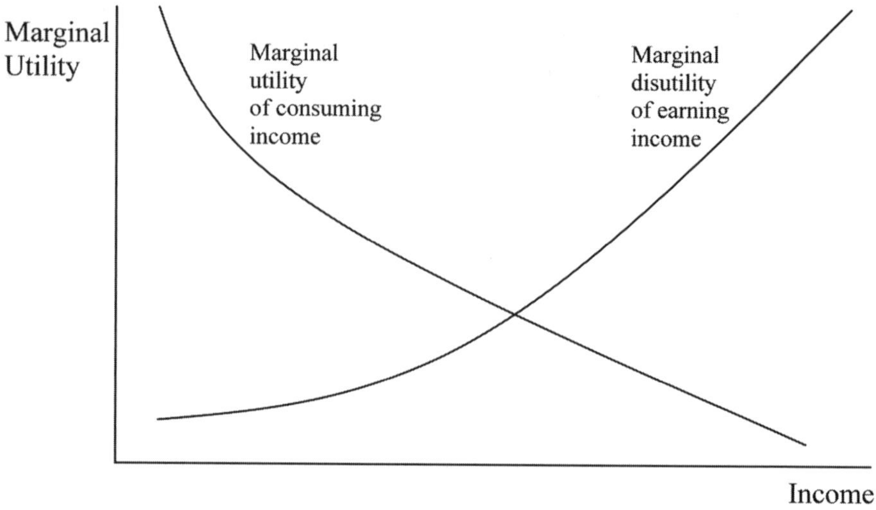

Figure 7.1: The Optimal Choice of Income

Chayanov quite rightly wrote that 'this is a logical development of the old positions of Gossen, Jevons' (Chayanov, 1999, 104). Chayanov adapted it from chapter five of Jevons's *Theory of Political Economy*. In the section entitled 'Theory of Labour' Jevons analyzed a utility maximizing model of labour supply of precisely the same essence as Chayanov's. And in the later section 'Balance Between Need and Labour', Jevons correctly concluded that in his model the response of the supply of labour to an increase in its reward was ambiguous: 'it is impossible to decide this question in an *a priori* manner' (Jevons, 1911, 180).

Chayanov also advanced an analysis of its comparative statics. However, he concluded that a rise in price of output must reduce the optimizing labour input; there was a negative relation between labour and its reward. In Chayanov's words '... a rise in payment for a unit of labour on the farm leads to a rise in annual output and in family well-being with reduced intensity of annual labour' (Chayanov, 1966, 84). In fact Chayanov was wrong and Jevons was right. Chayanov's analysis was logically erroneous. His 'peasant economy' problem may be characterized thus:

$$\text{Max } U(pq(L)) - D(L)$$

U = utility of consumption
D = disutility of labour
L = labour
$q(L)$ = output
p = value of output in terms of consumption goods

The response of labour to an increase in the value of output was:

$$\frac{dL}{dp}=\frac{pq'q\frac{U''}{U'}+q'}{-[pq'\frac{U''}{U'}pq'+pq''-\frac{D''(L)}{U'}]}$$

Given diminishing marginal productivity of labour (q”<0), diminishing marginal utility of consumption (U”<0) and increasing marginal disutility of labour (D”>0), the denominator was necessarily positive. The derivative therefore had the same sign as the numerator. And the numerator was ambiguous in sign. If marginal utility was constant (U”=0) the numerator was necessarily positive, and an increase in the price of output increased labour. But as soon as marginal utility was diminishing (U”<0), the numerator was possibly negative, and labour possibly declined in the face of a higher price of output.

Here is the classic ambiguity in the response in the labour supply, an ambiguity that resulted from the clash of the income and substitution effects. It can be understood in terms of Hicksian categories. If marginal utility was constant then the demand for leisure was purely a function of the opportunity cost of leisure, and the income effect for leisure was zero. The substitution effect must dominate. It was also the case that the amount of land that the ‘peasant enterprise’ was endowed with would have an ambiguous impact on the supply of labour. We can introduce land by letting consumption, C, be a function of land endowment, R, thus:

$$C=pq(\frac{L}{R})R$$

R = land endowment

It can be shown that response of L to R in the above maximization problem was ambiguous. Chayanov noted ‘from the moment’ of its appearance that his analysis was criticized by orthodox Soviet economists, but its logical errors seem never to have been picked by these hunters of bourgeois ideology. Their objection, of course, lay in the profound paradigmatical differences between Marx and Chayanov. To a Marxist, labour was value; to a Jevonian, labour was disutility.

Political Annihilation

Many the facts of Chayanov’s rout and destruction are now known, but questions of interpretation are still open. How far did his ‘recantation’ extend before his arrest in 1930? Jasny judged Chayanov to have climbed down on such issues as farm size. Indeed, in his article of 15 February 1929 (‘From Class Peasant Co-operatives to the Socialist Reconstruction of Agriculture’), ‘Chayanov seems to have gone beyond Stalin’, wrote Jasny, ‘when he declared in the same article, the future organization of agriculture is to be visualised not as a conglomerate of state and collective farms, co-ops and remaining independent enterprises, but as single socialist economies of whole districts' (Jasny, 1972, 202).

But how much Chayanov was opposed to large-scale agriculture has been debated. According to Shanin, there was no 'small is beautiful' message in Chayanov, only an objection to assuming bigger was always better. To Shanin, he recognized the need for large units of agricultural production. It is our contention that Chayanov did favour small peasant farm production before 1929. To him the nature of agricultural production – in particular the expense of transportation – dictated the limits to the enlargement of agricultural enterprises. Granted, larger agricultural enterprise had an advantage in wholesale and credit opportunities, as well as in the use of complicated equipment, or access to animal selection or agronomical advice. But in these fields the cooperation of small peasant enterprises would provide the peasantry with all the advantages found in large enterprises (Chayanov, 1917, 23–25).

We contend that a similar reversal took place over the capitalization of agricultural enterprises. In *Journey* 'the old idea of grain and meat factories' (Chayanov, 1977, 89) was dismissed, and inputs were overwhelmingly labour. By the late 1920s Chayanov was asserting that tractors, combine harvesters and trucks made immense 'grain factories' practical, and consequently he displayed enthusiasm for giant grain farms. What judgement of these reversals, if any, is appropriate?

Jasny passed a negative one. 'If this writer has a feeling other than deep pity for any one of those who capitulated to superior force, it is for Chayanov, all his talents not withstanding' (Jasny, 1972, 203). There may have been an anti-*Narodnik* bias in Jasny's judgment, as he was a Menshevik, and his *Names to be Remembered* was composed in large part from the names of Mensheviks. Further, Chayanov's statements on the eve of his arrest might be seen as an extension of his policy of co-operation with the regime (Chayanov, 1999, 110). He was successful for a while, as during NEP, Lenin was influenced by the idea of voluntary co-peasant operation. But, in the extreme times of late 1929 and the early 1930s, reality overcame even the worst expectations. Who was to know that there was to be no compromise with the regime?

In June 1930 Chayanov, along with Kondratiev and Yurovsky, was arrested on charges of sabotage and subversion. Stalin took a keen interest in their interrogations, and instructed the head of the Unified State Political Administration (OGPU, the political police) to: 'Run Messrs Kondratiev, Yurovsky, Chayanov etc through the mill … interrogate them as strictly as possible' (Stalin, 1995, 196). Chayanov, like Kondratiev, 'confessed' to joining a non-existent party, the Toiling Peasants Party (TKP). Their confessions ran to script: the TKP met regularly to plan an armed insurrection, which, with the help of foreign forces, would restore capitalism, and install a government headed by Kondratiev. Chayanov's particular duty was to advise the TKP on 'how to disrupt the entire economic life of the country in the event of foreign intervention' (that is, invasion) (Lih, 1995, 193).[6]

---

6 Another question: unlike the Mensheviks and the 'Industrialists', Chayanov and his fellow economists were never brought to trial. Why? Stalin believed that a trial was 'not without risk'. Risk of what exactly?

It is generally assumed that the 'TKP' was an OGPU invention, extracted by the defendants' strict interrogation by Yakov Agranov, 'one of the most feared sadists of the Lubyanka' (Barnett, 1998, 191), and a pioneer of the concoction of bogus conspiracies. We agree the accusations were fantastic, but under the terrible pressure of events, what dreamscapes might the thoughts of our fantasy author have galloped over, even before encountering Agranov?

Chayanov was released in 1932 and granted permission to work in an agricultural institute at one of the geographical extremities of the Soviet Union. He was forbidden to have any contact with other members of the institute, and experienced 'months of full solitude'. In a written plea to its director, he avowed that he 'wholly denied his former theory' and 'had brushed away all last remnants' of the 'petit bourgeois ideologist' that he once was: 'I give myself in full disposal to State and Party' (Bukhonova and Chilikova, 1997). This tragic document afforded him no shelter. He was rearrested in March 1937, sentenced on 3 October 1937 to the 'highest form of punishment', and shot the same day.

His wife Olga Chayanova was sentenced to ten years imprisonment, and re-arrested after her release. She last appeared in a final paragraph of the minutes of the AGM of the American Economics Association (AEA) of 1969. The secretary read a letter indicating that the widow of A.V. Chayanov was living in Russia on a very small income. In view of the fact that publication of Chayanov's book on peasant economy was issued in the AEA 'Translation Series' without a royalties payment, it was suggested that the AEA might want to make a small contribution to Madame Chayanov. Following a discussion it was agreed to make a contribution of $300.[7]

The Chayanov Boom

At least Madame Chayanov got something from the sudden resurrection of her husband's memory in the mid-1960s. In truth, the analytical core of the *Peasant Economy* was some very old Jevonian economy (with some serious analytic slips, too, as we have stressed). But for a time Chayanov was high fashion. So Chayanov's Jevonian analysis took a central place in Marxian works of anthropology (Sahlins, 1972), decorated with quotes from Althussser and other Marxian assortments of the decade. It was suggested that Chayanov could fruitfully be studied in accompaniment with the thoughts of Kautsky, Lenin and Mao. The folly of the times extended to grouping Chayanov – a classic neo-*Nardonik* advocate of decentralization – with the Bolshevik A.A. Bogdanov and the Menshevik V.G. Groman, and giving Chayanov equal credit with them for the input-output planning tool (a notion debunked in Belykh, 1989).

There also came to exist in the anthropology of peasants something known as the 'Lenin-Chayanov debate' (Schulman and Newman, 1991). Of course, Lenin and Chayanov never 'debated' anything. It is well-known that Lenin contested neo-*Narodnik* positions. As we have noted, Lenin in the 1890s attacked the *Narodnik* assumption of the non-existence of capitalist development in peasant agriculture. In

7 $1680 in 2007 prices.

reply, the *Narodiniks* of 1890s strengthened the thesis of the inherent advantage of peasant agriculture, a position, as we have argued, that was highly sympathetic to Chayanov.

It has been suggested that Lenin was 'very well disposed' to Chayanov, who seemed exempt from Lenin's bolts of rage. Thus Chayanov was a member of 'All-Russian Committee to Aid the Hungry' that had six of its members condemned to death on Lenin's orders. Chayanov was preserved, perhaps because of his membership of the Agricultural Commissariat. But that only begs the question how he managed to last so long there. Leonid Chertkov writes of Lenin ordering in 1921 that Chayanov should not be harassed 'because we need wise heads, we are left with too few of them' (Shanin, 1986, n. 26). The six less fortunate members of the Committee to Aid the Hungry were not in the event executed, but exiled to the likes of typhoid ridden Kazan, before being ultimately deported. Chayanov, in contrast, was dispatched to London to research in 1920, on an effectively 'all expenses paid vacation'. Is Chayanov one of those of whom the more one learns, the less one actually knows?

References

Avtonomov, V., Anan'in, O. and Makasheva, N., (2006), *Istoria ekonomicheskikh uchenii*, Moscow: INFRA.

Barnett, Vincent, (1998), *Kondratiev and the Dynamics of Economic Development: Long Cycles and Industrial Growth in Historical Context*, Basingstoke: Macmillan.

Belykh, A.A., (1989), 'A Note on the Origins of Input-Output Analysis and the Contribution of early Soviet Economists: Chayanov, Bogdanov and Kritsman', *Soviet Studies*, 61 (3).

Bukhonova, I.N. and Chilikova, E.V., (1997), 'Ia Okazalsia Vybroshennym Iz Chelovecheskogo Obshchestva: A.V. Chaianov v Kazhakstanskoi Ssylke', *Otechestvennye Arkhivy* (2).

Chayanov, A., (1917), *Chto takoe agararnyi vopros?* Moscow: Universal'naia Biblioteka.

Chayanov, A., (1921), 'Opyty izuchenia izolirovannogo gosudarstva', *Trudy vysshego seminaria sel'sko-khozyaistvennoi ekonomii i politiki*, Moscow.

Chayanov, A.V., (1925), *Kratkii kurs kooperation*, Moscow.

Chayanov, A.V., (1966), Basile Kerblay (ed.) *The Theory of Peasant Economy*, Homewood, IL: Irwin.

Chayanov, A.V., (1977), 'The Journey of my Brother Alexei to the Land of the Peasant Utopia', *Journal of Peasant Studies*, 4 (1).

Chayanov, A., (1986), *The Theory of Peasant Economy*, The University of Wisconsin Press.

Chayanov, A.V., (1989), *Krest'yanskoe khozyaistvo,* Moscow: Economika.

Chayanov, A., (1991), *The Theory of Peasant Cooperatives*, Ohio State University Press.

Chayanov, A., (1999), 'Chayanov in Berlin', Frank Bourgholtzer (ed.), *Journal of Peasant Studies*, 26 (4).

Ginev, V.N., (1977), *Agrarnyi vopros i melkoburzhuaznye partii v Rossii v 1917,* Leningrad: Nauka.

Kantor, M., (1927), 'Neonarodnichestvo v tiskakh protivorechii', *Bol'shevik*, (9).

Jasny, Naum, (1972), *Soviet Economists of the Twenties*, Cambridge: Cambridge University Press.

Jevons, W.S., (1911), *The Theory of Political Economy*, H.S. Jevons, (ed.), London: Macmillan.

Kojima, Shuichi, (2004), 'Comparing Chayanov and Kondratiev', *Japanese Slavic and East European Studies*, 25.

Kostrikin, V.I., (1975), *Zemel'nye komitety v 1917 godu*, Moscow: Nauka.

Kritsman, L.N., (1926), *Klassovoe rassloenie sovetskoi derevni*, Moscow.

Lenin, V.I., (1956), *The Development of Capitalism in Russia*, Moscow: Foreign Language Publishing House.

Lih, Lars T., Oleg V. Naumov and Oleg Khlevniuk, (1995), 'Introduction', in *Stalin's Letters to Molotov, 1925–1936*, Lars T. Lih, Oleg V. Naumov and Oleg V. Khlevniuk (eds), New Haven: Yale University Press.

Radkey, O., (1958) *The Agrarian Foes of Bolshevism*, Columbia University Press.

Schulman, M.D. and B.A. Newman, (1991), 'The Persistence of the Black Farmer: the Contemporary Relevance of the Lenin-Chayanov Debate', *Rural Sociology*, 56 (2).

Sahlins, Marshall, (1972), *Stone Age Economics*, Chicago: Aldine-Atherton.

Shanin, T., (1986), 'Chayanov's Message', in: Chayanov, A., *The Theory of Peasant Economy*, University of Wisconsin Press.

Spirina, M.V., (1987), *Krakh melko-burzhuaznoi kontseptsii sotsializma eserov*, Moscow: Nauka.

Stalin, J., (1995), *Stalin's Letters to Molotov, 1925–1936*, Lars T. Lih, Oleg V. Naumov and Oleg V. Khlevniuk (eds), New Haven: Yale University Press.

Chapter 8

Russian Émigré Economists in the USA

Vincent Barnett

Great strides have been made recently in understanding the history of North American economics in the first half of the twentieth century. For example the conflict between the American Institutionalist economists and their neoclassical opponents has received much more attention from scholars, leading to the development of the idea of interwar pluralism (Yonay, 1998). The links between the mathematization of economic theory and various military concerns such as games of strategy has also been explored to great effect (Mirowski, 2002). The role of émigré economists in developing both interwar and post-World War II concerns in North America has also been explored to some extent (Vaughn, 1994). However, this latter area still has significant gaps, at least in terms of the national origins of the various émigré groups that are analyzed, and might also benefit from more effort with regards to conceptual and thematic concerns.

The USA as a nation has prided itself in the fact that it was a country built upon a number of waves of immigration. The dream of emigration to the USA, and then being able to make a successful life for yourself no matter what your national origins were, was (and still is) a powerful force affecting North American culture. And the American economics profession in the first half of the twentieth century has long been recognized as containing a number of significant émigré theorists, some of whom are even winners of the Nobel Prize in economics. Hence it would seem reasonable to explore the influence of all of these particular economists conceived as émigré groups in more detail.

One obvious point of analysis is the countries of origin of the economists in question. Many émigrés to the USA in the interwar period came from continental Europe, but within this varied group of countries, many significant differences could be highlighted. For example, Karen Vaughn has investigated the impact of Austrian economics in North America, focusing in particular on Ludwig von Mises, but she also explained that before Mises, Joseph Schumpeter, Gottfried Harberler, Fritz Machlup and Oskar Morgenstern had been forced to leave their native lands by the march of Hitler's forces. Vaughn suggested that these latter four economists all obtained good academic positions in US universities and 'assimilated themselves nicely into the indigenous academic scene' (Vaughn, 1994, 62). The question naturally arises of what underlying conception(s) of economic theory they had brought along with them. As Vaughn showed convincingly, Mises had a particular Austrian view of market processes that was conceptually distinct from the neoclassical tradition of native-born American economists such as Irving Fisher.

One particularly unique country of origin for émigré economists was Russia/the USSR. Seen either as the very far edge of Europe, or even as constituting a special

Europe–Asian region of its own, Russia contributed to the pan-European exodus to North America (at least in individual personnel terms) as much as Austria or Germany did. According to Roger Backhouse, the émigré economists who entered the USA in the 1920s originated mostly from Russia (Backhouse, 2002, 207), suggesting that this particular exodus was of major significance to understanding interwar developments. Whether Russia had a particular intellectual tradition of its own in economics, different from but comparable to the homogeneity of the Austrian approach, is a question that requires further consideration in this context.

In order to begin to answer these questions, this chapter examines the exodus of Russian economists overseas after 1917 with a number of specific concerns in mind. Firstly, it simply documents some aspects of the overlapping work and experiences of a few of these economists as they tried to escape from Soviet Russia and make a new life for themselves in Europe and/or the USA. Most of the focus will be on the US-based émigrés, but a brief account of some European émigrés is included towards the end as a point of comparison. Secondly, it asks the question whether this group of émigré economists took with them a number of thematic and intellectual concerns vis-à-vis their economic theory, that is whether along with their physical emigration went a conceptual emigration which had important consequences for the development of North American (and indeed Western) economics after 1917. Put another way, to what extent was post-war 'American' economics the result of the fusion of some specifically Russian and/or Soviet priorities and attitudes with existing indigenous traditions?

Immigration into America

Simon Kuznets and Ernest Rubin have provided an analysis of the immigrant contribution to US population growth in the period from 1850 to 1940 as shown in Table 8.1.

Table 8.1: American Population Growth due to Immigration

Period	Percentage of US Population Growth Accounted For By Immigrants
1850–1860	22.9%
1860–1870	17.1%
1870–1880	10.8%
1880–1890	20.1%
1890–1900	8.4%
1900–1910	19.9%
1910–1920	2.9%
1920–1930	1.7%
1930–1940	-29.3%

Source: Kuznets and Rubin, *Immigration and the Foreign Born,* p. 3.

The dramatic decline of the percentage of total population growth that was due to immigrants after 1910, and an absolute decline in the immigrant population (by 2.61 million) across the 1930s, was explained by Kuznets and Rubin as a consequence of the change in immigration policy after World War One, augmented by the impact of the great depression after 1929. In general they described the USA as 'for a long time the frontier outpost, and more recently, the giant economic leader of the older civilization of Europe, the ancestral home of most of its population' (Kuznets and Rubin, 1954, 9). They identified 20-year long swings in both gross and net immigration to the USA, without conclusively deciding on whether this was a cause or a consequence of identified long swings in gross national product (Kuznets and Rubin, 1954, 4–5). Kuznets of course had first-hand experience of traversing the Atlantic frontier, as will subsequently be discussed in more detail.

Emigration from Russia

Emigration from Russia had a lengthy history going a long way back before the Bolshevik revolution in 1917. Throughout the nineteenth century many political exiles from the tsarist autocracy had fled overseas in order to escape the consequences of governmental attitudes towards their political beliefs. In the early part of the twentieth century various Russian Marxian groupings had set up camp in countries such as Germany and Switzerland, and some liberal émigrés could also be found in these countries (Williams, 1972, 31). However this would turn out to be temporary political exile rather than permanent emigration.

Another element in the émigré equation that is necessary to keep in mind is that there were a number of distinct periods of emigration of intellectuals out of the USSR, and that the factors involved in each case may have varied considerably. The first wave of post-revolutionary émigrés can be identified as being generated by the Russian civil war of 1918–20. This was a wave that included many anti-Bolshevik military personnel, but was not restricted to members of the White Army alone:

> They left Russia by many routes, the Black Sea, the western and southern frontiers, the White Sea and over the Far Eastern frontier. Not only the military forces, but large sections of the civilian population left the country in this mass exodus ... Hundreds of thousands of émigrés from Russia were scattered across the world ... (*MVD-MGB*, 1957, 1).

The geographical route of emigration that was taken by individual émigrés was of course relevant to their place of final destination. As well as the quantitative nature of the emigration from the USSR, there was also the qualitative aspect. One source emphasized that among those who fled the Bolshevik regime were some of the country's outstanding writers, academicians, statesmen and businessmen, including the composers Stravinsky and Rakhmaninov, the painters Chagall and Kandinsky, and the writers Nabokov and Zamyatin (Pipes, 1980, 326).

A notable case of forced emigration by the government occurred in the summer/autumn of 1922, when philosophers such as Nikolai Berdyaev and economic thinkers such as S.N. Bulgakov and S.L. Frank were arrested, charged with 'anti-Soviet activities' and then expelled from Russian soil. In this particular case of national ejection one source has outlined that:

> … at least 77 intellectuals, accompanied by their families, were expelled. Of them, 23 were economists, agronomists and cooperative movement leaders; 13 were philosophers, sociologists and legal scholars; 13 were scientists and technical experts; 11 were journalists and writers; six were historians; six were religious activists; and five were doctors (Zolotov, 2002, 3).

Another source identified the number of scholars and intellectuals expelled at this time as 'several hundred' (Williams, 1972, 247). The fact that, numerically speaking at least, economics-related personnel formed the largest subset with this particular grouping of émigrés as related by Zolotov (23 out of the 77 reported), suggests that this subject area was seen as the most politically sensitive of all by the Soviet authorities, even at this relatively early time. The New Economic Policy (NEP) (1921–29) had only been in operation for approximately one year when these particular intellectuals were expelled, suggesting that the relative openness that was trumpeted by the creators of NEP as an essential element of the new political attitude, had definite limits when it came to significant differences of opinion vis-à-vis policies of economic development.

The favoured national location of the 1922 exiles was Germany, where there were significant groups of Russian émigrés well entrenched. For example, a Russian Philosophical Society already existed in Berlin (Williams, 1972, 249). In terms of the nature of the émigrés themselves, they have been identified as the Westernized elite of a non-Western society (Williams, 1972, 372). It might reasonably be assumed that, being partly Westernized in terms of education, they would have been somewhat familiar with the culture and traditions of proximate European countries like Germany. It can also be hypothesized that Russian émigrés might have been less familiar with the culture and traditions of more geographically distant countries like the USA.

Russian Traditions in Economics

Before focusing on individual case studies of émigré economists, some general points about native Russian traditions in economics require consideration. Some previous studies have raised the question of whether indigenous currents in political economy that were present in Russia before 1917 were either transplanted overseas 'as they were', or were significantly transformed in the migration process (Kojima, 2004, 18). Others have suggested that:

> What in the context of the contemporary international academic community was a sudden large-scale movement of scientific personnel was facilitated by the convergence of international 'styles' of economic thinking and practice during the interwar years. The teaching of economics at the LSE was already, by the later 1920s, heavily stamped by Austrian, Swedish and American work; other major centres, especially Oxford, proved relatively open to an influx of Continental academics. The establishment of the University

in Exile (later the Graduate School) at the New School for Social Research in New York provided a custom-built home for refugees … (Tribe, 2001, 742).

This chapter will suggest that in fact, the work of the Russian émigré economists considered here was in part transformed by national dislocation (as suggested by Kojima), but it also contributed to actively transforming the existing set of currents that were encountered overseas (as implied by Tribe). But what were some of the most notable indigenous currents and themes in Russian economics before and just after 1917?

Firstly, mathematical economics and statistics (as represented by V.K. Dmitriev and A.A. Chuprov) had experienced significant development at the end of the nineteenth century and the beginning of the twentieth. The well-known school of Russian mathematicians influenced this aspect of pre-revolutionary economics to an important extent. Secondly, agricultural economics, as most notably represented by N.D. Kondratiev and A.V. Chayanov, received a major boost in the period leading up to 1917. Thirdly, business cycles theory, as represented by M.I. Tugan-Baranovsky and S.A. Pervushin, had flourished in the 1890s and beyond. And fourthly, various approaches to industrialization policy, for example as developed by D.I. Mendeleev, Sergei Witte and many others, had been an essential part of Russian economic thinking for a number of decades prior to 1917. The vast majority of Russian economists would have been quite familiar with the most significant aspects of these themes. The question naturally follows: did some of these currents and not others get transplanted overseas by Russian émigrés?

Another important factor was whether the particular émigré economists under analysis had received any education and/or training within Russia before their transfer overseas, or had emigrated at such a young age that their country of origin had little impact on their intellectual development. In this chapter the focus will be on those émigrés who did receive some level of education within Russia, and hence might be thought more likely to have absorbed the themes and approaches of their homeland, before having the opportunity of transplanting such themes elsewhere. Economists who emigrated at a very young age will not be considered in detail. Finally, the question of whether émigrés resided in any significant intermediate points of relocation, before finally travelling to the USA, requires some consideration. Alexander Gershenkron for example, spent some time in Vienna before heading for the USA, where he developed associations with Austrian economists such as Mises and F.A. Hayek (Craver, 1986, 11).

The following Russian-born economists who emigrated to the USA are discussed in chronological order, the person who was born the earliest being presented first.

Jacob Marschak (1898–1977)

Marschak was born in Kiev in 1898, studied mechanical engineering at the Kiev Institute of Technology and became a member of the Menshevik faction of the Russian Social Democratic Labour Party (RSDLP) at a young age. The Mensheviks were revolutionary socialists who had a number of significant disagreements with V.I. Lenin's Bolshevik faction of the RSDLP regarding the political strategy that

Russian Marxists should adopt, but shared a common reverence for many of Marx's historical doctrines. Marschak's membership of this faction suggests that he was very sympathetic to Marxist economics in general at this time, as other well-known Russian economists friendly to Marxism (such as Tugan-Baranovsky) were some way to the right of the Mensheviks in political terms. Arrow dated Marschak's conversion to Marxism at 1915, when he was only 17 years old (Arrow, 1986, 338). At the end of 1916 he was arrested by the authorities and not released until the February revolution in 1917.

As a result of the revolutionary upheavals Marschak served for a short while as Minister of Labour in the Menshevik government of Georgia, in which he opposed official recognition of the Bolshevik government in Petrograd. After the Bolshevik assumption of power in October 1917, he campaigned for Menshevik aims through 1918, but the Menshevik government eventually collapsed. Marschak then returned to Kiev, but quickly came to believe that (for him at least) politics was a lost cause. As a consequence of this he emigrated first to Berlin in 1919, then later on to Heidelberg. Marschak then embarked upon a second round of emigration out of Germany, first to Oxford in the UK and then finally on to the USA. He was thus 21 years old at the time of his initial emigration out of Russia.

In Berlin for six months Marschak attended the lectures of L.V. Bortkiewicz, and in Heidelberg he studied under E. Lederer, where he subsequently received a PhD in 1922. Germany was at this time home to a number of Russian Menshevik exiles. From 1924 to 1926 he worked as a newspaper reporter on economics-related topics for the *Frankfurter Zeitung*. He spent some time in the UK in 1927, and between 1928 and 1930 he became an important member of the Kiel Institute of World Economics headed by Adolph Lowe. When the Kiel Institute was dismantled as a consequence of the rise of Nazism, he went initially to the Oxford Institute of Statistics (1933–39), and then followed many members of the Kiel Institute to the New School for Social Research in New York. In 1943 Marschak became the head of the Cowles Commission in Chicago (Radner, 1987, vol. 3, 348), a research centre for the mathematical and statistical investigation of economics.

Marschak's early work in the 1920s was clearly indebted to his Russian Marxian origins. His first article published in 1923 focused on aspects of the socialist calculation debate, in particular it discussed the effect of monopoly on prices and how socialism as an economic system might yield improvements in pricing techniques. This suggests that Marschak was still sympathetic to some Marxian ideas at the time of his first emigration out of Russia. He also wrote an account of the 'new middle class' in 1926 using a structural-sociological approach. However in the 1930s, the focus of his work shifted towards the more recognizable concerns of the burgeoning econometric movement, with papers on topics such as the elasticity of demand and money conceived as an asset. It appears at first sight that, by the 1940s, Marschak had severed all his intellectual links with his Russian homeland and had made a complete shift to the mainstream American concerns of the Cowles Commission. The ideological interests of the socialist calculation debate were a world apart from the value-neutral statistical modelling being advocated by the early econometricians. However, it could be argued that this development was not so far away from the concerns of some Russian economists and statisticians as it might at first glance appear.

One of Marschak's first articles to fit squarely into the Cowles approach was 'Random Simultaneous Equations and the Theory of Production' written with W.H. Andrews, which presented a stochastic equation for the yield obtained from a given plot of land (Marschak, 1944, 144). The authors explained that a random parameter assumed different values with certain probabilities, this stochastic conception of economic variables being central to the new approach being developed in the Cowles Commission. For example in 1945 Marschak wrote:

> In economics, measurements must in general be statistical estimates because numerous factors exist that cannot and need not be identified separately and that combine themselves into 'random' influences. Economic propositions ... are in general statistical ... (Marschak, 1945, 379).

It is well known that the pioneering contribution in this respect was by T. Haavelmo. Or at least the Haavelmo paper was the pioneering work that introduced this approach to economics. In fact the stochastic approach to probability theory had a distinguished history in one particular country – namely Russia. The names associated with this approach – A.N. Kolmogorov, A.Ya. Khinchin and E.E. Slutsky – were people who any self-respecting Russian intellectual of the time would have known well.

The Russian tradition in probability was somewhat distinct from other currents such as the English biometric school, in that greater emphasis was placed on the concept of stochastic processes. As outlined by Jan von Plato, the mathematical study of stochastic processes with continuous time was started in the late 1920 in the USSR (Plato, 1994, 198). Plato further explained that:

> Until about 1930 the random processes studied in probability theory had been almost exclusively discrete in time ... Kolmogorov's first and very long paper of 1931 on continuous time random processes ... establishes a special measure theoretic framework for studying continuous time stochastic processes (Plato, 1994, 207–08)

Slutsky knew Kolmogorov's work quite well, as Slutsky himself had also worked on the theory of stochastic processes in Moscow in the 1920s (see Barnett, 2006). Did Marschak make a connection to this aspect of his Russian roots explicitly? Apparently he did not, as no references to either Slutsky's or Kolmogorov's works have been found in Marschak's publications. However according to Mary Morgan, Marschak actually studied for a time with Slutsky before 1917 (Morgan, 1990, 153, n. 17). Even without substantiating this personal connection with further evidence, it would seem unlikely that Marschak would not have known of Slutsky's work at all, even if only through the 1937 *Econometrica* English translation.

Another aspect of Marschak's involvement in the early Cowles programme was that this programme has been described as being 'ground zero of Walrasian market socialism in America' in the immediate post-war era (Mirowski, 2002, 166). Mirowski suggested directly that the Cowles faith in planning was partly derived from their shared European backgrounds and Old World cultural presuppositions (Mirowski, 2002, 168). Thus there were two prongs to Marschak's potential thematic transfer of émigré concerns, a more political aspect concerned with applying mathematical methods to achieve progressive policy aims, and a more technical aspect devoted to applying Russian mathematical concerns to develop American econometric methodology.

Simon Kuznets (1901–85)

Kuznets's belief in the crucial importance of emigration to the American economy was succinctly expressed in the preface to his joint-authored study of *Immigration and the Foreign Born* for the NBER, where the authors wrote:

> … immigration and emigration may well be the international flows that had the most profound impact upon the growth, and, for a long time, also upon the short-term movements of this country's economy (Kuznets and Rubin, 1954, v)

Kuznets was born in Pinsk in Russia in 1901. He was subsequently educated in Kharkov (at the Gymnasium and the Commercial Institute), was employed for a short while in the Bureau of Labour Statistics of the Ukraine, before finally emigrating to the USA in 1922. He was thus 21 years old at the time of his emigration. He obtained a first degree in 1923 and subsequently a PhD in 1926 both from Columbia University, and then became a member of the National Bureau of Economic Research (NBER) from 1927 to 1961 (Fogel, 2000, 1). A Soviet encyclopedia of political economy described Kuznets simply as 'an American economist', suggesting that such émigrés were officially disowned in the USSR (Sarychev, 1975, vol. 2, 321,), but he was more than this simplistic description implied. Kuznets's work as an economist can be divided into two main categories: business cycles/economic growth and national income. It can be argued that both of these areas of research are indebted in some (as-yet unspecified) fashion to the Russian and Soviet context from which Kuznets had originated.

Regarding the first category, the Russian contribution to business cycle theory is well known, as the names of Tugan-Baranovsky, Kondratiev and Slutsky immediately attest. Kuznets undoubtedly knew of this tradition of work extensively, and he frequently referred to Kondratiev and Slutsky in particular. For example in *Secular Movements in Production and Prices* of 1930 and elsewhere, Kuznets discussed the long cycle idea in some detail, suggesting that the repetitions available for analysis of long cycles were not of sufficient number to allow proper comparison (Kuznets, 1967, 264). Moreover, Kuznets also demonstrated knowledge of lesser-known Russian economists like V.A. Bazarov, whose work on 'curves of development' of capitalism had analyzed cyclical and secular trends using some original ideas imported from the natural sciences such as chemical equilibrium (Le Chatelier's principle) and wave mechanics (Barnett, 2004, 85–87). Kuznets's discussion of the declining rate of percentage increase of industrial growth in terms of a symmetrical logistic curve might well have been borrowed directly from Bazarov (Kuznets, 1967, 63–65).

Kuznets presented a theory of long-run economic growth (or what he called 'modern economic growth'), which recognized that at the level of particular industries, a tendency to retardation in growth rates might be found. According to the author of Kuznets's biographical memoir, the logistic curve provided a good fit to the growth pattern of a specific industry over its life cycle (Fogel, 2000, 7). The notion of 'secondary trend', or a cyclical swing of between 15 and 25 years, invented by Kuznets as an intermediate fluctuation between primary trend and business cycles, could also be seen to be indebted to Kondratiev's conception of economic conjuncture as being composed of long cycles, medium cycles and short cycles (Barnett, 1998, 106). Kondratiev's first account of this topic was published in 1922, with further expansions of these ideas written in 1925, 1926 and 1928. Kuznets wrote *Secular Movements in Production and Prices* in 1925–26, that is it was begun only three years after his emigration from Russia, and hence the impact of his pre-American experiences was likely still fresh in his mind.

A year or so later Kuznets was one of the first US-based economists to recognize the importance of Slutsky's 1927 article on the random causes of business cycles. Slutsky had been in contact with Mitchell's NBER, as an inscribed offprint of Slutsky's 1925 article on the stochastic asymptote and limit sent personally to Mitchell attested (CUSMC, Mitchell Papers, P-10). Someone at the NBER – possibly Kuznets himself given his language ability – prepared an English summary of Slutsky's 1927 article that stated that Slutsky's first thesis of the initial similarity of wavelike fluctuations had not been formulated rigidly or demonstrated mathematically. The summary continued:

> The inductive proof of the second thesis is in fitting sinusoidal curves to the models ... In order to get a good fit, however, a number of harmonics, superimposed had to be fitted (6 of them in one case), and even then the series had to be presented as consisting of discrete parts, with the groups of curves fitted accordingly different (CUSMC, Mitchell Papers, B131).

This apparently sceptical attitude, whether it actually emanated from Kuznets or not, did not prevent Kuznets from discussing Slutsky's 1927 article in print in his own article in 1929 (Kuznets, 1929).

With respect to the second category of Kuznets's work, national income, one of the first Russian efforts to measure this quantity was made by S.N. Prokopovich. Prokopovich published his 'Experiences at Calculating National Income in 1900' in the *Works of the Imperial Free Economic Society* in 1906. He calculated that the national income of all of Russia in 1900 was 8.9 billion rubles (Prokopovich, 1918, 26). Pioneering work in the area of the development of systematic national income accounting in the USA was accomplished by the NBER after 1920 (Zarnowitz, 1992, 165). Reading Kuznets's 1941 book on *National Income and Its Composition, 1919–1938*, it can be argued that some of underlying ideas employed in the initial chapter on the concept of national income itself owe a clear debt to his pre-NBER Russian context. For example Kuznets wrote:

> But if the market is considered as a complex of social relations of a certain type, and marketability as the characteristic of goods involved in them, it must be recognized that there are different kinds of market expressive of significantly different underlying social relations (Kuznets, 1941, 8).

The word 'marketability' had a direct Russian equivalent (*tovarnost'*) that was frequently employed in Soviet debates in the 1920s, and the idea of the market as a set of social relations had obvious Marxian paternity. Kuznets defined marketability as relating to the satisfaction, scarcity, disposability and relational involvement of a particular good. Other concepts employed by Kuznets such as 'national economy' (Kuznets, 1941, 50) are also direct translations of Russian phrases (*narodnoe khozyaistvo*), whilst the idea of 'family economy' (Kuznets, 1941, 10) could be seen as derivative of Chayanov's conception of the structure and motivating drive of peasant farming units. This might suggest a notion of the emigration of terminology or of underlying concepts, which occurred alongside the personnel transfer.

In general, the influence of Kuznets's pre-émigré experiences is more readily apparent on the first category of his work than the second, but it would seem unlikely that there was no influence at all of Kuznets's Russian origins on his underlying approach to economic analysis.

W.W. Leontief (1906–99)

Leontief was born in 1906 in St Petersburg, the son of a university professor. He studied at Leningrad University beginning in 1921 (at the very young age of 15) and he graduated in 1925. He left for Berlin the same year. As his reason for emigrating from Russia, Leontief subsequently declared that: 'I left the Soviet Union in 1925. I got in trouble with the government, actually. I had to go away in order to be able to work' (Leontief, 2007, 17). He also stated that there were political reasons for his departure, as he would frequently become involved in protests. At one point he was even arrested by the Russian authorities for his activities, his father being an organizer of factory strikes.

In Berlin Leontief studied with Werner Sombart and Ladislaus von Bortkiewicz, and then he became an important member of the Kiel school in the Institute of World Economics. After spending a year assisting in the planning of the Chinese railway network, in 1931 he travelled onwards to his final destination, the USA. In America he first joined the National Bureau of Economic Research in New York, but soon afterwards he left for the economics department at Harvard University, where he remained for the central part of his career until 1975 (Cave, 1981, 160–61). Hence Leontief spent only the first 19 years of his life in Russia. Even so the last four of these years constituted the first half of the NEP (1921–29), which was a crucial and very creative period for new developments in economic theory and policy, and hence some significant degree of contextual influence on Leontief's work cannot be ruled out *a priori*.

Leontief is, of course, most famous for his work on input-output analysis. Whilst the germ of this idea goes back to Francois Quesnay, it can be argued that the context of the USSR in the 1920s was where this idea had received its first detailed elaboration in practical terms. The Soviet effort to create a balance sheet of the entire national economy for 1923/24 was spearheaded by P.I. Popov from within the Central Statistical Administration (TsSU). Other Russian economists like A.A. Bogdanov and L.N. Kritsman have been selected as developing the input-output idea in 1921 (Belykh, 1989, 428), these in turn then influencing Popov via N.I. Bukharin. One commentator has written on the initial Soviet context of Leontief's work that:

> Early Soviet work devoted to compiling a balance of the national economy for the year 1923/4 has also been cited as an influence on Leontief's thinking … Leontief's review of this work appeared in Germany in October 1925 and, in Russian translation, in the December 1925 issue of *Planned Economy* … The present-day reader finds it hard to see the seeds of the input-output model in the short review, and Leontief himself disclaims the influence of the Soviet balance (Cave, 1981, 165).

Leontief's initial disclaimer of any Soviet influence occurred well before the Soviet collapse, and hence might be regarded as a little suspect, since political factors might have led Leontief to downplay any Soviet contribution to the context or content of input-output analysis. Together with the initial disclaimer, Leontief later cited his own work within the Kiel school on demand and supply as being more conducive to the fostering of the input-output approach, and also his knowledge of Quesnay (Leontief, 2007, 16–17).

This question certainly deserves further investigation. What exactly did Leontief's 1925 article on the Soviet balance contain? The following quotation is the opening paragraph:

> Among various problems which must be solved by contemporary Russian statistics, that of representing in numbers the total turnover of economic life is perhaps the most interesting as well as the most complex. As a result of many years' work by the Central Statistical Administration, the 'Balance of the Economy of the USSR in 1923/24' has appeared. The principal feature of this balance … is the attempt to represent in numbers not only the production but also the distribution of the social product, so as to obtain a general picture of the entire process of reproduction in the form of a 'Tableau economique' (economic table) (Leontief, 1964, 88).

Leontief related that within the balance, all goods had been divided first into three groups – industrial, agricultural and construction – and then into four – consumption, raw materials, fuel and tools of production. He emphasized that the problem of calculating the total income of a national economy had great importance for the methodology of composing statistics of production. Much later he admitted that national income analysis was being developed in the Soviet context of his youth, but he denied that anyone was thinking (at least early on) in terms of a statistical basis for economic planning (Leontief, 2007, 17). He also admitted that there was no real dichotomy between input-output analysis and national income accounting (Leontief, 2007, 18).

Despite Leontief's unconvincing denial of an early link between statistical analysis and planning methodology, the Russian and Soviet contributions to both statistical theory and statistical measurement had been significant both before and after the Bolshevik revolution in 1917. In his 1925 article on the Soviet balance Leontief also wrote that:

> Every statistical sum should be constituted in such a way that the relationship among the values of its component parts fully corresponds to the actual relationship of individual data included in the subject of statistical investigation (Leontief, 1964, 91).

Regarding the actual published balance table prepared by TsSU, Leontief declared how it showed that the economy of the USSR was organized in the main as a natural economy, and he concluded the 1925 article with the claim that the balance required further methodological discussion. This analysis does not sound as though Leontief was totally oblivious to the further elaboration of the balance approach, or that he would soon forget the importance of some of the techniques used in preparing the TsSU balance.

In more political areas of research, Leontief was not as virulently anti-Marx as some of his fellow émigré economists became in exile. In an article entitled 'The Significance of Marxian Economics for Present-Day Economic Theory' from 1938, Leontief commended Marx's contribution in a number of areas of analysis. Firstly, he praised Marx for developing a scheme describing the interrelation between the consumer and capital goods industries, something of at least indirect relevance to Leontief's own checkerboard balance approach. Secondly, he praised Marx for insightfully analyzing the long-run tendencies of the capitalist system, elements such as the increasing concentration of wealth and incessant technological progress (Leontief, 1938, 5). However Leontief was keen to emphasize the fact that Marx's contribution could only be evaluated in relation to its own period of creation, and hence it had been made obsolete in many areas by more recent contributions to economic theory. Leontief described Marx in conclusion as the 'great character reader of the capitalist system', and hence for Leontief the empirical and descriptive aspects of Marx were far more relevant to the modern economist than the outdated theoretical system that he had attempted to create (Leontief, 1938, 8–9).

Unlike some of his émigré colleagues, and perhaps prefigured by the type of economic analysis that he pursued, Leontief was not totally opposed to some forms of economic planning in market-type systems of control. As late as the 1970s, Leontief advocated the creation of a planning board in the USA that would use input-output techniques to develop indicative plans for various economic growth possibilities, and he accepted that the final choice in such a process would always be political. Leontief was perhaps the Soviet émigré who achieved the most in relation to mainstream Western economics, but the national origins of some aspects of his work should not be forgotten.

Russian Émigré Economists in Europe

As opposed to the three émigrés considered in detail above, a group of more politically orientated Russian émigré economists can be outlined, who were concerned more with participating in the ideological battle against Soviet power, rather than with further developing their purely economic expertise. This group were more likely to remain in Europe after emigrating, rather than travel onwards to the USA, and make a striking contrast to the US-based émigrés.

One of the most prominent of these émigré economists was S.N. Prokopovich (1871–1955), whose pioneering work on measuring national income was mentioned previously. In the late 1890s, Prokopovich had been a young socialist who came under the influence of Bernstein's revisionism, and he had consequently criticized G.V. Plekhanov's conception of a revolution that was to be controlled by a very small party, preferring instead to encourage workers to learn to organize for themselves. Prokopovich worked for a time in the Provisional Government in 1917 but left Russia in 1922. Subsequent to this exile, Prokopovich's 'economic cabinet' was set up first in Berlin and then transferred to Prague. In the 1930s this group published a 'Bulletin of the Economic Cabinet of Prokopovich' that subjected Soviet economic analysis and statistics to detailed examination from overseas. Prokopovich also provided an interesting theoretical account of the nature of Soviet economy, but it was more for his on-going empirical analyses that he was known.

Prokopovich's underlying argument regarding the state of the Soviet economy in the early period of Bolshevik control was expressed in relation to analyzing the principles of communism that had been implemented by 1922. He wrote:

> The whole history of the three years of communist reign proves that the dislocation of industry was due to the principles themselves and not to the inexperience and mistakes in the application of these principles (Prokopovich, 1924, 61).

By 'the principles themselves', Prokopovich meant the nationalization of industry and the centralization of economic control, which had (he suggested) yielded unambiguously negative results. A decline in labour productivity and the destruction of labour incentives had occurred together with a waste of industrial capital caused by a failure to continue re-investment. Prokopovich's solution was to reinstate private property in the means of production, which would serve to re-awaken economic initiative. In this conception the introduction of NEP in 1921 did not go far enough towards dismantling the principles of communism that had apparently been implemented after 1917. Prokopovich was one of the most significant of the émigré economists who remained in Europe in that his work engaged with Soviet economics at a very detailed level, and hence it was at the time a key source for alternative information about the precise state of Soviet development.

Another prominent émigré economist was P.B. Struve (1870–1944), who before 1917 was a leading member of the legal Marxist grouping. Struve's post-1917 economics was far less significant than that which he had published before 1917, and also less significant than that of Prokopovich after 1917, but he did provide some interesting general commentary on Stalin's 'economic revolution'. Struve's attitude by 1930 was ambiguous, sometimes mocking the 'blockade mentality' of a closed economy, but also recognizing that the five-year plans could result in increased industrial growth. He was particularly concerned to stress that the Soviet planning system could only function in association with political despotism and the use of continued coercion, and he described the five-year plan as a 'pump for accumulation and a machine for exploitation' (Pipes, 1980, 408). Like some other émigrés, dislocation from his homeland led Struve to a position of total hostility towards Soviet Russia, an attitude that sometimes blinded such people to the nuances of the Soviet position, and often made their post-revolutionary economics less original than their pre-revolutionary efforts.

As a general rule the Russian émigré economists who remained in Europe did not have the impact on Western economic theory that émigrés who ended up in the USA eventually did, except in terms of their general support for market-based systems of economy, against the economics of Soviet-style planning that was being promoted in the USSR. One possible reason for this was that the émigrés who remained in Europe tended to associate themselves with more political groupings, and hence focused much of their efforts on fostering Western opposition to Soviet power. Those émigrés who made their final destination the USA were less obviously political, and hence their main efforts were focused on contributing to the development of mainstream economic theory. However, as Shuichi Kojima argues in this volume, émigrés such as Prokopovich (and also B.D. Brutzkus) had an important influence on Western Sovietology, and hence were still significant figures in their own terms of reference (Kojima, 2008).

Conclusions

This chapter has suggested that a significant number of Russian émigré economists who travelled to America to make their homes took with them an intellectual and thematic baggage that was not easy to discard completely on arrival in their new places of residence. The existing concerns of their early Russian experiences had been crucial in setting the initial trajectories of their academic careers. These trajectories were certainly modified, and to some degree re-railed, by their later European and American experiences, but Western economics itself was also to a moderate extent transformed by the émigré concerns. It was argued that such concerns were in part political but also in part abstract and purely theoretical in nature.

Of course in some instances the concerns of Russian and of American economics in the 1920s and 1930s had been similar anyway, even without considering the influence of specific individual émigrés. For example, parallels between the approaches of Wesley Mitchell and Arthur Burns in America and Nikolai Kondratiev and Sergei Pervushin in Russia have been outlined previously (See Barnett, 1999). However, such similarities were actively reinforced by the émigré effect in America, just as Russian economics itself was being dramatically transformed by the onset of Stalinism in 1929 and the political purges of 1936–38. Thus to some extent the concerns of Russian economics before 1929 survived by proxy, ironically in the homeland of its future Cold War adversary itself.

Another perspective from which to view the impact of émigré economists is on the traditions and quality of the indigenous currents in economics that continued to develop within Russian borders after their dramatic exit. It could be argued that in losing very significant theorists like Marschak, Kuznets and Leontief, Russian economics was itself made markedly poorer as a result. Not only in terms of quality, but also in terms of various approaches to the subject, the potential capital of Russian economic theory was drastically curtailed by emigration. But one country's loss was another country's significant gain. Consequently, it is possible that the geographical location of individual human capital operates like a zero sum game, at least from an individual nation-state perspective.

Archive Sources

Columbia University Special Manuscript Collection (CUSMC), New York.

References

Arrow, K.J. (1986). 'Biography of Jacob Marschak', in C.B. McGuire and R. Radner (eds), *Decision and Organization*. Minneapolis: University of Minnesota Press.

Backhouse, Roger (2002). *The Penguin History of Economics*. London: Penguin.

Barnett, Vincent (1998). *Kondratiev and the Dynamics of Economic Development*. London: Macmillan.

——— (1999). 'Soviet Economists in Opposition and Overseas', in I.D. Thatcher (ed), *Regime and Society in Twentieth Century Russia*. London: Macmillan.

——— (2004). *The Revolutionary Russian Economy, 1890–1940: Ideas, Debates and Alternatives*. London: Routledge.

——— (2006). 'Chancing an Interpretation: Slutsky's Random Cycles Revisited', *European Journal of the History of Economic Thought*, September 2006: 411–32.

Belykh, A.A. (1989). 'A Note on the Origin of Input–Output Analysis and the Contribution of the Early Soviet Economists', *Soviet Studies*, vol. XLI, no 3: 426–29.

Cave, Martin (1981). 'Wassily Leontief', in J.R. Shackleton and G. Locksley (eds), *Twelve Contemporary Economists*. London: Macmillan.

Craver, Earlene (1986). 'The Emigration of the Austrian Economists', *History of Political Economy*, vol. 18, no 1: 1–32.

Fogel, R.W. (2000). 'Simon S. Kuznets', NBER Working Paper no 7787.

Kojima, Shuichi (2004). 'Comparing Chayanov and Kondratiev', *Japanese Slavic and East European Studies*, vol. 25: 1–25.

——— (2008). 'Exiled Russian Economists and the USSR: Brutzkus and Prokopovich', in Vincent Barnett and Joachim Zweynert (eds), *Economics in Russia*. Ashgate. (Chapter 9 below.)

Kuznets, Simon (1929). 'Random Events and Cyclical Oscillations', *Journal of the American Statistical Association*, vol. 24: 258–75.

——— (1941). *National Income and Its Composition, 1919–1938*. New York: NBER.

——— (1954). *Immigration and the Foreign Born*. Occasional Paper 46. NBER. With Ernest Rubin.

——— (1967). [1930]. *Secular Movements in Production and Prices*. New York: Kelley.

Leontief, Wassily (1938). 'The Significance of Marxian Economics for Present-Day Economic Theory', *American Economic Review*, vol. 28, no 1 (Supplement): 1–9.

——— (1964). 'The Balance of the Economy of the USSR', in N. Spulber (ed.), *Foundations of Soviet Strategy for Economic Growth*. Indiana: Indiana University Press.

——— (2007). 'An Interview with Wassily Leontief', in P.A. Samuelson and W.A. Barnett (eds), *Inside the Economist's Mind*. Oxford: Blackwell.

Marschak, Jacob (1944). 'Random Simultaneous Equations and the Theory of Production', *Econometrica*, vol. 12: 143–50.

——— (1945). 'A Cross Section of Business Cycle Discussion', *American Economic Review*, vol. 35: 368–81.

Mirowski, Philip (2002). 'Cowles Changes Allegiance', *Journal of the History of Economic Thought*, vol. 24: 165–93.

Morgan, Mary (1990). *The History of Econometric Ideas*. Cambridge: CUP.

MVD-MGB Campaign Against Russian Émigrés (1957). Possev Publishing House.

Pipes, Richard (1980). *Struve: Liberal on the Right, 1905–44*. Cambridge, MA: Harvard University Press.

Plato, Jan von (1994). *Creating Modern Probability*. Cambridge: CUP.

Prokopovich, S.N. (1918). *Opyt ischisleniya narodnaga dokhoda 50 gub. Evropeiskoi Rossii*. Moscow: SVKS.

——— (1924). *The Economic Condition of Soviet Russia*. London: King and Son.

Radner, Roy (1987). 'Jacob Marschak', in *The New Palgrave Dictionary of Economics*. London: Macmillan.

Sarychev, V.G. (1975). 'Kuznets', in *Ekonomicheskaya entsiklopediya politicheskaya ekonomiya*. Moscow: AN SSSR.

Tribe, Keith (2001). 'German Émigré Economists and the Internationalisation of Economics', *Economic Journal*, vol. 111 November: 740–46.

Vaughn, K.I. (1994). *Austrian Economics in America*. Cambridge: CUP.

Williams, Robert (1972). *Culture in Exile: Russian Émigrés in Germany, 1881–1941*. Ithaca: Cornell University Press.

Yonay, Yuval (1998). *The Struggle Over the Soul of Economics. Institutionalists and Neoclassical Economists in America between the Wars*. Princeton, N.J: PUP.

Zarnowitz, Victor (1992). *Business Cycles*. Chicago: University of Chicago.

Zolotov, Andrei (2002). 'Shipping Away a Generation', at www.chebucto.ns.ca/Philosophy/Sui-Generis/Berdyaev/essays/zolotov.htm.

Chapter 9

Exiled Russian Economists and the USSR: Brutzkus and Prokopovich

Shuichi Kojima

In terms of both vitality and originality, Russian economics experienced its first 'golden age' (Barnett 2005, 137) from the end of the nineteenth century to the First World War. The revolution had a great impact on Russian economics after 1917, in that economists came to face an unprecedented problem in the experiment of building socialism. Russian intellectuals faced a crossroads, and some chose to remain in Russia to cooperate with the Soviet government, while others left Russia of their own volition or were deported. Thus, after the revolution Russian economists were clearly divided into two groups, those remaining 'in-country', and those that were exiled. The former group played an important part in making Soviet economic plans and development strategies, particularly in the 1920s.[1] Exiled economists were more or less engaged in the academic study of the Soviet economy.

According to a recent study, 108 academic economists left Russia between 1917 and 1923 (Telitsyn 2000, 580). The main centres where they stayed were Paris, Prague and Berlin, but more than a few economists also stayed at London, Belgrade, Sophia and Harbin in China. In 1917–56, over 70 Russian economic journals were published outside the Soviet Union (Hale 1972, 526).

There was a great variety among exiled Russian economists. In terms of the character of their activities, they can be divided into four groups. First, political-oriented economists, for example Petr B. Struve in the Kadets, Viktor M. Chernov in the SRs and Aaron A. Iugov in the Mensheviks. Secondly, economists specializing in various fields within economics, for example Aleksandr I. Chuprov in economic statistics, Vahan F. Totomianz in cooperatives, Vladimir A. Kosinsky in agricultural economics and Mentor A. Bouniatian in business cycle. Thirdly, economists mainly engaged in studying the Soviet economy, for example Boris D. Brutzkus and Sergei N. Prokopovich. And fourthly, young economists educated at foreign universities, who later became American economists, for example, Wassily W. Leontief educated at Berlin, Simon S. Kuznets at Colombia, Evsey D. Domar at Harvard, Jacob Marschak at Heidelberg and Alexander Gerschenkron at Vienna.

It was exiled Russian economists who often shed the first academic light on Soviet socialism, something that had shaken the world in the twentieth century.[2]

1 For the 'nonconformist' economists remaining in Soviet Russia, see Jasny 1972, 89–211. The most prominent ones among them were Alexander V. Chayanov and Nikolai D. Kondratiev. For a comparison of their views, see Kojima 2005a, 1–25.

Their studies were not only influential to the perceptions held by Russians abroad of their own homeland, but also laid the foundations for Soviet studies in the West. The fact is that post-war academic Sovietology was greatly indebted to exiled economists.

In spite of this importance, the works of exiled Russian economists (except the above last group indicated above) are barely known even among specialists in the field of Russian history, let alone among those interested in the history of economic thought. Aimed at filling this void, this chapter will focus on two exiled economists, B.D. Brutzkus and S.N. Prokopovich, as they were the most representative specialists on the Soviet economy as mentioned previously. What was the picture of Soviet socialism depicted by these scholars? What kind of theoretical frameworks did they use to explain this significant historical phenomenon? What of the differences in their own views? What were their respective contributions to Soviet studies? These questions will be the focus of the following chapter.

The Careers of Brutzkus and Prokopovich

Before discussing Brutzkus's and Prokopovich's views, it is necessary to briefly look at their careers.[2] Boris Davidovich Brutzkus (1874–1938) was a Russian Jew, and belonged to a small group of scholars who believed in economic liberalism in Russia.[3] In his youth he was discriminated against in a Russian school, and was shocked by the *pogrom* in 1881–82. He specialized in agricultural economics at Novo-Aleksandr Institute for Agriculture and Forestry near Warsaw. At the Institute he was greatly influenced by a liberal agricultural economist, Aleksandr I. Skvortsov. Brutzkus at first studied Jewish settlement problems, and then moved on to the problems of Russian agriculture. In the Imperial period he argued in favour of the Stolypin agrarian reforms from the standpoint of economic liberalism. He remained in Russia after the revolution and gave lectures in 1920 criticizing the theory of socialism. Deported in 1922, he sought refuge in Germany. At the Russian Institute in Berlin until 1932 he was engaged in studying the Soviet economy, agriculture in particular, supported by German scholars, notably Max Sering. Among contributors to the debate on socialist economic calculation, Brutzkus was probably the only one who analyzed the Soviet economy systematically.[4] In 1935

2 For details of their careers, see Kagan 1989, 9–38; Rogalina 1998, 13–40; Iur'evsky 1955, 249–66; Bachurina 2005, 24–67; Kojima 2005c, 36–57.

3 Another leading scholar of economic liberalism was Lev N. Litoshenko, who was active until his death in a labour camp in Soviet Russia. For his career and view, see Kojima 2005b, 1–46. A detailed discussion on the weak tradition of economic liberalism in Russian economics can be found in Zweynert 2002, 416–27. According to a classical study of the history of Russian economic thought, one finds 'the most active individuals of Russian economic thought' among pro-socialist economists. See Tanaka 1967, 408.

4 Purely by accident, Brutzkus and Ludwig E. v. Mises presented the very similar criticism of socialism in the same year, 1920. Brutzkus in the disruption after the Revolution could not know the works by Mises. For a comparison of their views, see Morioka 1995, 63–68.

he moved to Jerusalem, where he taught agricultural economics until his death in 1938.[5]

Sergei Nikolaevich Prokopovich (1871–1955) was born into a noble family. In 1891 he was expelled from the Petrov Agricultural Academy in Moscow because of his student activities. In the same year he participated in an investigative trip to West Siberian villages suffering from the great famines of 1891–92. He later called this experience 'the social baptism that predetermined all my future' (See Kojima 2005c, 37). At this time he was influenced by a *Narodnik* sociologist, Piotr L. Lavrov, and also by *Narodnik* revolutionaries, while paying attention to Legal Marxism and the labour movement in Russia as well. After that he stayed in Western Europe for several years and investigated the labour movement there, during which time he joined the 'Union of Russian Social Democrats Abroad'. After returning to Russia, he developed some political activities, such as the establishment of the 'Union of Emancipation', and argued for economism in the Russian labour movement.[6] In 1917 he became the Commerce-Industrial Minister and later the Food Minister in the Provisional Government. After the revolution he also remained in Russia and played a central role in the public famine relief organization in 1921–22. He was deported from the country in 1922. Staying in Berlin, Prague and Geneva, he organized a research institute named the 'Economic Cabinet', where he investigated the Soviet economy until his death in 1955.[7]

Brutzkus and Prokopovich both belonged to the same generation, being born in the early 1870s. Both economists had the common experience of being exiled from Russia by the Soviet government in 1922. But their most significant common point is their concentration on studying the Soviet economy. As stated earlier, it was Brutzkus and Prokopovich who studied it most consistently and systematically. There were however some noteworthy differences between them in terms of their careers.

Firstly, these two economists varied in their stance toward Karl Marx. Among Russian economists of the same generation, there were not a few scholars for whom in their formative years Marx was a great influence, such as Mikhail I. Tugan-Baranovsky and Sergei N. Bulgakov. Prokopovich was also greatly influenced by Marx, but he knew more of the reality of the labour movement in Western Europe, and became increasingly aligned with Eduard Bernstein, so becoming famous as a representative of revisionist socialism in Russia before the revolution. In contrast, Brutzkus was generally critical of Marx, although he admitted that volume 1 of *Das Kapital* was of 'great significance' for the development of economics (Brutzkus 1923a, 42).

5 Brutzkus was on friendly terms with F.A. Hayek. Just before his death, Brutzkus sent a letter to Hayek, writing of the Nazi menace to European civilization and asking him to organize protests against the persecution of the Jews. See Kagan 1989, 36–38; Rogalina 1997, 158.

6 His wife, Ekaterina D. Kuskova was also an active journalist. The Prokopovich's were 'a close Russian counterpart to Sidney and Beatrice Webb', see Fisher 1958, 109.

7 Prokopovich had a special relationship with the University of Birmingham, see Kojima 2005c, 52–54. His young co-worker in this institute, Alexander M. Baykov, later became a professor and helped to found Soviet studies in the United Kingdom.

Secondly, before Brutzkus and Prokopovich were deported from Russia in 1922, the level of political activity separated one from the other. Brutzkus was very close to the liberal Kadet Party, but he was never involved in direct political movement except for a short time in 1917. He showed a deep interest in economic policy, but he continued to keep some distance from politics. In sharp contrast to him, Prokopovich, as a leading socialist, was engaged in political activity against the tsarist regime. In 1917 he even became one of the leading ministers in the Provisional Government. It was after his exile in 1922 that he ceased to be politically active. Post-exile he remained absorbed in academic studies, especially in investigating the contemporary position of the Soviet economy.

Thirdly, Brutzkus and Prokopovich differed in terms of the length of their academic careers. Brutzkus died earlier, in 1938, thus he could watch the Soviet Union only up to the period of the second five-year plan. On the other hand, since Prokopovich died in 1955, he was able to observe the Soviet economy for almost twice as long as Brutzkus. In his later books he discussed the fourth five-year plan, the development of nuclear weapons, and even the Cold War with the United States (Prokopovich 1956, 131–55).

Fourthly, a difference in their origins should be mentioned. Brutzkus was born as a Russian Jew. His life's work was the study of Jewish economic life, especially their settlement, and he searched for a way for Jewish people to live in Russia. Consequently he was always very cautious about the rise of Russian nationalism. On the other hand, Prokopovich had a noble origin, and was highly gifted as an organizer. He was always at the centre of various Russian movements both before and after the revolution. The above-mentioned differences in their careers would, in all likelihood, exert some influence on their views of Soviet socialism, so next Brutzkus's and Prokopovich's views on this topic will be examined.

Brutzkus on the Soviet Economy

Brutzkus's first discussion of socialist economy was a lecture given in Petrograd in 1920. It was published serially in a journal that was then banned, preventing its full publication. After being deported, he published the full text as a book entitled *Socialist Economy* in 1923. Later a German edition (1928) and an abridged English translation (1935) were published. After exile Brutzkus published many analyses of the Soviet economy both in German and in Russian, but his basic viewpoint was clearly stated in his first book, *Socialist Economy*. The characteristics of Brutzkus's study of the Soviet economy can be gleaned from the full title of the book: *Socialist Economy: Theoretical Considerations on Russia's Trial*. Firstly, he regarded the Soviet economy as an experiment, one of the compulsory introduction of Marxian socialist economy. Secondly, he approached it theoretically. Thirdly, he investigated Russia's historical circumstances that seemed suitable for this experiment.

Brutzkus regarded War Communism as a 'trial' of the socialist economy, later coming to see it as a prototype of Soviet socialism. Behind War Communism he found Marxian doctrine in a fairly pure form, including a unified state plan, the fundamental denial of market price and private property, value measurement made by working hours and the equal distribution of goods. He examined the plan of a socialist economy analytically, his starting point being the concept of a universal 'economic principle', meaning that the result of economic activities had to correspond to their cost. According to Brutzkus, in a self-sufficient natural economy, the relation of costs and results was relatively transparent, due to the small size of the economy and the rule of tradition. Under a capitalist economy, it came to have 'far more consistent and definite expression' in the form of price relations (Brutzkus 1923a, 14; Brutzkus 1928a, 16). But what form would it take within a non-market socialist economy?

The Soviet official view was that the exchange relations of labour became much more transparent in a socialist economy, so that the labour theory of value became all the more suitable as a means of calculation.[8] Criticizing the labour theory, Brutzkus explained that labour was an insufficient criterion of the value of goods in developed economies, being a poor measure of the relation of costs and results. The significance of economic calculation in socialism was, however, far greater than in capitalism because in a market economy, enterprises that could not recover costs went bankrupt. But a socialist economy, he argued, did not have such an automatic selection process at a micro level. Economic decisions were centralized, so any mistakes became fatal.

Moreover, Brutzkus pointed out the 'fundamental aspects of the problem', that the social demand for goods could not be decided *a priori* in developed economies (Brutzkus 1923a, 32; Brutzkus 1928a, 39). Common within markets was the fact that demand was aggregated. Since the market price indicated the degree of demand for commodities, it provided producers with accurate information on goods. But in an economy lacking a market mechanism, there was no access to such information. Therefore, all economic decisions depended on the subjective and arbitrary evaluation of bureaucrats. As a result there were no bounds to the waste of resources. In his view, economizing did not belong to the 'essence of socialism' (Brutzkus 1931b, 171), so there could be no bigger danger for socialist society than the 'decline of economic calculation'.[9]

Such was the central point of Brutzkus's criticism, which was *de facto* pioneering to post-war Soviet studies. This was also complemented by the following argument on subjective factors in socialist economies. In a market economy, production involved not only technical and mechanical work, but also the risk-taking of entrepreneurs, who had a vested interest in the outcome.[10] But the manager of a socialist enterprise,

---

8 Relying on the 'economic principle', Chayanov was also designing a model of a socialist economy at that time by drawing an analogy with the natural peasant economy. Brutzkus criticized him, arguing that this analogy was not valid in a socialist economy, taking human ability to control into account. See Brutzkus 1923a, 14; Brutzkus 1929, part 1, 425, part 2, 71; Kojima 1987, 221–62.

9 Brutzkus 1923a, 16. By the concept of 'decline of economic calculation', Brutzkus at an early stage outlined the 'knowledge problem' in a socialist economy. Hayek mentioned 'the extraordinary foresight' shown by Brutzkus. See Hayek 1935, x. Just before the collapse of the Soviet Union Brutzkus, who had stressed important functions of the market, was rehabilitated in Russia, and had a great impact on Russian economists. See Shirokorad 1990, 49 and 52.

10 Brutzkus 1923a, 64. On this point Brutzkus criticized the 'fetishism' of technology, the 'absolute dependence on technology', and the 'technological grasp of economy' seen in

being a bureaucrat, showed little concern for the profit and loss of the venture, for any reward was unrelated to the success of the enterprise. Risk and loss were easily shifted onto the state. Brutzkus maintained therefore that not only did bureaucrats lack accurate economic criterion and information within which to operate, but they also lacked the incentive and responsibility necessary to achieve managerial success. Since economic bodies were entrusted to such bureaucrats, chaos developed. Thus, Brutzkus found anarchy behind the outward appearance of the centralized system of socialism, leading him to conclude that socialism overcame the 'anarchy of the capitalist mode of production', by putting the national economy into a state of 'super-anarchy' (Brutzkus 1928a, 48).

As explained above, Brutzkus took a position opposing socialism in principle, while saying that Russia provided a stage suitable for experimenting with socialism. He never asserted the 'historical necessity' of the Russian revolution, but only the favourable circumstances of Russia that predisposed it to the revolution. The main ones he cited in his works were as follows.

According to Brutzkus, since the period when industries had developed under state protection and with foreign capital in the late tsarist era, remarkable concentration had occurred, that is the concentration of wealth amongst a small number of bourgeoisie on the one hand, and the concentration of industrial workers on the other (Brutzkus 1923a, 68; Brutzkus 1928a, 85–86). Russian heavy industries never developed organically and autonomously; nor could a middle class, as seen in West European society, be formed. Consequently, the gap between the rich and the poor was huge. Since democracy was less institutionalized under tsarism, any legal means by which workers could improve their political rights and economic interests were all but blocked. This strengthened the workers' combative posture. The regional concentration of Russian industries also made workers' organization and political struggle easier. This was why Russia suffered from periodic revolutionary crises. Finally, the tsarist system could not withstand the social strains caused by the First World War. It was the Bolsheviks who succeeded in leading the workers' revolution as they were 'in harmony with the spirit of revolutionary Marxism' (Brutzkus 1923a, 69; Brutzkus 1928a, 87).

West European peasants were often opposed to a workers' revolution. But Russian peasants, in Brutzkus's view, used the workers' revolution to realize their long-cherished ideal of redistributing land (Brutzkus 1929, part 2, 469; Brutzkus 1924, 301–08; Brutzkus 1925, 244–45; Brutzkus 1928b, 640–42; Brutzkus 1934a, 83). Russian peasants, with a less developed conception of property rights, took private land by force in order to redistribute it within rural communes, as soon as state power was dismantled by the revolution. This revival of communal forces once in decline was a result of the general collapse of people's daily lives brought about by the war. But this revival of communes, in Brutzkus's opinion, signified that 'the tendencies deeply rooted in Russian history appeared in sight again' (Brutzkus 1934a, 65). Additionally, the Bolsheviks regarded the peasant revolution as a useful way to destroy private property (Brutzkus 1923b, 29; Brutzkus 1929, part 2, 469).

Bolshevik thinking. See Brutzkus 1931a, 504; Brutzkus 1932c, 501; Brutzkus 1935, 139.

At first, the Bolsheviks thought that world revolution was indispensable for Russia to develop socialism, but Brutzkus denied this connection (Brutzkus 1923a, 70; Brutzkus 1928a, 88). In such an advanced country as Great Britain, greatly dependent upon world trade, world revolution would be necessary to oppose any possible economic blockade and to maintain the socialist system. By contrast in Russia, blessed with a vast territory and rich in natural resources, the degree of dependence on foreign trade was low. Russia was capable of 'almost perfect economic autarky' (Brutzkus 1923a, 71; Brutzkus 1928a, 89; Brutzkus [1937] (1995), 206), and therefore there was a chance to build socialism. Even if Brutzkus admitted that Russian society provided favourable conditions for revolution, his basic viewpoint was that the compulsory introduction of a socialist economy by state power had occurred. He thought this experiment would meet strong resistance from Russian society, in particular from the peasantry. Therefore, the 'trial' of socialism in Russia advanced along a winding path. He examined this path by dividing it into four stages – state capitalism, War Communism, the New Economic Policy (NEP), and the first five-year plan.

For several months after the revolution, capitalist organizations and managers were retained and controlled by the government (Brutzkus 1935, 99–101). But this trial of so-called state capitalism failed. Brutzkus found the main cause of this failure was the denial of capitalist legal principles by anarchical forces stimulated by the Bolsheviks. He emphasized that 'certain legal principles' were decisively important for a market economy to function.

Brutzkus understood War Communism mainly as a 'trial' of a socialist economy (Brutzkus 1935, 102–08). In his words, 'the logical system of natural socialism' attempted to establish itself. The market was completely denied, so the common denominator of market price had vanished, this being why bureaucrats had no accurate economic information. The 'super-anarchy' of production appeared, industries fell into paralysis, and the devastation of agriculture occurred due to requisitioning. The Soviet government also met with resistance from almost all social classes. The transition to NEP was thus unavoidable, while Brutzkus insisted that many economic institutions formed during this time survived to become the 'backbone' of the future Soviet economic system.

According to Brutzkus, the essence of NEP was the restoration of the market (Brutzkus 1929, part 2, 428–48; Brutzkus 1935, 108–22). The Soviet government made concessions in the economic field, so that the economy could be reconstructed. One restriction was that the 'commanding heights', such as large industries and transport, were held by the state. Another restriction was that the government never made political concessions to private economic behaviour. Small enterprises were not protected legally from the state, and in such lack of protection, Brutzkus saw the danger of NEP's disintegration. The Soviet government, he argued, began to pursue rapid industrialization after industrial reconstruction. The government's high benchmark for collecting the cereal crops necessary for industrialization could not be met, so the government closed rural markets and began to collect farm products by force. This led to the collapse of 'the last pillar' of NEP (Brutzkus 1935, 122: Brutzkus 1929, part 2, 472; Brutzkus 1931a, 505).

Brutzkus analyzed the five-year plans from two sides: achievement and sacrifice. The first five-year plan enabled Russia to make huge compulsory savings that would have been impossible under a market economy (Brutzkus 1931a, 507; Brutzkus 1935, 194). Most of the investment from these savings turned to the construction of industrial infrastructure and large-scale heavy industry. In terms of material output, the planned goal of developing heavy industries was achieved. What attracted his attention, however, was that such a quantitative expansion was only realized because of enormous sacrifice – he called it a 'pathological development' (Brutzkus 1935, 214; Brutzkus 1933, 418–19).

By far the biggest sacrifice was made by the peasantry (Brutzkus 1932a, 9; Brutzkus 1935, 174). According to Brutzkus, collectivization entailed hardly any technological changes, as the *kolkhoz* (collective farm) was a tool by which the government could collect farm products much more easily. So the peasants' resistance appeared in the form of a 'collapse of live-stock husbandry', as well as declining economic incentives, which led to a decline in agricultural production in general. Indeed, collectivization brought great success to the state's ability to collect farm products for a short period. However, it resulted 'in a long period of sickness for Russian agriculture' (Brutzkus 1935, 213; Brutzkus 1931a, 515; Brutzkus 1935, 154 and 174).

Thus, in Brutzkus's view, in 1931 the Soviet economy stood on the verge of total collapse. In his terms, the culmination of planned economy contributed to 'the disorganization of the economic system' (Brutzkus 1935, 164). The Soviet government came to know the 'correctness of the principle, 'no economy without economic calculation'' (Brutzkus 1932a, 87), and attempted to restore 'certain capitalist institutions', thus making a concession to economic reality (Brutzkus 1931a, 504; Brutzkus 1932a, 87; Brutzkus 1935, 165). For instance 'control by ruble', the *kolkhoz* market, 'Soviet trade', the piecework system, increasing the economic autonomy of trusts and enterprises, and limited individual farming were allowed. He argued that these concessions saved the system from final collapse. However, since the new policy was contradictory to the nature of the Soviet economy, the results were negligible (Brutzkus 1932a, 97; Brutzkus [1936] 1995, 201).

The Future of Soviet Socialism

How did Brutzkus see the future of Soviet socialism? In his view, the essence of the Soviet economy was an 'inner union between economics and politics', or the ultimate subordination of all economic life to politics (Brutzkus 1935, 231; Brutzkus 1929, part 1, 430; Brutzkus 1932a, 103), just as mainstream Sovietologists asserted after the war. The concentration of economic bodies in governmental hands meant that the failure of decision–making would lead to catastrophe. As such decisions were made by non-specialists under the conditions of the 'decline of economic calculation', this would be the main cause of the failure of the Soviet system.

As to the collapse of the Soviet system, Brutzkus presented one more line of reasoning. It was a political logic, which he called the evolution 'immanent in revolutionary socialism' (Brutzkus [1937] 1995, 219). Namely, that any dramatic change such as the Russian revolution necessarily entailed a violent civil war. So actually, the democratic system could not continue, and only the political oligarchy (who were able to concentrate power) could survive. Moreover, the oligarchy moved to a dictatorship very quickly. Under the subordination of economic bodies to politics, the dictator used economic power to strengthen his own dominance (Brutzkus 1931b, 171; Brutzkus [1937] 1995, 212). In this way productive forces came to be used for purposes that had no bearing whatsoever on people's material needs.

Brutzkus foresaw the collapse of Soviet socialism in the 1930s. In 1931 he wrote that, since the Soviet system was politically unified, its collapse would come from an 'internal disintegration of the power mechanism', where the movement of city workers and developments inside the Party would play the decisive role (Brutzkus 1931c, 448). Just before his death, he came to see this disintegration occurring due to a spontaneous inner explosion or an external disaster (Brutzkus [1937] 1995, 220). Since he had already pointed out the weakness both of property rights and the rule of law as characteristic, he foresaw that post-Soviet economic reconstruction would be very difficult (Brutzkus 1924, 302; Brutzkus 1925, 245; Brutzkus 1929, part 2, 469; Brutzkus 1932b, 221). These were Brutzkus's views, and attention is turned now to those of Prokopovich.

Prokopovich on the Soviet Economy

In total Prokopovich published six books on the Soviet economy after his deportation. His basic viewpoint was found in his German book *Russian national economy under the control of Soviet power* (Prokopovich 1944a). According to Prokopovich, Soviet power was an external factor to the historical development of the Russian national economy (Prokopovich 1923b, 73; Prokopovich 1927, 7; Prokopovich 1952, vol. 1, 18–19). The communist principle introduced forcibly by Soviet power collided with the Russian national economy, with both falling into enmity. His inherent concern was to 'objectively characterize the evolution of the Russian national economy under Soviet power' (Prokopovich 1923a, 5). A type of dualism formed his basic viewpoint.

The main characteristics of Prokopovich's approach were as follows. The Russian words *narodnoe khoziaistvo* (national economy) can also be translated into English as 'people's economy'. Firstly, in his publications Prokopovich paid special concern to the conditions of the Russian people, with many pages given over to understanding population and wages. The second characteristic was that Prokopovich captured the relationship between Soviet power and Russian economy in terms of the Marxian concepts of 'base' and 'superstructure'. Accordingly, he regarded the improvement of living standards due to an increase in productive forces as a 'necessity of national (people's) economy'.[11] He viewed Soviet economic policy from the viewpoint of this necessity, tending to take the transformation of the Soviet

11 Prokopovich 1934, 109. Prokopovich was arguing for 'economism' in the labour movement before the revolution.

system very seriously, while paying little attention to the structure and strength of Soviet power (Prokopovich 1923a, 5; Prokopovich 1952, vol. 1, 17–18).

The third characteristic was the descriptive and statistical character of his research. When beginning to study the Soviet economy, Prokopovich declared that his work was based on published Soviet materials. There was considerable false information in Soviet materials, but it was possible to approach the actual state of the Soviet economy through 'strict criticism as well as the continuous collation and comparison of data', because various parts of the national economy were closely connected (Prokopovich 1923a, 5; Prokopovich 1952, vol. 1, 17). He added that works written by non-conformist economists were also available, and he had been collecting Soviet economic literature for more than 30 years. For this reason, his research institute was one of the most important centres for information on the USSR in the world at this time (Iur'evsky 1955, 258; Barnett 2005, 129–30; Bachurina 2005, 127–28; Kojima 2005c, 49). As to his appraisal of the Soviet economy, changes can be detected in the 1920s and beyond. Examination of his views on the Soviet economy in the 1920s will corroborate these changes.

The Soviet Economy in the 1920s, 1930s and 1940s

Prokopovich adopted a very critical stance toward Soviet economic policy in the 1920s. He reiterated negative appraisals not only of War Communism but also of NEP. Like Brutzkus, he regarded War Communism as an 'experiment of communism'. In his view communist policy meant 'natural and technical command' from the centre, so it eliminated both any incentive to work and economic calculation (Prokopovich 1923a, 58 and 111). He claimed that such a 'total denial of every economic sphere' was the essence of communism, so economic collapse was not avoidable, something shown by Soviet Russia's experiences (Prokopovich 1923a, 24, 49, 57, and 145).

To prevent economic collapse, Prokopovich outlined that NEP was aimed at the 'improvement of productive forces, the increase in state revenues, and calming the discontent of peasants and workers' (Prokopovich 1923a, 126; Prokopovich 1923b, 54). Since the Soviet government tried to maintain its grip on the political dictatorship, however, NEP became a compromise between two conflicting principles. To circumvent this dilemma, a 'third economic policy' was needed. Its guidelines were as follows (Prokopovich 1923a, 154; Prokopovich 1927, 12): the 'complete renunciation' of communist principles; the release of private initiative from restraint; the establishment of private property; and 'the establishment of a European-type legal order'. In short, Prokopovich wanted free economic activities based on a private property system and a market economy under the rule of law. In the 1920s, expecting the rise of a younger generation in the Soviet Union, he was very optimistic about Russia's transition to such a system (Prokopovich 1923a, 148 and 154; Prokopovich 1927, 14–15).

In the 1930s, however, Prokopovich's appraisal of the Soviet system began to change. This was characterized by a shift from a critical attitude towards the Soviet system, to one that was more receptive, conciliatory and even sympathetic. Moreover, this change developed in two directions. One was a growing interest in economic planning, and the other was an increased attention to Russian nationalism. Prokopovich's earlier interest in planning has been alluded to, yet at this time he did not consider very seriously the problems of planning (Prokopovich 1923a, 7). It was in his book, *Idea of Planning and the Outcome of the Five Year Plan* published in Paris in 1934, that he first discussed economic planning in a more systematic way, with the worldwide interest in planning after 1929 in the background.[12] He cited the Soviet economy as only one form of planning. While countenancing in principle the advantages of a 'free economic system', he paid attention to the type of planning progressing in capitalist countries, the form that he viewed most seriously being the management plan operating in private enterprises.

Prokopovich based his discussion on the works of a German scholar often called 'the father of managerial economics', Eugen Schmalenbach, who explained the end of 'free economy' in terms of increased fixed costs in private enterprises. Prokopovich paid attention to the idea that developing heavy industry required large-scale investments, which in turn escalated the rate of fixed costs (Prokopovich 1934, 13–19; Prokopovich 1944a, 229–31; Prokopovich 1948, 36–37; Prokopovich 1952, vol. 2, 23–30). Owing to the rising rate of fixed costs, enterprises in industries such as petroleum, coal and metal could not match supply to market demand. Thus a state of 'chronic overproduction' appeared, free competition became difficult, and 'planning' between enterprises in these industries became inescapable. Such 'planning' between private enterprises, however, brought about the concentration of production, leading to the unequal distribution of national income. Prokopovich argued that state control should compete against this tendency, and his perception of the transition from 'free economy' to 'combined economy' was one of the reasons he came to support state intervention.

Besides the logic of economic development, another reason why he supported state planning was political democratization. In the nineteenth century, 'economic policy did not have a systematic character', being decided by the vested interests of various social groups (Prokopovich 1934, 70; Prokopovich 1944a, 225). But in the twentieth century, with the 'political influence of democracy' rising, economic policy was gradually liberated from the influence of interest groups. Economic policy also came to be given a rational foundation by studies of the national economy. He wrote that 'the state's energetic intervention in economy for the purpose of increasing national product and of the democratic distribution of national income' became one of the government's main concerns.[13] Thus, perspective plans for the development of a national economy were actually made in advanced capitalist countries. In the 1930s, planning based on rational economic policy became his new vision, with heavy industrialization and political democratization in the background.

12 Brutzkus wrote a critical review of this book. See Brutzkus 1934b, 440–42.

13 Prokopovich 1934, 70; Prokopovich 1944b, 225. Prokopovich was the pioneer in the studies of Russian national income as well. His work on national income was not only used by Gosplan, but also published in Moscow in 1930, notwithstanding that he had been deported from the country. Prokopovich also contributed an article on national income to the *Economic Journal* in 1926. See Prokopovich 1926, 69–82. J.M. Keynes was very interested in this article according to his letter. See Bachurina 2005, 34.

How then can the outcome of the first Soviet five-year plan be viewed? In Prokopovich's judgment it was a failure. Production did increase in heavy industries, but labour productivity and the quality of industrial products declined, and agricultural producers were destroyed by collectivization. In his opinion, the plan did not meet the needs of the national economy, as the political goal of 'building socialism' had priority over all others. Both socialized management and total planning were enforced by the government, without taking productivity into consideration. Furthermore, as a result of political priorities, a large number of incompetent engineers and workers were employed. The Soviet government came to believe in 'the creative role of violence' through the success of the revolution and civil war (Prokopovich 1934, 111; Prokopovich 1934, 64). In this way the politics of nationalization took precedence over economic rationality, and planning based upon political factors became arbitrary. Prokopovich believed that in such an underdeveloped country as the Soviet Union, planning had been introduced too early, while it was unavoidable in advanced industrial countries.

Prokopovich's approach to Soviet planning, however, changed again in the 1940s, and he came to regard economic planning as a worldwide trend, comparing the Soviet experience with planning in advanced industrial countries. He now considered the Soviet five-year plan to be one of 'grand designs' that originated in the Renaissance, which intended to control the course of history by human reason and will (Prokopovich 1944a, 282; Prokopovich 1948, 29; Prokopovich 1952, vol. 2, 7). However, in this new approach, because human knowledge was both limited and imperfect, the difficulty of controlling an economy would necessitate a continuous process of trial and error (Prokopovich 1952, vol. 1, 397–98; Prokopovich 1952, vol. 2, 13).

Although the practice of the Soviet planned economy for the previous 25 years showed a series of systematic defects, he argued that there were important results as well. Some important reforms of the Soviet planning system could be also expected after the Second World War. He said that the Soviet Union had much to learn from the experiences of advanced countries, because planning techniques had a 'basic tendency to become identical' (Prokopovich 1948, 51; Prokopovich 1952, vol. 2, 50). Prokopovich emphasized the need for the expansion of mutual learning between the East and the West, as the economists of convergence theory later argued. What then was the difference between Soviet and Western economic planning?

Firstly, relying on the work by G.D.H. Cole (1889–1959), Prokopovich stated that planning was not only more suitable but also easier in West European countries than in Russia. Secondly, referring to work by E.H. Carr (1892–1982), Prokopovich argued that the main focus of planning was decision-making over investment. It seemed that from this point of view he divided economic planning into advanced-country type and backward-country type (Prokopovich 1952, vol. 2, 49). In the planning of advanced Western countries, the principal object was opposing private monopolies, as well as countering economic crises. On the other hand, in backward countries like Russia, the main object of planning was the 'development of national productive forces, the struggle with illiteracy and low labour productivity, and the creation of national industries' (Prokopovich 1952, vol. 2, 49–50). As such, Prokopovich finally came to accept the Soviet five-year plans as having some validity.

Russian Nationalism

In the 1930s and later, Prokopovich's perception of the Soviet Union changed in one further direction, that of his increasing attention to Russian nationalism. Remarks emphasizing the national interests of Russia could already be found in a book from 1923, where he sounded an alarm by writing that Russia was likely to be a 'colony of West European industrial countries' owing to delays in reconstruction and paralysis of economic vitality (Prokopovich 1923a, 153–55; Prokopovich 1923b, 73–78). But it was in his previously mentioned German book, published in the midst of the Soviet-German War, that his nationalist viewpoint came to the fore. In the final chapter he made the following assertions (Prokopovich 1944a, 429–32).

Since the nobility had kept Russia trapped in serfdom and illiteracy for a lengthy period, it had become an extremely backward country in economic, social and cultural terms, which could not protect itself from competition with West European countries. Discontent amongst the people fuelled by this state of affairs had brought about the collapse of the tsarist system in 1917. After this, any revolutionary government would have to carry out a fierce struggle with Russia's backwardness. On this point the Soviet government had achieved outstanding success over the past 25 years. Even though Russia needed a strong hand and enormous sacrifices, 'the great economic result of the Soviet government' was 'especially brilliant and significant' when compared to pre-revolutionary Russia. The Soviet Union in 1944 was no longer the meeting point for international communism but was 'in the transition to the next stage in the economic, political and cultural development of the Russian nation'.

Prokopovich also wrote in books published in 1944 and 1952, that Russia had previously been a poor agricultural country and 'the colony of European industrial countries', but now it had completed the development of its industry to secure 'perfect economic and political independence' internationally (Prokopovich 1944b, 40; Prokopovich 1952, vol. 1, 54; Prokopovich 1952, vol. 2, 57). From such remarks, one could contend that Prokopovich's appraisal of the Soviet Union had changed in three respects. (1) He came to supplant the viewpoint of Russia's emancipation from West European control in his approach to the revolution. (2) He came to regard the struggle with Russian backwardness as the most important subject after the revolution, praising the achievements of the USSR.[14] (3) In his new perspective, the Soviet system itself was gradually transformed from a communist system to a national system.[15] Thus in the 1940s, Prokopovich came to accept the Soviet system from two points: first, his long-run perception of the transition from a free market economy to state planning, and second, his perception of Soviet Russia's nationalistic transformation.

14 In 1952 he clearly stated: 'I have always positively evaluated the Soviet government's policies that helped the advancement of the Russian national economy', Prokopovich 1952, vol. 1, 18.

15 Prokopovich in the 1940s was very similar to N.V. Ustrialov in the 1920s as far as they expected the Soviet system to change to one more in keeping with Russia's 'national interest', even though they had different frames of reference. See Pipes 1980, 351–56.

Comparing their Views

Thus far Brutzkus's and Prokopovich's perspectives of the Soviet economy show that both shared, to a certain extent, similar views in the 1920s. Both regarded War Communism as the introduction of the communist principle from above, explaining its collapse by the denial of economic calculation. Both pointed out the inadequacies of NEP, particularly in not taking the lack of legal protection of private enterprise seriously. Both desired Russia's transition to a 'free economic system' based upon private property and a market economy. These were the main points in common in the 1920s, although their views came to diverge in the 1930s. On examining their writings more closely, however, it would be clear from the beginning that both economists' stances differed, and even stood in opposition on more basic points. One can find the following basic differences.

The first and greatest difference pertained to their fundamental perception of the Soviet economy. Brutzkus saw the post-revolutionary Russian economy as an experimental ground for socialism. Therefore, he focused on policy implementation from above, and took Bolshevik thought very seriously. Contrary to this, Prokopovich viewed post-revolutionary Russia in terms of continuous conflict, an interpenetration and affinity between Soviet power and the Russian national economy, in particular paying attention to the latter's evolution. Behind this approach, there can be found a premise that Soviet power could cope with the problem of economic modernization. That was why his main concern was studying quantitative growth measures in terms of various economic indices such as population, national income and productivity.

The second difference was methodological. Brutzkus offered a strong theoretical criticism of socialist economy, analyzing the situation of the USSR as a concrete verification of his criticism. By taking a theoretical approach he depicted a clear, albeit slightly monistic, picture of the whole Soviet economy. On the other hand, Prokopovich took a documentary-descriptive approach. Most of his books on the Soviet economy consisted of chapters dealing with various branches, such as agriculture, industry, commerce and finance, but he presented no all-embracing conclusions. Furthermore, each chapter was filled with vast quantities of economic information based on Soviet materials. This was why his books were referred to as 'encyclopedias' of the Soviet economy (Rosen 1945, 101). Therefore, although his description was very detailed, it lacked the clarity of Brutzkus's approach.

The last but by no means the least difference concerned their ideas about the future of the Soviet economy. Brutzkus attached great importance to the principles of socialism on which the Soviet system was being built, and he foresaw the failure of this 'experiment' and the collapse of the Soviet system. As to reconstruction after the collapse, Brutzkus foresaw many difficulties. On the whole his view of the Russian future lacked optimism even though he was hostile to the Soviet system. In contrast, Prokopovich did not consider the Soviet system to be inflexible and rigid. Particularly from the 1930s, he came to anticipate the evolution and gradual transformation of the Soviet system. The expected development predicted was Soviet Russia's transition to a more national system with more rational planning. He even presented some policy proposals assuming that the Soviet system could be reformed. In short, he saw an optimistic future for the Soviet Union. Why did these two economists view the Soviet Union in such different ways?[16] Behind these differences it is necessary to highlight some background information.

Firstly, Brutzkus died earlier, having viewed the Soviet Union only in the chaotic period of the 1930s, unlike Prokopovich who continued observing the Soviet Union until the mid-1950s. Prokopovich observed a Soviet Union that had defeated Nazi-Germany in the Second World War, and had then gone on to become a superpower. It is not so difficult to imagine that the Soviet government's inclination to Russian nationalism during the war made a deep impression on him. Since the 1930s, many Western intellectuals came to share a perception of the contemporary age as the 'change from market to plan', and Prokopovich represented this view among exiled Russian intellectuals. Secondly, the differences in their views can be subtly attributed to differences in their backgrounds and careers. Brutzkus could not sympathize with Russian nationalism to the same extent as Prokopovich, while Prokopovich could not accept Brutzkus's critical attitude toward Russian peasants. The contrast of their appraisals of Russian history in general, and the history of Russian people in particular, is stark.

Thirdly, it seems that there was a difference in the political values that these scholars held. It would be natural for Brutzkus, embracing the values of economic individualism, to take a critical stance toward the Soviet system, which seemed to him incompatible with the concept of individual freedom and responsibility. On the other hand, Prokopovich who, in his formative years, had been greatly affected by the *Narodniki* and by Marx, continued to hold the viewpoint of a social democrat after exile. Remaining sympathetic with the Russian people (*narod*), and being convinced of the 'development of productive forces', he placed his hopes in the transformation of Soviet society.

Conclusion

This conclusion will examine Brutzkus's and Prokopovich's views of Soviet socialism in terms of contemporary Soviet/Russian studies. When reading their works closely, it is apparent that they showed viewpoints very similar to representative perceptions of the Soviet Union after the Second World War. It could be said that the theoretical frameworks that Brutzkus and Prokopovich presented pioneered post-war Soviet studies. Brutzkus considered the roles played by socialist doctrine and political power more seriously than others, arguing that the 'experiment with socialism' was being enforced consistently by Soviet power in Russia after the revolution. The scholars who constituted the mainstream in Sovietology soon after the war also adopted the same approach. They argued that in the Soviet Union, a strong state had been trying to transform and control Russian society by using all means possible, and they regarded the Soviet system as an unprecedented one in world history, expecting its total collapse. Brutzkus and the mainstream scholars had these points in common.

---

16 It must be added that in spite of various differences, Brutzkus and Prokopovich kept friendly relations with each other. See Brutzkus' letters to Prokopovich and his wife in Rogalina 1997, 145–60.

On the other hand, Prokopovich saw post-revolutionary Russia in terms of the interrelationship between Soviet power and the Russian national economy. His view was that the latter's evolution would gradually change the former in the long run. Such a viewpoint was very close to the revisionist one, competing against the mainstream in post-war Soviet studies. Revisionists stressed the modernization of Soviet society, seen for example in industrialization, urbanization, improved education, increasing social mobility and an increase in interest groups. They emphasized the gradual change of the Soviet system and its ability to adapt. Some revisionist economists insisted on a convergent tendency between Western and Eastern economic systems through the combination of market and plan. Similar viewpoints can be found in the later writings of Prokopovich. Both he and revisionist social historians paid much attention to the role of Russian workers and peasants. Since these notions were based on pluralistic thinking, they had a strong positivistic and descriptive tendency. Accordingly they could not, unlike Brutzkus and the mainstream scholars, portray such a clear-cut picture of Soviet socialism.

Soviet socialism greatly shook world history in the twentieth century, but at present we have no full-scale and academic examination of the history of its perception.[17] In such an examination, which may well be written in the future, Brutzkus's and Prokopovich's contributions should be highlighted as pioneering.

References

Bachurina, O. (2005), *Ekonomicheskoe nasledie S.N.Prokopovicha i ego obshchestvenno-politicheskaia deiatel'nost' v emigratsii*, St Petersburg: Nestor-Istoria.

Barnett, Vincent (2005), *A History of Russian Economic Thought*, London and New York: Routledge.

Brutzkus, Boris D. (1923a), *Sotsialisticheskoe khoziaistvo. Teoreticheskoe mysli po povodurusskogo opyta*, Berlin.

——— (1923b), 'Ob evoliutsii zemel'noi politiki sovetskoi vlasti', *Ekonomicheskii vestnik*, vol. 1, 27–43.

——— (1924), 'Die russische Agrarrevolution', *Zeitschrift fuer die gesamte Staatswissenschaft*, vol. 78, 301–45.

——— (1925), *Agrarentwicklung und Agrarrevolution in Russland*, Berlin.

——— (1928a), *Die Lehren des Marxismus im Lichte der russischen Revolution*, Berlin.

——— (1928b), 'Das Dorf des russischen Nordens in der Revolution', *Berichte ueber Landwirtschaft,* N.F., vol. 7, 607–42.

——— (1929), 'Narodnoe khoziaistvo sov. Rossii, ego priroda i ego sud'by', *Sovremennye zapiski*, no 38, pp. 401–32 (part 1); no 39, 428–74 (part 2).

——— (1931a), ' "Piatiletka" i ee ispolnenie', *Sovremennye zapiski*, vol. 46, 503–20.

17 For the history of Japanese perceptions of the Soviet Union see Kojima 1988, 21–49.

——— (1931b), 'Neuere Buecher ueber Sowjetwirtschaft', *Archiv fuer Sozialwissenschaft und Sozialpolitik*, vol. 65, 162–77.

——— (1931c), Review of Kal Kautsky, *Der Bolschewismus in der Sackgasse* (Berlin, 1930), *Archiv fuer Sozilalwissenschaft und Sozialpolitik*, vol. 66, 447–48.

——— (1932a), *Der Fuenfjahresplan und seine Erfuellung*, Leipzig.

——— (1932b), 'Die Probleme der Kollektivierung der baeurlichen Landwirtschaft in Sowjetrussland', *Berichte ueber Landwirtschaft*, N.F., vol. 16, 216–43.

——— (1932c), Review of Aaron A.Iugov, *Piatiletka, Sovremennye zapiski*, vol. 48, 500–01.

——— (1933), 'Vzlet i raspad Sovetskogo planogo khoziaistva', *Sovremennye zapiski*, vol. 51, 417–31.

——— (1934a), 'Die historischen Eigentuemlichkeiten der wirtschaftlichen und sozialen Entwicklung Russlands', *Jahrbuecher fuer Kultur und Geschichte der Slawen*, N.F., vol. 10, 62–99.

——— (1934b), 'Review of Sergei N.Prokopovich', *Ideia planirovaniia i itogi piatiletki* (Paris, 1934), *Sovremennye zapiski*, no 55, 440–42.

——— (1935), *Economic Planning in Soviet Russia*, London: Routledge.

——— [1936] (1995), 'Plan i rynok v khoziaistve sovetskoi Rossii', in Kagan, V.I. (ed.), *Sovetskaia Rossiia i sotsialism*, St Petersburg: Zvezda, 181–204.

——— [1937] (1995), 'Sovetskaia Rossiia i sotsialism', in Kagan (ed.) *Sovetskaia Rossiia i sotsialism*, St Petersburg, 205–23.

Fisher, George (1958), *Russian Liberalism*, Harvard University Press.

Hale, N.A., (ed.) (1972), *Half a Century of Russian Serials*, part III, New York: Russian Book Chamber Abroad.

Hayek, Friedrich A. (1935), 'Foreword', in Brutzkus, *Economic Planning in Soviet Russia*, London, vii–xii.

Iur'evsky, E. (1955), 'O S.N. Prokopoviche', *Novyi zhurnal*, no 42, 249–66.

Jasny, Naum (1972), *Soviet Economists in the Twenties*, Cambridge University Press.

Kagan, V.K. (1989), *Boris Brutskus*, Jerusalem: M. Sominsky.

Kojima, Shuichi (1987), *Studies in the History of Russian Agricultural Thought*, Kyoto: Minerva (in Japanese).

——— (1988), 'The Changing Japanese Perception of the Soviet Union as seen in Postwar General-Interest Magazines', *Konan Journal of Social Sciences*, vol. 2, 21–49.

——— (2005a), 'Comparing Chayanov and Kondratiev', *Japanese Slavic and East European Studies*, vol. 25, 1–25.

——— (2005b), 'Russian Liberal Economists and Agrarian Question in the 1920s', *Konan Economic Papers*, vol. 46, no 1, 1–46 (in Japanese).

——— (2005c), 'A Biographical Sketch of an Exiled Russian Economist, S.N. Prokopovich (1871–1955)', *Konan Economic Papers*, vol. 46, no 2, 33–64 (in Japanese).

Morioka, Masashi (1995), 'Boris Brutzkus on the Socialist Economy', *Ritsumeikan Kokusai Kenkyu*, vol. 7, no 4, 38–79 (in Japanese).

Pipes, Richard (1980), *Struve. Liberal on the Right, 1905–1944*, Harvard University Press.

Prokopovich, Sergei N. (1923a), *Ocherki khoziaistva Sovetskoi Rossii*, Berlin.

——— (1923b), 'Novaia ekonomicheskaia politika', *Ekonomicheskii vestnik*, vol. 1, 44–78.

——— (1926), 'The Distribution of National Income', *Economic Journal*, vol. 36, 69–82.

——— (1927), 'Desiat' let opyta', *Russkii ekonomicheskii sbornik*, vol. 11, 5–15.

——— (1934), *Ideia planirovaniia i itogi piatiletki*, Paris.

——— (1944a), *Russlands Volkswirtschaft unter den Sowjets*, Zurich.

——— (1944b), *Die natuerlichen Hilfsquellen der UdSSR*, Zurich.

——— (1948), *Der vierte Fuenfjahrplan der Sowjetunion 1946–1950*, Zurich.

——— (1952), *Narodnoe khoziaistvo SSSR*, 2 vols, New York.

——— (1956), *Sbornik statei. Posmertnoe izdanie*, Paris.

Rogalina, Nina L. (1997), 'Pis'ma B.D. Brutskusa k E.D. Kuskovoi i S.N. Prokopovichu', *Voprosy ekonomiki*, no 11, 145–60.

——— (1998), *Boris Brutskus: Istorik narodnogo khoziaistva Rossii*, Moscow: Moskovskie uchebnik.

Rosen, J. (1945), 'Die Entwicklung der russischen Volkswirtschaft', *Schweizerische Zeitschrift fuer Volkswirtschaft und Statistik,* vol. 81, 96–101.

Shirokorad, Leonid D. (1990), 'O B.D.Brutskuse i ego rabote: Problemy narodnogo khoziaistva pri sotsialisticheskom stroe', *Vestnik Leningradskogo Universiteta*, ser. 5, vyp. 4, 46–55.

Tanaka, Masaharu (1967), *Studies in the History of Russian Economic Thought*, Kyoto: Minerva (in Japanese).

Telitsyn, V.L. (2000), 'Ekonomicheskaia mysl' rossiiskoi emigratsii pervoi volny', in Vinogradov, V.A. (ed.), *Ekonomicheskaia istoriia Rossii XIX–XX vv. Sovremennyi vzgliad*, Moscow: ROSSPEN, 580–91.

Zweynert, Joachim (2002), *Eine Geschichte des oekonomischen Denkens in Russland 1805–1905*, Marburg: Metropolis.

Chapter 10

The Debate on the Law of Value in the USSR, 1941–53

Michael Kaser

Three important economists notably contested Stalin's pronouncements on economic theory in the aftermath of the Second World War, Nikolai Voznesensky, Evgeny Varga and Vasily Nemchinov.[1] The first paid for his opposition with his life. Varga and Nemchinov were merely removed from their academic positions, with the latter contributing to the resuscitation of Soviet economics after Stalin's death. Stalin's successor, Nikita Khrushchev, authorized public discussion of both men, despite the closeness of his own ideas on economics to those of Stalin. In a parallel debate, Nemchinov was resolutely opposed to Lysenko's theory of heredity. Lysenko returned to the shadows when Stalin died, but went back to vigorously defending his position in 1958 while Khrushchev was in power. In February 1965, Lysenko was dismissed and Soviet biology resumed on the path of world science.

Voznesensky had initiated a Soviet economic reform according to principles that were conducive toward an empirical use of value and profit in planning, but Stalin had disavowed Voznesensky's policies (and, as part of the suppression of the 'Leningrad Affair', had him executed in 1950), while Khrushchev, in turn, declined to adopt them. The reform of wholesale prices in 1949, a cornerstone of the reforms promoted by Voznesensky, was continuously postponed under Khrushchev: the 1955 price lists, which should have been revised in 1960, would not to be put into effect until 1967. Nemchinov supported Liberman's proposal to re-introduce the concept of profit into economic management. Khrushchev procrastinated with respect to the reform, first in 1962, then again in 1964, but Alexei Kosygin, his successor as Chairman of the Council of Ministers, partially adopted it in September 1965.

Nemchinov's stand against Lysenko was only officially justified several months after Nemchinov's death, the opinions advanced by Varga having been rehabilitated a few months previously. Voznesensky was rehabilitated by Khrushchev in his 'secret report' to the XXth Party Congress in 1956, and an account of Voznesensky published in 1958 made these facts public. However, his economic theories and policies were not recognized until 1963, the year in which his former assistant Gennady Sorokin published an apology backed by supporting statements prepared by the historian Vasily Kolotov (Kolotov and Petrovochev, 1963).

1 Revised version of a text first published in French as 'Le débat sur la loi de la valeur en URSS – étude rétrospective 1941–1953', *Annuaire de l'URSS 1965*, CNRS, Paris, 1966, 555–69.

Writing a Manual of Political Economy

The arrest of leading 'bourgeois' economists, notably N.D. Kondratiev and L.N. Yurovsky in 1930, had been a salient signal that the officially-sanctioned discipline was to be confined to studying what the socialist state chose to do. The appointment of Lev Leontiev, Ostrovityanov and Varga as Corresponding Members of the USSR Academy of Sciences in 1939, may be seen as preliminary to ending that dogmatic prohibition, which was announced in an anonymous article of 1943, stating that the 'law of value' (a law regulating exchange relations by labour value) was authorized for consideration within the context of socialist economics. That article, published in the theoretical organ of the Soviet Communist Party *Pod znamenem marksizma* (*Under the Banner of Marxism*), no. 7–8 1943, started with a critique of the contemporary state of Soviet economic policy.

As revealed by subsequent debates, almost all of the action took place around the lack of a new manual of political economy. The previous such manual dated back to 1928 (edited by Iosif Lapidus and Konstantin Ostrovityanov); the 1943 article called for a new text, and a draft was to be at the heart of the intervention made by Stalin on economics in 1951. The work (edited by Ostrovityanov, Lev Leontiev and others) was published in 1954. No manual could have been published under the conditions that prevailed in the 1930s, and the 1943 article implied this when it condemned the 'voluntarism' that denied an objectively-directed development of the production process. In this context, 'voluntarism' had to be considered as a notion akin to the 'teleological' approach to drafting the first five-year plan in the mid-1920s, namely that Soviet planners should formulate very ambitious development goals under the slogan: 'There is no fortress that the Bolsheviks cannot storm'.

Those in the opposite camp were termed 'geneticists', who postulated that development planning projected and adapted past trends and experiences. As Alec Nove related: 'an eminent Soviet scholar who had known both men said to me "Bukharin and Preobrazhensky, however much they differ on other matters, were both agreed that the law of value would have no place under socialism"' (Nove, 1974, 183–203). Even less concern was being placed on 'economic laws' by the late 1930s, when 'teleological' planning itself was reduced to brief summaries of long-term targets such as for steel and engineering. The material balances system (tabulations of inputs and outputs by product group) was abandoned until re-established by Nikolai Voznesensky after taking the helm of Gosplan (the State Planning Commission) at the end of 1938 (Sorokin, 1963, 150–53).

In 1939, the XXIIIth Party Conference had assigned the Soviet economy the task of 'attaining and surpassing the per capita production level of the principal capitalist countries'. Behind the propaganda component were at least quantifiable and interdependent targets. Both then (see Zelenovsky, 1941, 17–25) and later Soviet commentators perceived the third five-year plan as a decisive return to long-term planning, over approximately three five-year periods, in order to link objectives to existing potential. The 1941 Genplan may be considered a reiteration of the Genplan abandoned in January 1933. The earlier long-term plan had also sought to quantify the objectives contemplated by resolutions adopted at the XVth and XVIIth Party Conferences (1926 and 1932 respectively).

From 1940 to 1942, Stalin convened select meetings of economists and planners to discuss the preparation of a manual of political economy. Stalin attended at least one of them and may have attended others: he doubtless informed the participants as to his standpoints, having formulated the elliptical concept as '*sebestoimost' bez stoimosti*' (intrinsic cost without extrinsic value) at the first meeting. This would appear to have indicated his view that it was possible to present a theory of the embodiment of labour in goods (which, as a Marxist, Stalin could hardly have denied under a socialist regime), but the concept of 'value' could no longer be expressed where trade relationships were exclusively a function of work performance. It was reported that Voznesensky remained silent during this meeting and he was later condemned for a 'mixture of voluntaristic opinions with respect to the role of plans and the state in Soviet society and for making a fetish of the law of value, which should supposedly preside over a distribution of labour between the various sectors of the Soviet economy' (Suslov, 1952).

A crucial meeting took place at the start of 1941, at which Stalin seems to have allowed himself to be convinced, or claimed to be convinced, of the possibility of permitting the concept of 'value' to be applicable to socialism. A comment by one of the participants, Lev Leontiev, indicates that 1941 was the decisive date:

> Above all, it is obvious that it was particularly naïve to assign a date, such as for example 1941, to the 'introduction' of the law of value in socialism. It implies that the Soviet people had started and continued to build socialism without the law of value, that they mastered this law without realizing it, rather like that Molière character who did not suspect that he spoke in prose (Leontiev, 1961, 4).

Leontiev was assigned to write that manual. As a specialist in ideology, he was the most qualified of the invitees to the meetings: he had been on the staff of the Marx-Engels-Lenin Institute from 1930 to 1935 and from 1935 to 1943 was a member of the *Pravda* editorial board. Ostrovityanov may have been consulted, as the co-author of the previous manual. Indeed, their careers evolved in parallel during the course of the years between the benchmarks of 1949 and 1953.[2]

Voznesensky, who was in all likelihood the third person to have shared in developing the new theory, later wrote his own draft (destroyed after his execution), which accorded the law of value an even greater role than had been authorized for the 1943 text. Stalin would not have played any direct role himself and it seems unlikely that the text could be attributed to Stalin, as Nove suggested (Nove, 1963). After publishing his theories on Soviet political economy in the abridged party history of 1938, the reading of which became a national obligation, Stalin settled for letting the economists he had selected make their own way until he returned with his *diktat* of 1952.

Leontiev's draft was approved at a meeting in 1942. The Polish Oxford economist Włodzimierz Brus, who was in the USSR during this period and in close contact with Soviet economist colleagues, commented on that meeting:

---

2 Leontiev was the Academic Secretary of the Academy of Social Sciences of the Party's Central Committee, and Ostrovityanov was the Academic Secretary of the corresponding division – political economy, philosophy and law – of the USSR Academy of Sciences

> The documents relating Stalin's conversations with the economists (concerning the preparation at that time of a manual on political economics) were never published. The anonymous article (1943) was distributed to institutions of higher education as a draft (Brus, 1961, 170).

Lev Gatovsky, another prominent economist who attended those meetings, had also promptly reversed his published opinion between articles of 1930 and 1931, excluding in the latter any objective nature to the law of value. Jack Miller described Gatovsky as distinguishing 'between the phenomena (Appearance) and the laws of structure and process which they obey (Essence) … as distinct from the superstitious acceptance of the "blind forces of the market" in capitalism and other forms of what Hegel called the "customary tenderness to *things*"' (Miller, 1953, 407). Miller argued:

> The notion itself of value (i.e. exchange value as distinct from use value) does not exist outside production for the market, commodity exchange and trade. By definition there is no room for it in a socialist economy, for under socialism the community is expected merely to distribute and allocate the social product … There is no room for selling and buying or seller and buyer (Miller, 1953, 352).

Aleksandr Notkin (Institute of Economics, USSR Academy of Sciences) and Nikolai Tsagalov (Moscow University) were Gatovsky's principal supporters and denounced the affirmation vigorously:

> This formulation can mean nothing other than an assertion that in socialist society the purpose of reproduction and consequently the setting up of the balance-connections of this reproduction is to be subordinated to consumption tasks … However, it does not follow from this that the entire system of socialist reproduction has to be built up from the point of view, directly, of consumption (Miller, 1953, 412).

This latter objective of a socialist economy had been posited by Stanislav Strumilin, that 'the fundamental objective of production becomes consumption' (Strumilin, 1937). This brought him an accusation of being counter-revolutionary in 1937 (Zauberman, 1948, 7), but by the end of that decade he was again *persona grata* at economists' meetings and his principal critic, Notkin, was excluded.

Thus, Leontiev, Ostrovityanov and Varga were all appointed as Corresponding Members of the Academy in 1939, whereas Notkin was absent from the 1940–42 meetings, albeit regaining participation for the second round of meetings in 1951. Notkin's 1961 self-criticism for not recognizing the existence of objective economic laws during the 1930s indicated an earlier lack of sympathy with the then reformers. After declaring that the fundamental laws of socialism included the 'law of planned and proportionate development' he stated:

> As a continuation of the primacy of politics and political tasks, we judged that the optimum increase in accumulation and consumption could only play a secondary role and that it could not be considered as a characteristic feature of socialist reproduction. This point of view emerged and was approved in the concrete reality of the transitional period of the economic development of the USSR (Notkin, 1961, 20).

It seems clear that the principal economists at the first series of meetings were Leontiev, Ostrovityanov and Voznesensky. In 1943, once the draft article was published, Leontiev was named Assistant Chief Editor of the journal *Novoe vremya*, Ostrovityanov was appointed to a Chair at Moscow University and Voznesensky was elected a member of the USSR Academy of Sciences. These appointments were not necessarily recognition of their services with respect to writing the draft, but did at least confirm that these three economists were authorities in the matter and politically in good standing.

Ideological Reassessments on the Eve of the War

Developing an ideologically acceptable text took four years, from the XVIIIth Party Congress in March 1939, to final publication in 1943. Part of this delay was caused by the disorganization that resulted from the German invasion in June 1941, although certain changes in economic management appeared in practice as soon as Stalin had made his decision in 1939. That decision appears to have been taken in February, before or during the XVIIIth Party Congress, which focused on economic business. Work was once again started to develop an annual plan, indeed Voznesensky's published report presenting the plan to the conference was remarkable in its own right. The (unpublished) plan documents were thus complete for the first time since 1937 (Kozin, 1938, 79), because no overall plan seems to have been prepared for 1938, 1939 or 1940 (Jasny, 1961, 184).

Also in 1941, the Central Statistics Directorate (TsSU) reverted to its original name that was lost in 1930 when the term 'statistics' suffered the same fate as the 'law of value'. Gosplan's statistical work was assigned from 1931 to the Central Administration for Conservation of Economic Records (TsUNKhU), on the pretext that plan preparation and plan fulfilment reporting were the necessary functions of a planning authority (Grossman, 1960a, 17). Strumilin had been arguing for the re-establishment of systematic statistical reporting and analysis since 1936 and the adoption of his ideas by the 1941 meeting implies that he participated in it. As practised in the 1930s, the reporting of key economic variables could be developed as 'balances' describing the production and distribution processes, either *ex ante* for planning or *ex post* for plan fulfilment and record-keeping. Instruments of government policy, such as taxation, were applied to these balances but projections do not seem to have been made of economic variables (other than national accounting aggregates), which were not plan indicators.

The reorganization effected by Voznesensky during the war gave a greater role to the state and academic organizations at the expense of Party organizations. Thus, a decree of 16 August 1941 to approve the plan for the fourth quarter of the year put the name of the Council of the People's Commissioners before that of the Central Committee, a reversal of previous usage. In May 1942, a general assembly of the Academy of Sciences prepared a plan for establishing closer relations between science and industry, pursuant to which during the course of the year, Academy commissions were attributed numerous planning functions in the eastern regions. A remark made in 1958 by the then Chairman of Gosplan on lack of cooperation between his agency and the Academy reflected the post-war suspension of the participation of external advisors in the planning process (Kuzmin, 1958). The need to implement emergency measures following the invasion delayed other changes that may have been contemplated in 1941, but the economists/reformers are noteworthy for having improved the state planning apparatus under Voznesensky, and for having re-established connections with academic research institutions.

Post-War Frontiers for Political Economy

The authorized boundaries of social science in the Soviet Union, severely restricted after 1929, were enlarged as soon as the war was over (Barnett, 2005, 118–33). At the start of 1946, the Department of Political Economy and Law of the Academy of Science called for more theoretical studies in those disciplines and condemned the 'predominance of concrete elements of description at the expense of theoretical generalizations'.[3] Leontiev developed his concept of the 'objective necessities' of any economic mechanism: he made the law of value 'the key … to all the economic categories of socialism', and contended that economic calculation was necessary as long as the work that created the value required by remuneration was based on results, namely under 'socialism' as distinct from 'communism' (Leontiev, 1947, 47–61). Zauberman warned at the time that:

> A closer analysis of Leontiev's reasoning reduces his 'objective necessities' to propositions which hardly state more than is already implied in their logical assumptions. It would be erroneous to think that Soviet economic thought has moved during the last five years any nearer to the tenets of the 'genetic school' which met its tragic end at the threshold of the 1930s. The theory of value has remained at the stage which it reached on its re-admission five years ago (Zauberman, 1948, 3).

The contribution made by Voznesensky to the debate on value in his *The War Economy of the USSR during the Patriotic War* (Voznesensky, 1948) was summed up by his assistant, Gennady Sorokin, in a belated obituary of 1963 (Voznesensky was executed in 1950):

> Voznesensky stated that socialist planning required knowledge of the economic laws of production and distribution, and their sagacious use, in order to obtain a proportionate development of the economy … Scientific socialism, he wrote, cannot deny the role of the law of value, fixing retail prices or the evaluation of losses and profits in a socialist economy (Sorokin, 1963, 153).

Ostrovityanov (under the influence of Voznesensky) conceded the importance of a monetary evaluation of 'socially necessary work', as Marx had referred to it, and as interpreted by Voznesensky as the work actually effected in a planned economy (Voznesensky, 1948, 149). Lev Gatovsky acknowledged that planning 'eliminated

3 'In the Department of Economics and Law', *Vestnik Akademii Nauk SSSR*, no. 3 1947, 201–205.

the antithesis' between actual work and socially necessary work but made no further concession (Gatovsky, 1948, 50–69).

Others took advantage of the opportunity provided by the acceptance of the law of value to revise the concept of capital, the Marxian value of which resides in incorporated work. Strumilin appreciated the time factor (as he termed it) of capital in terms of increasing the productivity of work, with the growth rate of productivity representing the discount rate over time (Strumilin, 1946). Vitaly Sobol preferred a re-evaluation of assets and Notkin and A.A. Konius attempted, though not without reservations, to reintroduce the concept of 'obsolescence' under socialism, thereby incorporating technical progress into the determination of long-term value (Sobol, 1947). Strumilin developed this point in a paper which internal evidence indicates to have been written in 1947 or 1948, but which was only published in 1964 in a collection of his works (Strumilin, 1964). He wrote that the concept of obsolescence 'enables us to consider the value of all products of work as a magnitude transformed over time; however, contrary to what occurs in the "theory" of the spontaneous growth [of capital], such a magnitude is a decreasing and not an increasing function of time' (Strumilin, 1964, vol. 4, 111).

In that study, he quoted Voznesensky's 1947 book, but only to cite a fact and not an opinion. Since Strumilin seems not to have published anything significant between 1948 and 1954, a fair conclusion is that his ideas were no longer in favour after Stalin's revocation of any 'transformed law of value'. This eclipse contrasts with the ascendancy he exercised during the first years of Stalinist political economy, as one of the leaders of the 'teleological' group (Kaufman, 1953).

Evidence of Voznesensky's interest in planning with units of value, as opposed to the simple physical balances, which he had inherited from the 'teleological' approach, may be found in the measures he took immediately after the war. In March 1946 the Supreme Soviet adopted a five-year plan for the Reconstruction and Development of the USSR from 1946 to 1950. Presented as a legislative act, it differed from both the previous plan, the third five-year plan for 1938–42, and the ensuing plan, the five-year plan for 1951–55, both of which were formulated as resolutions of a Party Congress (respectively the XVIIIth and the XIXth Congresses) and neither of which were reformulated as state documents. It was not entitled the 'fourth five-year plan', although it was retrospectively so termed in the 'foreword' to the party directives on the fifth five-year plan, published in 1952. The promulgating act included a provision for the subsequent establishment of detailed five-year plans for the various ministries, which indicated both the haste with which the law must have been drafted and the desire to establish a comprehensive programme.

The plan provided for the abolition of rationing of bread by autumn 1946, and for all other goods by the end of 1947. The catastrophic harvest of 1946 delayed the first stage, but in December 1947 rationing was lifted and, linked with a drastic monetary reform, the level of retail prices was aligned with that of money wages. Radical deflation permitted the use of an 'income and outlay balance of households', an innovation that had been introduced by Voznesensky just before the war (reviving national accounting techniques that had been abandoned in 1930). During that same December, the planning institutions were thoroughly restructured. The preparation of 'material balances', that is, accounts of inputs and outputs for specific products in physical units, was assigned to the newly-created Gossnab (State Committee for Supply) and the forecasting and promotion of technological changes to another new entity, Gostekhnika (State Committee for Technology).

Gosplan (renamed a 'committee' instead of a 'commission' to highlight the policy change) was to be exclusively responsible for planning in monetary terms and for 'national economic proportions' (distribution of the national product between consumption and accumulation) and for the forecasting of consumer purchasing power. Gosplan became solely concerned with projections and programming the following August, when the statistics administration was made autonomous. In 1947 and 1948, a series of amalgamations reduced the proliferation of economic ministries that had occurred during the hostilities and in the months immediately following the war. Gosplan then prepared the first major wholesale price reform since the second five-year plan, as 'planning prices' had been little changed since 1936. The so-called 1926–27 constant prices, which had been long under criticism, were replaced on 1 January 1949 by a new set of planning prices (Kaser, 1950).

In Voznesensky's thinking, the confrontation of new theories and practice was far from envisaging either a market mechanism within planning or recognizing the possibility of planned management within a competitive economy. The arguments published between 1943 and 1948 distinguished between the manner in which the law of value functioned under socialism and under capitalism; the former being a 'transformed expression' of the latter. Zauberman formulated that contemporary Soviet interpretation as:

> The law of value in socialism … (a) acts under the conditions of the state ownership of the means of production, thereby precluding the exploitation of man by man and the transformation of values into capital; (b) acts as part of an overall plan that avoids the disastrous effects of the laws of capitalism such as market anarchy and industrial crises; and (c) avoids the need for equalizing profit rates in the system (Zauberman, 1948, 2).

Varga contested this distinction in his book *Transformations of the Capitalist Economy after the Second World War* (Varga, 1946). Although Varga discussed the possibility of the use of planning in monetized economies, his obverse acceptance of a money mechanism in planned economies seemed ideologically dangerous. At a conference held in May 1947 to discuss his book, Varga declared:

> … we are still partially under the influence of the obsolete concept that while we have a planned economy, anarchy will always and invariably dominate in capitalism. I believe that the problem cannot be posed in such terms. Let us consider the war period: the state had to undertake planning. Later … in 1947, something like a 'Gosplan' *sui generis* appeared in certain capitalist countries. In England, for example, the plan would determine how much coal or steel was to be produced (Varga, 1948).

Soviet commentators implied that Stalin allowed Varga to disseminate his opinions as a provocation, no doubt directed against Voznesensky. A member of the Institute of World Economy and International Relations (which was soon to be disbanded following the criticism of its Director, Varga) at the conference just noted, proposed that Stalin encouraged Varga as well as his opponents. This could explain Varga's resistance under a constant barrage of attacks and without declared support from any highly placed personality.

Reversals in Economic Theory

Overall, Stalin favoured direct, physical objectives and controls at all levels, from the formulation of the central plan to the production of each state enterprise. Voznesensky had introduced a price-setting procedure based (although still imperfectly) on cost formulae and through which the decisions made by both the planners and the executing agents (such as enterprise directors) could be checked; in principle, it was the same for the collective farms. In 1952, Stalin denied that in exchanges between state corporations a transformed law of value was being applied in socialism, because in the state sector goods were distributed by instruction, although in the collective farm sector application of the law of value was permitted:

> The task is to extend these rudiments of products-exchange to all branches of agriculture and to develop them into a broad system, under which the collective farms would receive for their products not only money, but also and chiefly the manufactures they need (Stalin, 1952, 103–104).[4]

For the state sector, the re-establishment of planning in physical units after Voznesensky's dismissal in 1949 can be deduced from a critical article that was published in January 1950 and entitled 'Improve the Journal *Planovoe khozyaistvo*':

> Issues of planning for the various branches of production are not well dealt with in the journal. The post-war five-year plan was essentially devoted to the development of the oil, metallurgy and electric power industries. The development of these branches of the industry is a substantial determinant of the structure of production within the national economy and of its rate of development (Okhotnikov and Podkuron, 1950).

Determining 'proportions' and the rate of growth by means of targets for metallurgy and energy is, of course, the opposite of a macroeconomic policy based on relative cost/benefit. When the criticism of *Planovoe khozyaistvo* was published, the first reversals of Voznesensky's domestic policy were already under way, although the two opposing theses continued to appear until autumn 1949. The proceedings of the conference of November 1948, published in *Voprosy ekonomiki*, No. 8, 1948, showed that Sorokin unambiguously defended Voznesensky, who was then working on his never-published *Political Economy of Communism*.

The conflict between Varga and Voznesensky was exposed more clearly in an article by M. Myznikov in *Planovoe khozyaistvo*, no 6, 1948, entitled 'The Distortions of Marxism-Leninism in the Works of E. Varga'. Myznikov's association with Voznesensky is patent: he contributed to the Gosplan journal for the first time (no 11, 1938) a few months after Voznesensky was appointed Chairman and he frequently cited Voznesensky's book as an authority in opposition to Varga; he disappeared from

4 The quotation is from *Economic Problems of Socialism in the USSR*.

the review's editorial committee and its circle of authors shortly after his superior was dismissed. Stanislav Strumilin and Lev Gatovsky also joined the criticism of Varga for suggesting that the 'bourgeois' state planned its economy even in peacetime. Strumilin attacked UK economic policy under Herbert Morrison's 'free planning' at length in *Izvestiya Akademii Nauk (Otdelenie Ekonomiki i Prava)*, no 2, 1947, which was an allusion to an article on the economic plans of the British Labour government published in the newspaper of the British Embassy in Moscow, *Britansky soyuznik* (*British Ally*), 7 November 1946 (Strumilin, 1964, vol. 4, 335–37).

In 1952, Stalin would criticize the policies of both Varga and Voznesensky. While Stalin presented the contradiction in terms of production goods and consumption goods (since his priorities for the plan focused on ensuring that the annual increase in the one would surpass that of the other), the same reasoning could obviously also apply to choice of any type of potential production. It was only in 1964 that the 'law of the preferential growth of heavy industry' was denounced as one of Stalin's 'erroneous dogmas', although its application had figured in the contest between Khrushchev and Malenkov in 1954–55.

The present author has related the abandonment of Voznesensky's domestic policy following his dismissal to Soviet policy with respect to the Council for Mutual Economic Assistance (Comecon) (Kaser, 1965, 29–38), and Leonard Schapiro has placed it in the context of East–West relations. For Schapiro, Stalin had moved closer to those who felt that a capitalistic crisis was imminent, believing that the Marshall Plan, the Korean War, and the arms race were nothing more than 'wisps of straw' to which capitalists hung on to. In Stalin's own words: 'the disintegration of the single, all-embracing world market must be considered as the most important economic sequel of the Second World War' (Stalin, 1952, 31), resulting partly from the 'economic blockade of China, the USSR and the people's democracies in Europe which did not join the Marshall Plan' and 'the fact that … these countries have grown closer in economic terms by establishing economic cooperation and providing mutual assistance to one another' (Stalin, 1952, 35–36).

Maksim Saburov, Voznesensky's successor, quickly adopted a policy that was radically opposed to his predecessor's. A policy of annual reductions in retail prices resulted in the weakening of an incomes policy that could deploy economic incentives within the environment of a stable general price level. On 1 January 1950, and again on 1 July, wholesale prices were significantly reduced, an action which was contrary to Voznesensky's policy of setting wholesale price relatives in approximate conformity to those of costs, and which required a return to subsidization for production goods. The second of these price deflations was specifically attributed to Stalin's initiative. During the course of 1950, numerous medium-term sectoral programmes were introduced and the extant five-year plan was virtually abandoned. In November, Georgia, Stalin's native republic, published its own six-year agricultural plan. In August and September, four major dam and canal projects, none of which had been included in the plan,[5] were announced, exerting strains on the supply plan until in

5 Another unannounced hydroelectric project was that using Lake Sevan in Armenia, about which the present writer learnt from a Russian fellow traveller during a three-day train journey in October 1949 from leave in Tbilisi back to his post as Second Secretary in the

1953 they were reduced in scope and in one case even abandoned. It also seems that the preparatory work for a new five-year plan was suspended and no drafts were published before August 1952.

In November 1951, Stalin convened a conference, attended by more than 200 economists, historians, philosophers and jurists to discuss the texts that were published the following year in his *Ekonomicheskie problemy sotsializma v SSSR* ('Economic Problems of Socialism in the USSR'). He demanded the establishment of a select committee which was to include not only the authors of the manual and members of the majority, but also the minority that had virulently criticized the project. The completed manual was to be submitted to the Central Committee within one year.

A vast conference, with approximately a thousand participants, was convened by the USSR Academy of Sciences in January 1953 to discuss Stalin's writings. Ostrovitiyanov criticized his own errors and those of a certain number of other economists who had disseminated and praised the 'pernicious, anti-Marxist book' written by Voznesensky, yet cited only secondary personalities (Kozlov and Gladkov). Nemchinov did not align himself as closely with Stalin as Ostrovityanov did, because during the last session the latter 'specifically criticized certain shortcomings in the formulations used by the academician V.S. Nemchinov in his report'.[6]

The XIXth Party Congress in October 1952 resolved to adopt these documents as a basis for a new Party Programme, the editorial commission for which was to be chaired by Stalin. It was rumoured that he convened another meeting of economists for 5 March 1953 (that is, within the one-year deadline he had set). This conference never took place, as it had been convened for the day on which Stalin died.

The Context of Stalin's Dismissals

It would be too simplistic to attribute the dismissals of the intellectual leaders of economic thought and policy, 1948–51, solely to variance with Stalin's ideas. But, on the other hand, they were not arbitrary: they took place in the particular political context of the period. Voznesensky was the President of the Leningrad City Planning Committee (*gorplan*) and Vice President of the City Executive Committee (*gorispolkom*) while Zhdanov had been the First Secretary of the Party's City Committee (*gorkom*); he was appointed Chairman of the USSR State Planning Committee (Gosplan) in December 1937. In March 1941, when he entered the Politburo, his principal assistant, Maksim Saburov, took charge, but he returned to lead Gosplan in 1944. Stalin appointed him to the Foreign Affairs Commission when its remit was extended to include, beyond the scope of its title, economic policy and domestic politics. Thereby in the government's internal and external economic policy, Voznesensky held a position parallel to that held by Zhdanov with respect to the domestic and foreign communist parties.

British Embassy, Moscow; the informant believed that the tunnels were for testing nuclear weapons.

6 The reports were published in *Pravda*, 8–11 January 1953.

In February 1948, Kosygin, later (following Khrushchev's fall in October 1964) to become Chairman of the Council of Ministers, was appointed Minister of Finance; he replaced Arsenii Zverev, who had been responsible for that portfolio since 1938 and who was to become in the 1960s one of the principal opponents of the reform of planning and price-formation proposed by Nemchinov. The indications are that Kosygin sided with Zhdanov and that in his financial functions he supported Voznesensky in reforming prices and abolishing subsidies to heavy industry.

Zhdanov was at the peak of his influence at the start of 1948, but died in August of the same year. Kosygin, until he was transferred from the Finance Ministry to the Light Industry Ministry at the end of December, was listed by name, along with Voznesensky, at all major political events.[7] It is not known whether Voznesensky approved Stalin's 'Plan for the Transformation of Nature', a vast project launched on 20 October 1948 to plant forest belts in arable zones, but abandoned after Stalin's death. That grandiose scheme does not fit with Voznesensky's general policies and possibly indicates a certain weakening of his authority. A parallel case in foreign policy is patently the rupture with Tito at the beginning of that year, to which Zhdanov was opposed.

The political events that include Voznesenky's fall took place in mid-February.[8] On 24 February 1949, *Pravda* omitted publishing a list of the leading personalities invited to the Bolshoi Theatre, as it had done in the corresponding issue of 1948.[9] On 5 March it was announced that Molotov and Mikoyan were leaving their respective portfolios of foreign affairs and foreign trade and, according to a statement made on 12 March from the Supreme Soviet, 5 March was also the date on which Voznesensky was dismissed as Chairman of Gosplan (and on 7 March dismissed as Vice Chairman of the Council of Ministers). Varga retracted a large number of his opinions in a letter to *Pravda* on 15 March.

At the XXth Party Congress (in February 1956), Khrushchev declared that after the war the so-called Leningrad affair occurred. As it has now been proven, that affair was completely fabricated. The innocents who paid with their lives included, among others, Voznesensky, Kuznetsov, Rodionov and Popkov. Kuznetsov and Popkov had succeeded Zhdanov as the First Secretaries of the Party Committees in Leningrad (in 1944–46 and in 1946–49 respectively), and Rodionov chaired the RSFSR Council of Ministers. Similar alignments can be traced in the academic sphere.

For example, Nemchinov opposed Lysenko's idiosyncratic biological concepts, made official doctrine by Communist Party decree in August 1948, just before Zhdanov's death, and was dismissed from the management of the Timiryazev

7 Specific instances were a dinner in honour of a visiting Czechoslovak delegation (*Pravda*, 15 December 1948), the delegates elected by the party's urban and regional conferences in Moscow (ibid, 18 December) and Leningrad (ibid, 24 December). Kosygin's transfer was announced in *Pravda*, 29 December 1948.

8 The convocation for the Supreme Soviet – at which Voznesensky's dismissal was announced – was decreed on 14 February. Another indication of political change was the arrest, on the same day, of Anna-Louise Strong, a pro-Soviet American journalist who was editor of *Moscow News*, the English-language newspaper.

9 Voznesenky's name was included in various protocol lists in *Pravda* on 22 January and on 2 and 4 February 1949.

Agricultural Academy. Nevertheless, he was not persecuted and was appointed to chair the Council for the Study of Productive Resources of the USSR Academy of Science in 1949. That Council had been chaired since 1946 by Strumilin, who had been recalled to Gosplan in 1943 and remained there until 1951. From 1946 to 1951, Strumilin was also an active member of both academic and state planning bodies. Ostrovityanov was appointed Director of the Institute of Political Economy in 1946 and remained there until 1953, when he was replaced by Dyachenko (who at the same time became a Corresponding Member of the Academy of Sciences).

Those who, based on a list published in the *Great Soviet Encyclopedia*, would have taken part in November 1951 in discussions with Stalin about the manual of political economy included Ostrovityanov, Leontiev, Gatovsky and Laptev (who would succeed Dyachenko at the Institute of Political Economy and precede Plotnikov, who was Zverev's deputy minister during Stalin's final years and following his death). Notkin, from the same Institute, was Stalin's scapegoat when he condemned the extension of commercial relations that was to result from the sale of Machine-Tractor Station equipment to collective farms. But he seems not to have suffered any reprisals as a result of his opinions and eventually saw Khrushchev implement his proposal in 1958. As already noted, Varga in 1948 lost his own Institute, but joined the staff of the Institute of Political Economy and the Editorial Board of *Voprosy ekonomiki* in 1948 and remained there until 1956.

The one mysterious personage criticized by Stalin in his 1952 text, and hence also during the meeting of 1951, was 'L.D. Yaroshenko'. Of all the economists who were criticized he was the one who was most virulently attacked, but nothing else was heard about him, either before or since. There is no trace of his writings, other than the one Stalin attributed to him. In 1953, in a comment on Stalin's denunciations, Isaac Deutscher observed that:

> It may well be that Stalin crudely exaggerates the simple-mindedness of the 'young cadres' and thus sets up imaginary whipping boys whom it is easy to belabour in controversy. It is difficult to believe that the 'young cadres' should be unaware of the experiment of War Communism, which was nothing but an abortive Bolshevik attempt to abolish the market economy (Deutscher, 1953, 353).

Because Yaroshenko proved to be an invention of Stalin's,[10] the indulgent treatment of the academics who did not align themselves with Stalin's thinking, implies that the factors behind Voznesensky's execution were more political than economic.

Conclusion

By eliminating the progress made between 1943 and 1948, Stalin inflicted a serious blow to economics in the USSR from which it could not recover until after his death in 1953. In the relatively freer atmosphere for discussion of the post-Stalin decade,

10 Vsevolod Holubnychy (Institute for the Study of the USSR, Munich) was the first to speculate on this in a discussion with Alec Nove (University of Glasgow), who recounted it to the present writer.

debate on the law of value could explicitly incorporate the demand as well as the supply side into price determination and culminated in five academic conferences between December 1956 and January 1958 (Grossman, 1960b). By then a significant stage in the transition of Soviet economics from Marx to Marshall was complete.

References

Barnett, Vincent (2005), *A History of Russian Economic Thought*, London: Routledge.

Brus, Włodzimierz (1961), *Ogólne problemy funkcjonowania gospodarki socjalistycznej*, Warsaw: PAN.

Deutscher, Isaac (1953), 'Dogma and Reality in Stalin's "Economic Problems"', *Soviet Studies*, April.

Gatovsky, L. (1948), 'The Planned Socialist State – Source for Developing the Soviet Economy', *Planovoe khozyaistvo*, no 2.

Grossman, Gregory (1960a), *Soviet Statistics of Physical Output of Industrial Commodities,* Princeton, New Jersey: Princeton University Press.

——— (ed.) (1960b), *Value and Plan: Economic Calculation and Organization in Eastern Europe*, Berkeley and Los Angeles: University of California Press.

Jasny, Naum (1961), *Soviet Industrialization 1928–1952*, Chicago: Chicago University Press.

Kaser, Michael (1950), 'Soviet Planning and the Price Mechanism', *Economic Journal*, vol. 60, March.

——— (1965), *Comecon: Integration Problems of the Planned Economies*, London: Oxford University Press.

Kaufman, Adam (1953), 'The Origin of the Political Economy of Socialism', *Soviet Studies,* vol. 4.

Kolotov, V. and Petrovochev, G. (1963), *N. A. Voznesensky (Biograficheskii ocherk)*, Moscow: Politizdat.

Kozin, M. (1938), 'Instructions and Procedures in Formulating National Economic Plans', *Planovoe khozyaistvo*, no 7.

Kuzmin, I. (1958), *Izvestiya*, 5 April.

Leontiev, L. (1947), 'On Questions of the Political Economy of Socialism', *Planovoe khozyaistvo*, no 6.

——— (1961), *Ekonomicheskaia gazeta*, no. 8.

Miller, Jacob (1953), 'A Political Economy of Socialism in the Making,' *Soviet Studies*, vol. 4 (April).

Myznikov, M. (1948), 'The Distortions of Marxism-Leninism in the Works of E. Varga', *Planovoe khozyaistvo*, no 6.

Notkin, A. (1961), *Tempy i proportsii socialisticheskogo vosproizvodstva*, Moscow: Izdatel'stvo ekonomicheskoi literatury.

Nove, Alec (1963), *The Soviet Economy: An Introduction*, London: Allen and Unwin.

——— (1974), ‘Some Observations on Bukharin and His Ideas’, in Chimen Abramsky and Beryl Williams (eds), *Essays in Honour of E.H. Carr*, London: Macmillan.

Okhotnikov, A. and Podkuron, P. (1950), *Kultura i zhizn’,* 11 January.

Sobol, V. (1947), ‘On the Question of Valuing Capital Assets’, *Planovoe khozyaistvo*, no 4.

Sorokin, G. (1963), ‘A Leading Communist Party Activist in Economics: On the 60th Birthday of N.A. Voznesensky’, *Voprosy ekonomiki*, no 12.

Stalin, J. (1952), *Economic Problems of Socialism in the USSR*, Moscow: Foreign Languages.

Strumilin, S. (1937), *Planovoe khozyaistvo*, no 9–10.

——— (1946), *Vestnik Akademii Nauk SSSR*, no 3.

——— (1964), *Izbrannye proizvedeniya*, Moscow: AN SSSR, vol. 4.

Suslov, Mikhail (1952), *Pravda*, 24 December.

Varga, E. (1946), *Izmeneniya v ekonomike kapitalizma v itoge vtoroi mirovoi voiny*, Moscow: Politizdat.

——— (1948), *Planovoe khozyaistvo*, no 6.

Voznesensky, N. (1948), *Voennaya ekonomika SSSR v period otechestvennoi voiny*, Moscow: Politizdat, 2nd edn.

Zauberman, Alfred (1948), ‘Economic Thought in the Soviet Union’, *Review of Economic Studies*, vol. 16.

Zelenovsky, A. (1941), ‘The Immediate Tasks of Gosplan’, *Planovoe khoyaistvo*, no 1.

Chapter 11

Soviet Economics after Stalin: Between Orthodoxy and Reform

Pekka Sutela

Joseph Stalin died on 5 March 1953. This heralded the beginning of a new era in Soviet history, one in which economics was to play a much greater role than during the Stalinist decades.[1] Soviet history finally ended in the collapse of *perestroika*, an attempt to reform socialism fundamentally. This attempt was, in its final years, informed by ideas and indeed advice from many of the best Soviet economists available. To this extent therefore, *perestroika* was the last test of the practical potential of Soviet economics. Though it would be a huge simplification to equate the practice of *perestroika* with the views of economists, as obviously their various views were bound to differ, in the end the collapse of Soviet policy to a degree at least signalled the failure of economists. Since approximately 1990, the Russia of Boris Yeltsin used the ideas and advice of a new generation of economists, many of them students and junior colleagues of the economists of *perestroika*, and set policy goals thoroughly different from those that had predominated before. For these reasons, selecting the years 1953–89 for consideration in this chapter offers a suitable time frame for an analysis of Soviet economics. But it also helps to choose an analytical framework.

Economics had a peculiar role under Soviet socialism. On the one hand, Soviet Communists proudly declared a kind of scientism. Contrary to the assumed anarchy of market capitalism, socialism was created, developed and managed consciously, based on a unified doctrine called Marxism-Leninism. Socialism in this view had a maker, Marxism-Leninism, acting through the Communist Party to lead the country. Socialism was seen as a unique society as it was based on a doctrine and therefore the success or failure of socialism was also the crucial test of the theory.

Such scientism also included critical potential in a number of dimensions. Did the existing socialism correspond with the doctrine? When problems arose, was the doctrine or its failed application to blame? Who, in fact, decided what the true doctrine was? Was it given forever, or could it be changed, and if so, by whom? How did one distinguish the true doctrine from bogus ones? Furthermore, what was

1 Pekka Sutela, Head, BOFIT, (Bank of Finland Institute for Economies in Transition); Docent in Economics, Helsinki School of Economics and Business Administration. All opinions are those of the author and do not express the views of the Bank of Finland. This chapter builds upon my earlier work on the subject: Sutela (1984, 1987, 1991) and Sutela and Mau (1998).

the relationship between the new doctrine of socialism and the received one about capitalism? Were the concepts and theories of Karl Marx relevant in conceptualizing socialism? Could interpretations change in the light of more recent experience?

On the other hand, such critical potential was blunted by the fact that more than being simply a doctrine, Marxism-Leninism was an ideological belief system serving the needs of power, prestige and legitimacy of the leading party, personified in its political elite. The normal scientific criteria did not and could not hold true here, any more than they hold in any other ideology. An accurate method for distinguishing between true and false statements could not exist, not even that of referring to a higher authority, as such authority could change, as happened after 1953. But when it came, de-Stalinization did not equal a shift away from socialism, instead it equalled a shift inside socialism. Some elements of ideology had to change, others could not.

The potentially troublesome issue of the 'true' doctrine changing with time had arisen previously. As Ethan Pollock (2006) has shown in his study of Soviet post-war 'Science Wars', Joseph Stalin not only had genuine intellectual pretensions, but was privately scornful of the more extreme views on 'proletarian science'. He was also realistic enough to admit that his own views had changed over time. What Stalin had written in the 1920s was not necessarily still true in the 1940s. But, if that was possible, who could tell when it was the case – especially after 1953, when Stalin was no longer available to arbitrate?

Contrary to early Bolshevik beliefs inspired primarily by Kautsky and Lenin, managing the Soviet economy soon proved a demanding task that was not suitable for 'any cook', as Lenin had dreamed. Already in the nineteenth century, orthodox socialists had come to think of the society of the future as a giant piece of social machinery, a single factory like the German postal service or the Prussian army, to cite some of the early characterizations (Sutela 1984, 17–40). In this Kautsky–Lenin view of a centrally managed economy, it was a complex but basically deterministic organization under unified command. In a peculiar contrast with what was indicated above, it would need no other social sciences other than social engineering writ large. That might be called economics, which had to have one primary characteristic: to be useful in a technical sense as a guide to centrally managing the economy.

Over the decades of Soviet socialism, calls by political leaders for a practically useful economics were frequent, actually being the usual demand made. Soviet economics therefore had to be something quite different from the Marxian critique of bourgeois society. No critical analysis of Soviet reality was called for. On the contrary, the potential of Soviet economics as social engineering was truncated by the needs of ideological purity and political correctness. The political leadership might need new proposals, but it would not give away the privilege of deciding what was appropriate and what was not. Contrary to the Stalinist years, economic views did not condemn people to prisons and camps after 1953. Still, censorship remained and the limits of the permitted fluctuated over time. The fact that everything was written with an eye on censorship must be remembered when reading Soviet economics. Each institute had an *osobyi otdel*, specific department caring for ideological purity and state security.

Of course, actual central management never followed the Kautsky–Lenin model. It was born quickly, with much improvization and including the unintended consequences of poorly prepared decisions, rather than any prior strategic planning. The outcome was nothing like the Prussian army, and the issues of property rights, incentives and information were never resolved in the way foreseen early on. Actual central management not only did not correspond with the Kautsky–Lenin model, it also functioned quite badly. Unnecessarily so in fact, in the sense that it could have functioned better, even while remaining within the definition of socialism declared by 1936. Economists were expected to come forward with proposals for improvement, and they were ready to do so in the early 1930s, when the first experiences of practical central management gave rise to a surprisingly candid discussion on issues like prices and incentives (Sutela, 1987). The durability of central management as it was first established was shown by the fact that many identical proposals for improvement were repeated over and over again from the early years until the 1980s. These concerned, in particular, pricing formulas and incentives. And there were economists who remained prominent in these discussions over almost all these years. Stanislav Strumilin was the most prominent, but others like Aleksandr Birman and Shamay Turetsky should not be forgotten.

Any such proposals for improvement were handicapped by many factors. It was never easy to judge where the limits of appropriateness were, and it was always easy to use accusations of political incorrectness to gain debating points or more serious advantages. This was not only a matter of ideology, political correctness and censorship, it was also a matter of the availability of statistics, other empirical data and the possibilities of field research. As late as in the 1980s, political leaders like Yuri Andropov and Mikhail Gorbachev lamented the lack of relevant research on the Soviet economy and society. What they failed to emphasize was that the party they headed had the prime responsibility of having made such studies impossible. Also, some of the questions they raised were impossible to answer. There was no way of assessing the exact share of military expenditure in the Soviet economy. Resources and products were heterogeneous in character, and no ideal price system was available to assess the importance of differences in quality. This was emphasized by Yury Yaremenko (1981) in one of the most original monographs ever produced by a Soviet economist. He also had the questionable honour of being the last chief economic advisor of the last Soviet president. A later collection of interviews and discussions (Yaremenko, 1999) shows how hopeless, even desperate, that job was, but also how deep was the disappointment that socialism could not be salvaged. That was the final predicament of Soviet economics.

These facts help to explain some of the prominent features of the economics of Stalin's time, and the way in which they continued in the post-Stalin period. The often-neglected waves of pre-reform proposal discussions in the 1930s (Sutela, 1987) are one of them. But so is Molotov's reputed ban on price debates by economists in 1938. Stalin deemed it appropriate to order an official textbook of Marxist-Leninist Political Economy of Socialism in 1936. But the book only came out in 1954, after Stalin had personally resolved some of the doctrinal issues involved (Pollock, 2006), and even then it could only maintain its monopoly position for a few years. In the 1930s a young Leningrad mathematician, Leonid Kantorovich, was asked to solve a production optimizing task at a veneer plant. He did that to great acclaim, having invented the mathematical method of linear optimization in the process. This was to bring him the Nobel Prize in economics many years later. But when he, in 1942, had generalized the task onto the level of national economic planning, no publishing permit was forthcoming. What had been a fruitful proposal for improvement on the plant level had come too close to the prerogatives of political planners on the national level. Still, the borders between improvement and political decision-making remained contested until Stalin's death. He had to defend the priority of politics in economic policy-making even in his very last published writings.

Inevitably, the realm of appropriate economic discussion widened after Stalin's death, not least because there was a consensus at the highest political levels that many things had to change in Soviet society. For economists, this made proposals of reform possible, even welcomed, and the Soviet economics of 1953–89 is best analyzed in terms of reform discussions. A reform here means a conscious change implying a relaxation or re-interpretation of at least one such feature of the economy that had previously been regarded as a part of the definition of socialism. The definition adopted here is a relatively stringent one, and excludes most of what Soviet economists actually wrote in their everyday work. Most of that would only be of interest to the narrowest of experts in enterprise or branch-level issues. But as Vladimir Mau (1990; 1993; 1995) has shown, relevant questions on issues such as property rights and incentives did arise even in the seemingly arid writings of (say) agricultural economists.

The discussion to follow is strictly focused. It concentrates mainly on matters relevant for allocation, or on what Soviet economists called the economic mechanism. On the other side, this discussion bypasses issues of property rights, for instance.

The analysis below does not follow a chronological order. Still, the discussions described took place in real time, and some of the political background has to be outlined. There is also another relevant issue, that of generations. Up until the 1960s, some of the active key figures, like Stanislav Strumilin (1877–1973) and Viktor Novozhilov (1892–1970), had at least some pre-revolutionary education. But they had also gone through all of Soviet history with its ups and downs. Largely due to repressions, almost all the participants of the relatively free and wide-ranging economic debates of the 1920s were absent by 1953, but some witnesses remained. The first, usually strongly anti-reformist, generation of political economists, were mostly men who had risen within Stalin's revolution. With little education or independence of mind and a history of risk-avoidance, they preferred doctrinal purity and political servitude to innovation.

If people like Strumilin and Novozhilov had memories of the pre-revolutionary period, many of the reform-minded economists to be discussed below were born in the 1930s. Their formative youthful experience was the 1956 Party Congress, with Nikita Khrushchev's strong anti-Stalinism. More widely their lives were patterned by the 'thaw' era of de-Stalinization, improved living standards, some democratization and hopeful vistas for the future. Their contribution was to offer theories on how the Soviet system should function, which they equalled with how it could be reformed. After the depressing years of Leonid Brezhnev's rule of stagnation after 1965, *perestroika* seemed to offer a new possibility of building a better socialism. Such beliefs were not shared by the next generation, that of Yeltsin's advisors. They were born around 1956 and had their formative experience under Brezhnev, coming to believe that stagnation was the essential nature of socialism. Soviet socialism could not be reformed and therefore reforms should not be attempted. The transition to capitalism, not an improved socialism, was their choice. Some of them had also made a rare Soviet contribution to studying the socialist system as it really was, not as it should be.

Varieties of Soviet Economics

Soviet scholars and administrators produced a number of classification schemes for the various branches of economics concerning the Soviet system. For our purposes a division into three will suffice. Highest on the level of ideological importance and political correctness was the Political Economy of Socialism (PES), a constituent part of the Marxist-Leninist belief system and a 'scientific' basis for economic and other policies. It was meant to provide for socialism what Marx had done for capitalism. But if Marx had written a critique of capitalism, PES was a justification of socialism and communist policies. As already mentioned, creating PES originally took the form of writing a textbook, a process commenced in 1936 but only finalized in 1954. War obviously intervened, but the project itself was a minefield of scholarly and political challenges. It suffices to enumerate only some of them.

Marx had emphasized the historical specificity of capitalism. But could his theories and concepts have any relevance for socialism? Marxism-Leninism found a way out of this problem: by developing a specific theory of capitalism, Marx had also provided the fundamentals of a general doctrine applicable to all societies. In capitalism, the anarchy of markets means that the laws of the economy function spontaneously, independently of the will and consciousness of people. They were in this sense 'objective'. Socialism was a centrally managed system, established, developed and managed purposefully. But were there objective laws in socialism? If the answer was yes, what was the difference between capitalism and socialism? If not, were policies really unbound by any objective necessities? This question was never resolved in a satisfactory way.

Which of the Marxian categories were relevant for socialism? Was the law of value one of them? What was the relationship between capitalist exploitation and the socialist need for profits? Did the communist party belong in the category of productive or non-productive activities? To the last question the answer since the mid-1930s was: non-productive. What was the division of labour in the development of PES between the highest political and ideological leadership and professional economists? This relationship always remained blurred.

For these and other reasons, PES remained a perplexing topic. It cannot be simply dismissed as an ideological belief system utterly devoid of interest, because it was a vehicle for developing and communicating policy ideas and interpretations. Neither can it be just seen as a scholastic pastime perhaps of interest in theory, but unimportant in practice. To take an example much debated from the 1950s until the 1980s: it matters for practice whether the essence of socialism ('the basic category' of

PES) was seen as the planned character of development (which was then more or less successfully implemented), or the satisfaction of human needs (for which markets might actually be useful). After the monopoly of the 1954 textbook collapsed, there were competing interpretations of these and other issues, which were very important from the Marxist-Leninist viewpoint, but also were of practical importance.

It was possible to distinguish trends of thought of varying degrees of conservatism and reform. Though the divisions are far from neat, scholars working at universities, responsible for the education of the youth, tended to be more conservative than their colleagues at the academy, responsible for research. The party ran a network of research institutes and contrary to what one might think, they were not always a bastion of old ways of thinking. In the Khrushchev years, with old party ideologists like Otto Kuusinen and up-and-coming ones like Yuri Andropov involved, the party ideologists pushed strongly for very moderate reform. During the Brezhnev years, under the likes of Mikhail Suslov and Sergey Trapeznikov, the line of the party institutes changed thoroughly. But then again, in the *perestroika* years, under Vadim Medvedev and others, the party institutes again became proponents of modest reforms. Vladimir Faltsman (1995), a leading expert on the economics of growth and investment, has provided (in an outspoken booklet with a print-run of 200 copies) a rare glimpse of the lives, personages and institutes of Soviet economists since the 1960s.

Actually, the reign of pure Stalinism was as short as the monopoly of the 1954 textbook. The differences inside PES were never great, and they were often more a matter of scholasticism than of major contrasts in practical implications. But every now and then they did have interesting policy implications as well. This caused some headaches for the communist party, posing itself as the guardian of orthodoxy both inside the country and internationally. In the 1970s in particular, facing challenges ranging from domestic debates to Chinese and euro-communist critiques, an attempt was made to produce another monolithic textbook expounding official orthodoxy. The attempt failed; the political economists were simply not able to agree.

Given the scientific claims of Marxism, it is not surprising that the goal of scholarly agreement was not only shared by the defenders of orthodoxy. Aleksandr Yakovlev, the main ideologist of *perestroika*, later described how in the late 1980s: 'an illusion was created that what needs to be done is to gather as full and reliable information as possible, analyse it strictly scientifically and (then) act in a corresponding way – in that case everything will go in the necessary direction, an honest and reasonable policy will be formed. This is an illusion which I also shared' (Yakovlev 1994, 205).

The reformability of Soviet socialism, based on free discussion and well-informed policies, was thus believed in by most in a naïve way until the very end. The number of convinced opponents of the system was very small, there were no major economists among the open dissidents, and perhaps surprisingly, no major unpublished manuscripts emerged from economists' desks after what had been unpublishable became possible to publish. Self-evidently, what the economists wrote was influenced by the existence of censorship and the pressures of orthodoxy, but there is no evidence that their inner thoughts were completely differently from what they published. In fact, several prominent proponents of *perestroika* have until today continued to argue that a better socialism would have been possible – had *perestroika* not collapsed for reasons totally independent of the advice that the reformist economists offered.

The importance of the generational change outlined above cannot be overemphasized. The older generation of political economists, people whose names are probably best forgotten, were forever stamped by their formative experience of cleansing academia of less-than-perfect Stalinist scholars. For them, PES was a form of class struggle, and though the history of economic institutes during the Stalinist years remains to be written, many must have compromised themselves in serious ways. From the point of view of serious scholarship, they were a major case of adverse selection. But as in other walks of intellectual life, there was a 'generation of the 1956 party congress' in PES as well, people – almost all of them men – who were attracted to economics because it mattered for a better future. Leonid Abalkin, Pavel Bunich and Vadim Medvedev were just three of the most prominent names in this category.

In fact most Soviet economists never pondered the categories and laws of PES; they were preoccupied with more mundane matters. Some of their work was disseminated widely, much was restricted to internal institutional use, or just published in obscure editions. None of this work has been properly analyzed, though a few peaks appeared. One of them was Yevsey Liberman, a professor of economics of the engineering industry in a Kharkov engineering institute, who became a celebrity with a series of articles stretching over almost ten years, advocating better use of profit and incentives in planning. Though they did point out the need for what were later to be called hard budget constraints, these articles were generally devoid of deep economic contents. But importantly, Liberman was used to start and maintain the public discussion leading up to the 1964 economic reform programme usually identified with the name of Aleksey Kosygin, the Prime Minister, but sometimes with the name of Liberman as well.

Another less well-known set of examples were the internal memoranda that institutions like the Economic Research Institute of the State Planning Commission wrote for the political leadership. Such institutions had the best access to empirical data, enabling them to detect various emerging problems, and acted as whistleblowers inside the administration (Lewin, 2005; Faltsman, 1995). This type of work also still awaits a substantial analysis. Another interesting example might be agriculture, on which a rich set of memoranda must exist. Some of them have been used by Gaidar (2006) with good effect.

In the Soviet Union, this literature was called applied (*prikladnaya*) or branch-specific (*otraslevaya*) economics. While it is unclear what was actually being applied, or how the problems of a specific economic branch were put in a more general setting, analyses of this part of Soviet economics would clarify the extent to which planners and policy makers had materials for a relevant understanding of the Soviet economy. This would tell us much about the whole system as well.

Another variety of branch-specific economics was the analysis of foreign countries, for which there were several institutes, using both secret and publicly available information. Any honest analysis of developed market economies must have shown how the goal set by the 1961 Party Congress of economically overtaking the USA in 20 years, was increasingly distant. The rich availability of analysis on such fellow socialist countries as Hungary, Poland and Yugoslavia must have alarmed some analysts not only about the 'dangers of revisionism', but also about the possibility of different socialist solutions. In this light it is not surprising that a major analyst of European socialist economies like Oleg Bogomolov became something of a celebrity as a Social Democratic politician during *perestroika*.

A key member of the early Yeltsin economic policy team has told (Hoffman, 2002, 89–92) what an impact the arrival of a photocopy of *The Economics of Shortage*, the seminal book by Janos Kornai, had on young oppositional Leningrad economists in the early 1980s. It became 'the Bible', opening eyes to the way in which central management really worked. Kornai (2006, 250–51) related this story, but he also told of a debate with a conservative Soviet economist who could not admit that shortages were a systemic feature of central management. But by 1989 he noted, with obvious satisfaction, that Moscow economics students also knew his arguments very well – but their teachers did not (author's personal observation, Moscow, March 1989). Another Central European economist with a major impact in the Soviet Union, but earlier on, was Wlodzimierz Brus.

Finally, a third kind of Soviet economics must be discussed. Mathematical economics had deep roots in Russia, including Yevgeny Slutsky and Wassily Leontief (see Vincent Barnett's chapter in this volume), but the starting point of the Soviet school of optimal planning was the 1942 manuscript of Leonid Kantorovich (1965, xvii), finally published in a thoroughly revised form. Kantorovich's approach was that of social engineering writ very large. If it was possible to optimize the cutting of veneer into pre-ordered sizes and shapes, then was national planning not also a matter of optimizing? There was a goal function to be maximized, set by the political process and consisting of a pre-ordained selection of commodities to be produced. And there were the constraints: the availability of various resources as well as the technologies determining how they might be transformed into commodities. Kantorovich's major contribution was to show how such a task could be solved in a linear case. Further, he showed that in the process, shadow prices arose for each of the resources and products. They could be used to direct a profit-maximizing plant into fulfilling the given plan task. There could thus be two kinds of central management. In the case of direct centralization, plants were given plan tasks in the form of the numbers of tons and pieces to be produced. But indirect centralization was also possible by giving instead of quantities, the plant prices, wage rates and other plan-derived value indicators, plus a behavioural rule like profit maximizing. In simple models at least, the resulting allocations would be identical. The indirect approach seemed to offer relative benefits. At least it gave the plants a semblance of initiative and self-determination.

The Kantorovich approach became known as optimal planning. In truth, it faced a number of challenges, which were soon raised in Soviet discussions. Was this obviously technocratic approach the correct one? Perhaps the political authorities had goals other than maximizing production (or welfare, in more challenging applications)? Was the originally static optimizing approach in line with the ethos of a developmental state, as the Soviet Union had defined itself? Were the daunting informational and computing requirements implicit at all solvable? Was the whole approach an import of 'bourgeois' thinking into the USSR, as some claimed? What, in fact, was the relationship between PES and optimal planning? Was optimal planning a technocratic challenge to the primacy of politics in PES, or rather a way of implementing that primacy?

The history of optimal planning, both as a theoretical construct and also its practical applications, has been thoroughly discussed in the literature (Ellman, 1973; Zauberman, 1976; Cave, 1980; Sutela, 1984). There is no need for repetition. Instead, a more fruitful approach is to look at Soviet economics as a whole between orthodoxy and reform. This will give a more nuanced picture than the stark contrast between a completely conservative PES, and a totally reformist optimal planning, that is sometimes presented in the literature.

Stages of Economic Reform

A distinction has been made between proposals for improvement or pre-reform proposals on the one hand, and actual reform proposals on the other. The difference was that the former proposals respected all the characterizations of the centrally managed economic system, as was defined in the prevailing ideology. Reform proposals, on the other hand, relaxed at least one such characterization. To the extent that reform proposals were accepted, the definition of the centrally managed economic system changed over time.

The distinction was not as difficult to maintain as it might seem. The character of PES as part of a unified ideology implied that definitions of the 'true' socialist economy abounded in official documents like the communist party programme and party congress decisions. Basically the definition remained stable from the early 1930s to the late 1980s, reflecting the lack of any true reform of the Soviet economy. This contrasted with the Hungarian, Polish and Yugoslavian cases. Still, reform proposals were made in the Soviet Union by economists belonging to all currents of Soviet economics, as outlined above.

For a more detailed analysis, it is useful to divide socialist reform discussions into five phases. Most socialist countries went through all the phases in roughly chronological order. This was also true of the Soviet Union, though, like in all countries, some phases were more pronounced than others. First, as already mentioned, there was the pre-phase of reform, which started almost immediately after the establishment of the centrally managed system. Here the intention was to rationalize the functioning of the system, trying to make it work like the large-scale social engineering system it was supposed to be. Already the Soviet literature of the 1930s was surprisingly rich in various projects for rationalization. Prices, a necessary feature of any large-scale economic system, were to be made to reflect costs and benefits better. Incentives were to be made more efficient, and accounting and data management was to be improved. Examples of this are many.

But even the most ambitious of such proposals left the defining characteristics of central management intact. In the optimal planning framework of Kantorovich, referred to above, the product mix was determined exogenously, that is by the political authorities. The overall maximizing approach was well in line with the 'growthmanship' ethos that the USSR had introduced into world practice. It was only if not only the primacy of political decisions, but also the arbitrary character of such decisions, were introduced into the definition of socialism, that pre-phase discussions became part of reform discussions proper. This would not be without foundation, as technocratic planning was a disputed concept in Stalin's times, explicitly abandoned by the dictator himself in his 1952 pamphlet on political economy (Stalin, 1952).

But there was also the recurrent call for useful economics, and after Stalin's death, only the optimal planners had a coherent set of proposals for eliminating the efficiency, equity and growth losses that arbitrary decision-making entailed. They had three main weapons at their disposal. The first one was Kantorovich's book, finally published in 1959 (Sutela 1991, 34–35). Another was the work of Viktor Novozhilov (1970, 1972), and the third one that of Vasily Nemchinov (1964). Kantorovich provided the underlying theory, whilst Novozhilov showed, among other things, how that could be reconciled with Marxism. Nemchinov offered leadership, but with a keen eye for practical applications.

Different developments were possible starting with the basic optimal planning approach. There were economists and planners who saw the new mathematical methods and the use of computers as a way of furthering centralization, as they facilitated using and controlling much larger information flows. Others went the other way, drawing truly reformist conclusions, as we shall see below. But some of the rationalizing proposals also had far-reaching consequences. One example concerned the partitioning of the economy.

The Kautsky–Lenin image of socialism as a single large factory could not literally be true: the factory in question was too large for that. Traditionally it had been partitioned for the purposes of practical management on the basis of industrial branches. Branch ministries had much of the concrete economic power in the country, as plants were either directly or indirectly subordinated to them. Planners mainly made the investment decisions, while the political leadership had the supreme power. But this was not the only feasible way to partition the economy. One alternative, region-based organization, was tried and abandoned in 1957–65. Another alternative was to try and combine the branch- and region-based approaches. Economists at the Novosibirsk branch of the Academy of Sciences worked in that direction in the 1970s, but these were technically very difficult and politically controversial proposals (Sutela 1984, 127–32).

The most wide-reaching among such proposals was to be called goal-oriented planning. Why start from existing technological divisions of labour? Why not take as the starting point the satisfaction of different social needs, or the tasks to be performed? This approach was common in military and strategic planning. If the task was to reach the moon, establishing a space programme was the right approach. Why not adopt the same approach to rural development, urban planning, housing and health? This was called planning by clusters. Soviet economists called it planning by complexes.

This would have major consequences. Branch ministries could perhaps be abolished. There would be less of a ratchet or 'planning from the achieved level' effect, and there would be innovative and changing ways of organizing the economy. Bureaucratic conservatism would give way to dynamism. Perhaps even, to keep the management task manageable, those parts of the economy not directly serving any of the complexes could be left unmanaged, guided by markets. This conclusion was however explicitly drawn very late. But what had started as a pre-reform exercise in rationalization, had produced a proposal for a Chinese-type dual-track approach.

Phase I of Reform Discussions: Decentralization

Reform proper meant that at least one of the defining features of central management was challenged. In the Soviet Union, this tended to be the existence of plant-specific compulsory plan targets. Plans including them were often called addressed; those without, parametric or normative (that is, based on norms). In pre-reform discussions, ministries were accused of petty tutelage based on overly detailed and ever-changing addressed targets. In phase I reform discussions, the addressed targets were to be abolished. Plants would just be guided by such value-based norms as prices, interest rates and depreciation coefficients. This was where reform discussion had advanced to by the early 1960s.

The theoretical backbone was provided by Kantorovich's optimal planning. Shadow prices derived from a central plan could be similar for all plants. This was symmetric with the law of one price in simple markets. There would be no need for commandeering and petty tutelage. Efficiency and the output mix aimed at by planners would be reached, as rationally behaving plants would obey the information provided by shadow prices. This idea was the main one in Soviet reform economics all the way until the late 1980s. It was the basic economic thinking of the generation moulded by the de-Stalinizing 1956 Party Congress.

The last article of Vasily Nemchinov from 1964 was, Mikhail Gorbachev claimed almost 25 years later, the main inspiration of *perestroika*. It outlined what Nemchinov called a *khozraschet*-economy, perhaps best translated as a cost-accounting economy (Sutela, 1991, 62–67). In essence, this was to be a dual-track economy. Most production would be based on state orders allocated in a competitive process. This would include few obligatory targets. Otherwise, plants would be guided through stable norms, and they would be free to have horizontal contracts with other plants. There would be wholesale trade for investment goods. Any production in excess of state orders could be sold freely, though mostly at fixed prices. No free markets, post-plan competition or private property was envisaged. A younger economist, Nikolai Petrakov (1971) went further, wanting to change the relative roles of market demand and state orders in allocation. He was duly criticized for having proposed market socialism (Sutela 1984, 1991).

Optimal planners had thus infringed into the area traditionally belonging to PES. Some political economists, usually from the older generation, were scandalized by their proposals. Others, from the younger ones, tried to develop their own reform-minded views under titles like 'planned socialist markets' and 'commodity-money relations'. The difference was that under socialism, prices and other values were planned, not market-based. This followed from the axiomatic fact that political and economic power had to be unified, and in the hands of the state. The most important proponents of these views were Leonid Abalkin (1973) and Vadim Medvedev (1966). Later they, like Petrakov, were among the failed advisors of Mikhail Gorbachev.

Phase II of Reform Discussions: Market Pricing

Phase II of reform discussions began when prices, at least most of them, were not centrally set, but were market-based. Diagnosing the turning point is not easy, as the censorship-generated lack of clarity in much of Soviet writing makes the border between parametric pricing and dual-track planning imprecise. What share of prices was actually to be centrally set? What was to be the relative role of state orders and market demand? This had to be left unclear to be able to publish.

In theoretical economics, Viktor Volkonsky (1967) was probably the best example of a Soviet market economist in the 1960s. As theoretical constructs, Kantorovich's shadow prices were equivalent to general equilibrium market prices. Volkonsky did not shy away from writing that proving the optimality properties of competitive prices was 'the greatest achievement of world economic science' – no traces of a 'proletarian science' here. But, again in the spirit of high theory, he also knew the issues raised by business fluctuations and lumpy investment decisions, even hinting at the possibility of open unemployment in the Soviet Union. There were also economic journalists like Gennady Lisichkin arguing in favour of markets, and economists like Raimundas Karagedov putting the Hungarian reforms forward as the model for the USSR also.

But the most important person in this context is the already mentioned Nikolai Petrakov. Though not a mathematical economist himself, he was a leading young economist in the optimal planning school, and was among those drawing the most radical conclusions from the approach. Due to censorship considerations, his writings were hardly a model of clarity. He was very strongly criticized publicly, and in the early 1970s he experienced a publishing ban. In an article from 1970 in the journal *Novyi mir*, then the main forum for radical reformism, he broke ground by abandoning the Kautsky–Lenin image of the socialist economy as a single factory. Logically, but in contrast to much optimal planning work, he also denied the existence of a unified social objective function, calling for a pluralistic political process instead. This was needed for the creation of new information, Petrakov argued, following the Austrian economists. Planning should not be left to planners alone: they had their specific interests, which they served by using rationing, not equilibrium prices, to allocate scarcity. By extension, this also applied to the party leadership, but that could not be put into print, not even in *Novyi mir*, which was struggling for existence. Neither could Petrakov call for private property. Still, he combined economic and political radicalism in a rare way. Similar democratic arguments in favour of markets reappeared in the Soviet Union only much later, in the late 1980s, in the writings on Gavril Popov, Nikolai Shmelyov and Leonid Abalkin.

The pro-market writings of the late 1980s missed many of the insights of Petrakov and Volkonsky. Leonid Abalkin, for instance, argued that there were no separate capitalist or socialist markets, but at the same time claimed that, because in the USSR markets would exist in a socialist environment, no unemployment or exploitation would arise from them. Even worse, the 1987 Law on Socialist Enterprise, which had been drafted by the most prominent reform economists of the day, argued that enterprises were both commodity producers and subordinated to higher administrative bodies. This implied that most prices would remain centrally set. Whether this was what Abalkin, Abel Aganbegyan, Pavel Bunich, Petrakov, Popov and Stanislav Shatalin actually proposed, or a political dictate by bureaucrats ignorant of economics, remains for future historians to settle. What is known now is that the proposal which the economists put forward in 1986, was based on the traditional optimal planning ideas of centralized pricing and stable norms (Sutela 1991, 151–54). The *perestroika* of Mikhail Gorbachev thus used the best advice that Soviet economics had to offer. The failure of *perestroika* was thus also the final failure of Soviet economics.

An extra detail was offered by the reception of a small article by Larisa Piyasheva writing under a pen name (Sutela and Mau, 1998, 52). Piyasheva argued that there could be no markets under socialism, as this would be like being a little bit pregnant. A much more famous economic journalist, Otto Latsis, countered by arguing that optimal planning theory had shown, after all, that indirect centralization was both possible and desirable. The views of the 1960s were thus still used in defence of Gorbachev's policies.

Phase III of Reform Discussions

The next and final stage of reform discussion followed when in addition to commodity and labour markets, the need for capital markets was also recognized. Outside the USSR, this argument seemed to arise from two sources. Either one claimed that market allocation led to higher efficiency than bureaucratic decision-making, or one argued that hard budget constraints could only be imposed if the paternalistic umbilical cord between plants and state administration was thoroughly weakened. As long as the debate remained within the socialist reform discussion framework, private property could not be proposed. Therefore, substitutes were sought in two directions: self-management, or impersonal owners like pension funds.

In the USSR, phase III never reached any depth comparable with the debates in Hungary and Poland. Self-management did have a small number of proponents during the last years of Soviet rule; among the economists, Pavel Bunich was the most important. Others included a few social science and law scholars. Arguably, this thinking did have some impact on the 1987 Law on Socialist Enterprise, which instituted work-place elections of managers and enterprise self-management. But in reality, arguments in favour of self-management only became vocal after 1991, when they were turned into nationalist and communist arguments against a transition to a normal market economy. A few optimal planners became advisors to opposition parties. Most withdrew. Only a few changed their patron from Gorbachev to Boris Yeltsin. It was their students and junior colleagues who became central in the Yeltsin administration.

From Reform to Transition

The Soviet Union was a latecomer to economic reform discussion. Kantorovich's optimal planning framework was the sole major theoretical invention, and that was an early one. Fifty years later, the same framework was still used as a basis for policies. Not surprisingly, as the framework was devoid of any actual macroeconomics, and learning from existing practice always remained meagre, these policies failed thoroughly. After 1989 the issue was no longer socialist reformism, but a transition to a market economy. The speed of the collapse in socialist reformism had several causes. Central European experience and the evident failure of *perestroika* were, together with political dynamism, perhaps the main reasons for this.

Soviet economics also disappeared almost without a trace. The leading academic economists – Abalkin, Bogomolov, Dmitry Lvov, Petrakov, Yaremenko and Stanislav Shatalin – turned themselves and the Economics Department of the Academy of Sciences into embittered critics of Yeltsin's policies, but with little impact. Only a couple of economists of their generation lent their support to the Yeltsin regime, but they had no policy role whatsoever. The sole exception was Yevgeny Yasin, an optimal planner who served as the economic minister for many years and became the grandfather of modern Russian liberalism. Among the students of the academic economists, Sergey Glaziev was the only one to rise into some prominence as an opposition politician. Most others joined the Yeltsin economic policy team as politicians or advisors. As the word is understood elsewhere, the USSR only left one prominent senior academic economist to Russia. He was Viktor Polterovich, an internationally published expert on equilibrium and disequilibrium models, who only became a Member of the Academy at a ripe age. The process of educating a new generation is still ongoing. There were, naturally, extremely prominent Russian-born economists working elsewhere, early emigrants from the Soviet regime. No major studies written but left unpublished during the Soviet period have emerged afterwards. But then, with a couple of brilliant exceptions, dissident thinking was never strong in the USSR.

This still remains something of a puzzle. The recurrent purges of the profession from the 1920s to the 1950s must explain much. Even afterwards, the pressure for ideological orthodoxy was a strong one. It was not for nothing that people working in the more ideologically loaded branches were called '*popy*' or priests. Perhaps the optimal planning framework offered too easy an outlet for reformist thoughts. It, like others, had to show its consistency with PES, but independent thinking was not completely suppressed, in theoretical economics at least (Ellman, 1973; Zauberman, 1976).

What Remains?

Is there any reason (apparent from the purely historical one) for anybody to be interested in Soviet economics in the period 1953–89? The story of the economists' interaction with economic, political and ideological authorities still remains to be written. It would shed much light on the way in which the Soviet system actually worked. But seen from the point of view of economic science, the answer has to be more modest. In an earlier assessment (Sutela and Mau, 1998) we offered two examples that might be of interest. One was the views of Boris Mikhalevsky, Stanislav Shatalin and Aleksandr Anchishkin on economic growth and technical change. The other was the work that a few young economists were doing on the bargaining economy as opposed to command economy, generally much more popular as a description of the Soviet system. Among these economists were Pyotr Aven, Yegor Gaidar and Vitaly Naishul, each of whom played their role in the Yeltsin regime. Did the bargaining versus command economy view impact on transition policies? Perhaps not, but that also remains to be studied.

But the inheritance of optimal planning also lives on in unexpected ways. One example is Putin (1997), a candidate dissertation written completely in the spirit of the 1970s and 1980s. If optimal planners had their role in the Gorbachev regime, and their students in the Yeltsin years, perhaps the Putin dissertation reminds us of the fact that decades-old doctrine taught in provincial universities might also matter.

References

Abalkin, L. (1970), *Politicheskaya ekonomika i ekonomicheskaya politika*, Moscow: Mysl.

——— (1973), *Khozyaistvennyi makhanizm razvitogo sotsializma*, Moscow: Mysl.

Cave, Martin (1980), *Computers and Economic Planning*, Cambridge: Cambridge University Press.

Ellman, Michael (1973), *Planning Problems in the USSR*, Cambridge: Cambridge University Press.

Faltsman, Vladimir (1995), *Rossiiskie nauchnye shkoly: zapiski ekonomista*, Moscow: Akademiya narodnogo khozyaista pri Pravitelstve Rossiikoy Federacii, Delo.

Gaidar, Yegor (2006), *Dolgoe vremya: Rossiya v mire: Ocherki ekonomicheskoi istorii*, Moscow: Delo.

Hoffman, David E. (2002), *The Oligarchs: Wealth and Power in the New Russia,* Oxford: Public Affairs.

Kantorovich, L.V., (1965), *The Best Use of Economic Resources*. Oxford: Pergamon.

Kornai, Janos (2006), *By Force of Thought: Irregular Memoirs of an Intellectual Journey,* Cambridge and London: The MIT Press.

Lewin, Moshe (2005), *The Soviet Century*, London: Verso.

Mau, Vladimir (1990), *V poiskakh planomernosti,* Moscow: Nauka.

——— (1993), *Reformy i dogmi 1914–1929*, Moscow: Delo.

——— (1995), *Ekonomika i vlast,* Moscow: Delo.

Medvedev, V.A. (1966) *Zakon stoimosti i materialnye stimuly sotsialisticheskogo proizvodstva,* Moscow: Ekonimika

——— Medvedev, V.A. (1983), *Upravlenie socialisticheskim proizvodstvom*, Moscow: Politizdat.

Nemchinov, V.S. (1964), *O dalneyshem sovershenstovanii planirovaniya i upravleniya narodnogo khozyaistva*, Moscow: Ekonomika.

Novozhilov, V.V. (1970), *Voprosy razvitiya socialistichoy ekonomiki*. Moscow: Nauka.

——— (1972), *Problemy izmeneniya zatrat i rezultatov pri optimalnom planirovanii*, Moscow: Nauka.

Petrakov, N. Ya. (1971), *Nekotorye voprosy upravleniya socialistcheskoi ekonomikoi*, Moscow: TsEMI.

Pollock, Ethan (2006), *Stalin and the Soviet Science Wars,* Princeton and Oxford: Princeton University Press.

Putin, Vladimir Vladimirovich (1997), *Strategicheskoe planirovanie vozproizvodsta mineralno-syryevoy bazy regiona v usloviyakh formirovaniya rynoschnykh otnoshenii*, St Petersburg: RGB.

Stalin, J.V. (1952), *Ekonomicheskis problemy socializma v SSSR*, Moscow: Gosudarstvennoe izdaltestvo politicheskoy literatury.

Sutela, Pekka (1984), *Socialism, Planning and Optimalitys: A Study in Soviet economic Thought,* Helsinki: The Finnish Society of Sciences and Letters.

——— (1987), 'Economic Incentives in Soviet Pre-War Economic Thought', in Hedlund, Stefan, (ed.), *Incentives and Economic Systems*, London and Sydney: Croom Helm.

——— (1991), *Economic Thought and Economic Reform in the Soviet Union*, Cambridge: Cambridge University Press.

Sutela, Pekka and Mau, Vladimir (1998), 'Economics under Socialism: the Russian Case', in: *Economic Thought in Communist and Post-Communist Europe*, Hans-Jürgen Wagener (ed.), New York, Routledge

Volkonsky, V.A. (1967), *Model optimalnogo planirovaniya i vzaimos-vyazi ekonomicheskikh pokazatelei*, Moscow: Ekonomika.

Yakovlev, Aleksandr (1994), *Gorkaya chasha*, Yaroslavl: Verkho-Volzhkoe knizhnoe izdatelstro.

Yaremenko, Yury (1981), *Strukturalnye izmenenie v socialisticheskoi ekonomike*, Moscow: Nauka.

——— (1999), *Ekonomicheskie besedy*, Moscow: Centr issledovanii i statistiki nauki.

Zauberman, Alfred (1976), *Mathematical Theory in Soviet Planning*, London: Royal Institute for International Affairs and Oxford University Press.

Chapter 12

From Marxist Economics to Post-Soviet Nationalism

Andrey Zaostrovtsev

Since the early 1990s, Russian economists have encountered Western economic theory or mainstream economics in its contemporary manifestation. Market-oriented reforms demanded a new way of thinking that embraced not only a denial of Marxist-Leninist political economy (read: the propaganda of the superiority of the communist economy), but also required an understanding of the principles of operation of a market economy. However, from the time of its first appearance in post-Soviet Russia, Western economics encountered the resistance of numerous academicians who had not been able or willing to study Western economic theory, and who started to recognize how little they had in common with their 'bourgeois' colleagues.

The resistance to mainstream economics started from the first appearance of the 'bourgeois' (dismal) science in contemporary Russia. Not having been able to prevent it from entering the universities' curricula, the traditionalists first tried to find a place in the classrooms for the teaching of various types of hastily written texts labelled as 'political economy' or 'basic economic theory'. These writings had little in common with political economy or basic economics as understood by modern Western economists, but they helped some Soviet professors to defend their positions within economics faculties, because they were widely taught and occupied the academic timetable. The second set of reasons why a resistance movement emerged was ideological and psychological in nature. Many Soviet and post-Soviet political economists were honestly convinced of the scientific value of their traditional concepts, and it would be a significant blow for them to recognize that they do not meet contemporary scientific standards at all.

However, the main goal of this chapter is not to describe the resistance to economics and the concrete actions of the opposition camp, rather its central aim is to draw the attention of the reader to the increasing trend towards nationalism and isolationism in present-day Russian economic thought. This trend in economic thinking must be seen in the context of political developments in today's Russia, with the country moving in the direction of authoritarian rule. As is well known, this type of organization of society (especially in the Russian tradition) is not compatible with individualistic patterns of thought that form the background of modern mainstream economics.

Economic Thought Versus Economic Analysis

The distinction between economic analysis and economic thought was introduced by Joseph Schumpeter in his *History of Economic Analysis*. He understood the former mainly as a set of analytical tools meeting professional standards, whereas he characterized the latter as a 'collection of all opinions and wishes on economic issues (especially on economic policy) available in public consciousness at that particular time and place' (Schumpeter, 1954, 52). Consequently, he refused to include the works of Marxist authors like Lenin, Trotsky and Stalin in his monumental book.[1]

If Schumpeter's distinction is followed, it is obvious that in contemporary Russian economics, a conflict between economic thought and economic analysis has emerged. As of yet, the discussion is not so much about scientific publications, as about the syllabi of economics education at universities. And that might be seen as quite natural. In order to attempt to refute the tools of mainstream economic analysis, the highly formalized language in which these tools were formulated had to be used. They cannot really be convincingly rejected by abstract reasoning in the old style of Soviet political economy.

As for the university syllabi, the conflict between traditional political economy and modern economics took quite concrete forms. From the early 1990s onwards, Russian university syllabi, tailored in the old Soviet manner of the political economy of capitalism and socialism, started to be gradually superseded by courses of mainstream micro- and macroeconomics. This process started spontaneously and was not immediately institutionalized. The degree to which this transition succeeded at different faculties depended firstly on the power relations between enthusiasts of Western ideas and the adherents of traditional syllabi, and secondly on the amount of Western funding.

It certainly would be an exaggeration to speak of the triumph of mainstream economics in Russia in the last decade of the twentieth century. Only in the newly established educational institutions were courses of economics modelled on Western examples. This was mainly due to the fact that in these institutions, the interest groups of traditional Soviet economists had little chance to exert any influence on the curriculum. The teaching of Western-style economics was also aggravated by considerable deficiencies in qualified staff. Moreover, the 'New Russian economists' who appeared in the mid-1990s, and who conducted research exclusively in the field of modern mainstream economics, did not take much notice of the representatives of traditional political economy. They rarely read their criticisms and sometimes even had little idea of the existence of traditional political economy at all.

In 2001 the important journal *Voprosy ekonomiki* published a special report 'On Economic Science, Education and Practice in Russia in the 90s' (Ekonomicheskaya nauka …, 2001). It noted that the pressure aiming at a prompt introduction of

---

1 The prominent Russian expert on the history of economic science Vladimir Avtonomov has successfully applied Schumpeter's distinction between economic analysis and economic thought to the history of Russian economic thought: '… In the years of *perestroika* and market reforms, thought (both liberal and conservative) completely dominated over analysis' (Avtonomov, 2001, 47).

Western standards into economic science had led to a significant split, and also to the disorientation of the academic community. According to the report, the teaching community had reacted in three ways to the challenge of Western economics:

- First, a revival of conservative tendencies and a denial of Western science as something alien and even hostile.
- Secondly, the uncritical adoption of Western economics.
- Thirdly, the search for a third way or a synthesis of Soviet political economy and Western economics, despite the huge differences between these traditions.

One important reason for the rejection of mainstream economics was that, as a result of the intrusion of Western approaches, many professors in the economic faculties of traditional (that is: not newly founded after 1990) universities found themselves languishing on the shelf. In the 1990s, it had already become unacceptable to lecture on the political economy of capitalism, let alone of socialism, on the basis of textbooks of the previous epoch. But the introduction of new educational courses required considerable efforts of self-education, even as far as intermediate courses on micro- and macroeconomics were concerned.[2]

A glance at the publications of the traditional political economists revealed that they almost never referred to international economic literature. One of the main reasons for this was that the mathematical language in which mainstream economists tended to formulate their ideas, was an insurmountable entry barrier to the economists trained in the Soviet style. In this way, the conflict between traditional Soviet political economy and Western mainstream theory emerged out of the fact that a generation of economists whose main task was to propagate the ideas of Marx-Engels-Lenin and the resolutions of CPSU congresses, proved unable to acquire the technical skills necessary to understand the content of theoretical papers in an average international economics journal. A second entry barrier was command of the English language, but this barrier was somewhat lower and has lost much of its importance in the most recent period (at least for the younger generation).

Moreover, old university professors felt that the ground was being cut from under their feet – their academic degrees and their previous publications were turning to dust. Although they managed to keep their national reputation and their official posts, the opening of Russia to Western influences showed them that the outside world did not actually regard them as economists, and that even within international Marxist discourse, they did not play any important role.[3] In order to cope with this situation,

---

2 The situation of the early 1990s was characterized by Rustem Nureev and Yurii Latov as follows: 'The representatives of the older generation of the scientific community ideologically repudiated Western "economics" without even knowing its most basic rudiments. The younger generation differed from the older only in lacking this "allergy" to "economics," but not in having any real knowledge' (Nureev and Latov, 2002, 23)

3 For example, there is only one reference to Soviet Marxists in the list of literature and in the article *Marxist Economics* in the *New Palgrave* (Glyn, 1987, 394–95), and this reference refers to a work published in 1928. In 1999, an *Encyclopedia of Political Economy* appeared, and the two articles dedicated to Marxist political economy do not mention any Soviet political economists (O'Hara, 1999, 707–16).

Soviet political economists tried to erect a new type of ivory tower. The cornerstone of this tower was the appeal to preserve political economy as the fundamental course (or at least one of the fundamental courses) in teaching economics. In December 1996 a conference under the ambitious title 'Economic Theory on the Threshold of the XXI Century' was held in Moscow and in St Petersburg, at which the general conditions of economic research and teaching were discussed. The conference provided clear evidence that a considerable number of the teaching staff at Russian economics faculties had rejected modern economics before they had really acquired an understanding of it (Osipov, 1998). Further discussion occurred in various economics journals. *Rossiskii ekonomicheskii zhurnal* for example represented the point of view of those who attempted to re-assert old-style political economy and counteract the spread of mainstream economics (Zaostrovtsev, 2005).

The New National Economics

The shift of a number of adherents of traditional Soviet-type political economy to nationalism was to some extent stimulated by a discussion that was launched after the Russian Ministry of Education had approved a new educational subject called 'national economy' in 1999. University courses on 'national economy' were mainly of a descriptive nature, characterizing the organization and the function of the Russian economy (state regulation, public finance, the banking system and foreign trade) and discussing some problems of reform.

When this subject was officially introduced in 1999, there was little scientific foundation beneath it. Thus there emerged the need to define what 'national economy' was really about, that is, in what respect it differed from mainstream economics on the one hand, and from traditional political economy on the other. In this situation, the conservative camp immediately tried to fill the niche with an outspokenly nationalist theory of the Russian national economy.

Dmitrii Zemlyakov was among the first to notice this opportunity. His article on 'The Discipline "National Economy": Methodological and Theoretical Foundations' contained reasoning about the crisis of economics in which – in typical fashion for a traditional Soviet economist – he criticized its abstractness, its atomism, the dominance of formal models and also the lack of historical understanding. He therefore argued that it was necessary to supplement mainstream economics by a theory of the national economy, which should investigate the special regularities of an individual society in its concrete historical situation.[4]

Regarding the methodology of the new science, Zemlyakov suggested the application of the ideas of all non-marginalist schools, including Marxism, the historical school, old and new institutionalism and evolutionary economics. It was obvious from his criticism of the atomistic foundations of modern economics, that he strongly objected to understanding public interest as the result of aggregated individual interests. Holism was not mentioned directly, but it was apparent that

4 In this respect, he was not an innovator. In 1996, Viktor Ryazanov had already put forward the idea of creating an economic theory entirely dedicated to the specific laws of the Russian national economy (Ryazanov, 1996, 83).

it was the methodological basis of the new nationalist doctrine. Zemlyakov also left no doubt about the ideological foundations of the new subject. As he explicitly stated, it provided university teachers with a long-awaited possibility of propagating the notion of the outstanding importance of Russia's economic security, and to train specialists with an etatist (state-directed) view of national economy (Zemlyakov, 2000, 80).

The nationalist current of Russian economic thought was further developed by Dmitrii Sorokin, who emphasized the historical nature of political economy. Very much in line with the German historical school of the nineteenth century, he argued that it was possible to speak about the political economy not only of particular countries (Russia, countries of Western Europe, the USA and China), but also of different stages in their historical development (Sorokin, 2001, 80). As a result, political economy should consist of various theories that were valid for different regions and times: it had gained 'nationality', and within each nationality it also specified an 'epoch'.

Etatism and holism were prevalent in Sorokin's conception, as the Russian state must regain control over public interests in general, and over the mercenary interests of groups and individuals in particular. Consequently, progress and development should be measured in social terms rather than in narrowly economic ones. As Sorokin argued, due to a number of non-economic factors (geographical, natural, climatic, national and geo-political), the decisive feature of the Russian economic system was that it was unable to function without the active participation of the state (Sorokin, 2001, 80).

It was difficult not to notice a drift to nationalism also in Leonid Abalkin's thought. Abalkin was one of the most famous Soviet political economists and an important state figure in the epoch of *perestroika*. He believed that the Russian system of moral values, and the type of culture based on these values, had led to the recognition of economic problems different from those prevailing in the West. For example: 'The denial of the concept of 'economic man' (*homo economicus*), and of attempts to consider him separately from society and from his environment, can be considered as a distinctive feature of the Russian view of life' (Abalkin, 2001, 10).

Abalkin understood the focus on the role of the state as the control centre of the national economy to be the second feature of the so-called Russian school of economic thought. Abalkin, who in the 1970s had been one of the key advocates of 'socialism with a human face' and who decisively influenced Gorbachev's economic policy, had now turned into an active propagandist of the philosophy of Nikolai Danilevsky, who was a leading Russian nationalist in the nineteenth century (Danilevsky, 1869). The following Abalkin statement, made in an article dedicated to Danilevsky's legacy, gave the clearest evidence of his nationalist turn:

> It is very important for us to re-establish etatist thinking and to overcome its deficiencies ... And we can solve this problem because thoughts about the country and the historical destiny of Russia have been incorporated into the genes of our people. Etatist thinking should become a principle of real policy and real behaviour … (Abalkin, 2002, 126).

The related idea of the 'nationalization' of economic theory was most consistently developed by Viktor Kulkov. He shared the opinion that the traditional approach of political economy had advantages over mainstream economics when it came to analyzing the national economy, although he was the first to identify a basic contradiction in the traditionalists' position. He argued that it was not only mainstream economists, but also the post-Soviet traditionalists, who tended to assume the existence of absolute economic laws. The only difference was that the mainstream, following in the lines of Adam Smith, prescribed market relations with eternal validity, whereas the post-Soviet traditionalists, following Marx, began from the existence of generally valid developmental laws. Kulkov emphasized that both ways of reasoning had been opposed by the German historical school (Kulkov, 2004, 61).

According to Kulkov, 'updated dialectics' and holism should become the methodological pillars of a future economic research programme. According to the principle of holism, the nation had common interests and common goals of development that were irreducible to a set of individual desires. The author then passed to what he called 'particular forms of reflection on the national factor in economic theory' (Kulkov, 2004, 66–67), and he identified five general features of Russian economic thought as follows.

The first was the *national style of research*. According to Kulkov's interpretation, this style of research was widespread in Russia in the second half of the nineteenth century and in the first two decades of the twentieth, when Russia was dominated by the ideas of the German historical school. In particular, Russian economists had always been especially interested in the philosophical and in the moral background of economic phenomena. They tended to broaden the subject by including spiritual and other non-economic factors, and due to the anthropocentric orientation of Russian thought, they had tended to trace back the value of goods to human labour alone.

The second was a *national orientation*. Here Kulkov emphasized the special role of the labour paradigm of value. If the Western individualistic consumer society corresponded with the neoclassical paradigm based on utility, then many characteristics of the labour paradigm were relevant to Russia as it had developed not as a consumer society, but as a society of producers. Thirdly, Kulkov raised the question of the existence of *particular national economic laws*. The author considered the natural, climatic, geographical, geopolitical, socio-cultural and historical conditions of Russia to be unique, and the more considerable the national peculiarities of a country were, the more significant were national economic laws. Thus the economic laws of Russia included: state regulated development, the dominance of state property, moderate social differentiation and the mobilized economy. The existence of these laws limited the laws of the market economy, and might even invalidate them in certain instances.

Fourthly, the article proclaimed the *uniqueness of Russian economy and society*. The author emphasized that it was crucial not to speak of a 'national model' but instead of a 'national economic system'. The term 'national model' implied that there was a certain standard model of which there were national versions (as for example national models of market economy). In contrast, the term 'national economic system' expressed the idea that national economies were not only versions of a standard model, but also were driven by specific national economic laws.

Finally, national peculiarity concerned the *goals of national economic development*. They included an increase in competitiveness of the national economy, the achievement of an advanced technological level, the preservation of territorial integrity and the establishment of a common free market zone, the maintenance of national economic security, and the achievement of ethno-economic harmony within the conditions of a multinational state. According to Kulkov, some of these goals might come into conflict with general economic ones (or create limits to macroeconomic growth), but they could not be ignored in view of the ultimate interests of the country (Kulkov, 2004, 70).

Thus, in contrast to the majority of his like-minded colleagues, Kulkov denied the existence of general developmental laws and concentrated instead on national specificity. Also, there were almost no references to Marxian dialectics, the labour theory of value and the relation between productive forces and the relations of production. Rather, the Russian economy was represented as a unique system developing according to its own laws. Economic man as a rational calculator disappeared, and was replaced by 'Russian economic man'. His characteristic features were support for collectivism, etatism, social measures and stability (Kulkov, 2004, 70). If the nature of the Russian people essentially differed from those of the West, then it followed that Western economic laws did not apply in Russia. Under these assumptions, it was concluded that a national economic theory was needed that was valid only for the specific conditions of Russia.

X-Type and Y-Type Economies

One of the most serious challenges within contemporary Russian economics, and one of the most remarkable examples of the approach that could be called 'soft nationalism', was formulated by Svetlana Kirdina, a representative of the Novosibirsk socioeconomic school.[5] The approach of this school gravitated towards what is usually called 'old' institutionalism in Western economics. In the author's foreword she wrote that it was necessary to provide an antithesis to the economic imperialist approach of G.S. Becker and J.M. Buchanan (Kirdina, 2004, 4). What Kirdina presented instead was an exercise in 'sociological imperialism' or an attempt to apply the analytical tools of sociology to economic problems. It goes without saying that methodological individualism was replaced with methodological holism. Consequently, the author also rejected new institutional economics, which she regarded as inappropriate for analyzing Russia's economic reality.[6]

5 Another well-known representative of this school is Olga Bessonova. Her recently published work also provides an overall idea of the school's views (Bessonova, 2006). However, Kirdina's work demonstrates a more radical rejection of the Western model (market economy and democracy).

6 'Foreign neoinstitutionalism does not provide sufficient means to analyse basic 'carrying' institutional structures of the Russian economy fully and comprehensively ...' (Kirdina, 2004, 37).

Kirdina's own conception was based on the notion of 'institutional matrices'.[7] Accordingly there were two types of institutional matrices applicable to the world, each of which had its own basic institutional patterns that differed in a fundamental way. These are presented as shown in Table 12.1.

Table 12.1: X-Type and Y-Type Systems

Sphere Of Operation	**X-type**	**Y-type**
Economic Sphere	Redistributive[8] or centrally regulated	Market-based institutions
Political Sphere	Centralist political structure	Institutions of a federal political structure
Ideological Sphere	Communitarian ideology, the main content of which is the domination of collective, common values over individual ones; the priority of 'We' over 'I' in the ideological sphere.	Institutes of subsidiary ideology fixing the dominant meaning of individual values; the priority of 'I' over 'We' in the ideological sphere.

Kirdina believed that the X-matrix pattern was dominant in Russia and the majority of countries in Asia and Latin America, whereas the Y-matrix pattern was dominant in the majority of Western European countries and the USA.

The differences between the basic institutes of X- and Y-economies were presented in the light of their five functions. The first difference concerned property. Whereas in the Y-economy the institution of private property dominated, X-economies were characterized by the dominance of conventional property, according to which: 'society as a whole is recognised, openly or latently, as the owner of key resources and production facilities' (Kirdina, 2004, 90).[9] The second difference related to the dominant pattern of interaction between structural elements. In the Y-economy the dominant pattern was market exchange, whereas in the X-economy it was redistribution. Goods were accumulated in a 'pool' and then distributed in accordance with political and social goals. Thirdly, in the X-economy competition was replaced with co-ordination. How far the distinction between X- and Y- economies was based on holism became clear when Kirdina argued that coordination 'regulated

7 'Institutional X- or Y- matrices that present a stable complex of institutions in the most important spheres of the social system (economic, political and ideological), contain genetic information that ensures reproduction of the relevant type of societies' (Kirdina, 2004, 75).

8 This term she took from Karl Polanyi.

9 It should be mentioned that 'society' in this context really means 'state'. In contrast to the institution of private property, there are no once and for all established borders in property rights between subjects here; these borders are conventional and defined at the 'supreme level'.

the efficient use of scarce resources, manufactured goods and delivered services for the benefit of the economy as a whole' (Kirdina, 2004, 91–92). A fourth difference concerned labour motivation.[10] The function of hired labour and material incentives in the X-economy was taken by 'service labour'. The fifth and final distinction regarded the feedback system in which the economic system adjusted to changes in the environment. In the Y-economy feedback was provided by profit and loss, whereas in the X-economy it was provided by proportionality.

X-economies and Y-economies could, according to Kirdina, borrow certain properties from each other while keeping their institutional core, although a complete replacement of X-matrix with Y-matrix was not possible (at least for a large country). Rather, changes in the basic institutions were likely to result in the destruction of the society as a whole. A typical example was the fate of the Roman Empire (Kirdina, 2000, 201–202). Basic to Kirdina's position was a refusal to consider the market economy as superior to non-market ones, and thus she did not consider the transition from non-market to market economies as progress or modernization.[11] To her both systems were of equal merit, and each of them was effective in its appropriate place. This explained their stability within historical time. Given such an approach, the current Russian authoritarian model was certified as a valid one with an almost infinite lifespan.

The Economics of Holy Russia

The most radical representative of Russian nationalist ideology among economists today is Oleg Platonov, and he heads an organization called the Russian Civilization Institute.[12] The clearest expression of Platonov's economic views can be found in two books of the series called 'Holy Russia, Large Encyclopedia of the Russian Nation' (Platonov, 2002; Platonov, 2006b). The essence of his reasoning can be found in the foreword to a volume on 'The Russian Economy' that was published in this series.[13] In contrast to Kirdina, Platonov understood the Russian economy as a completely specific phenomenon, as an expression of a civilization that was morally superior to the West.[14] He suggested that the main feature of Russian civilization that distinguished it from the West was the importance of spiritual and ethical priorities

10 The author uses the term 'compulsion', although its validity for the systems that the author calls Y-economies seems to be doubtful.

11 '… Market economies are not considered as inevitable and the only proper way for all countries' (Kirdina, 2004, 45).

12 This Institute was founded in 2003 in order to dessiminate the ideas of Ioann Ladozhsky who occupied the post of metropolitan in the Russian Orthodox church and was well known for his furious clericalism and nationalism. One of the members of the Institute Council is Igor Shafarevich – the world-famous Russian mathematician and nationalist.

13 Recently Platonov published the book 'Russian Economy without Globalizm' where his economic views found further development (Platonov, 2006a).

14 Platonov parenthetically identifies communal types of economy, to which, apart from Russia, he refers to such countries as Japan, China, Korea, and Taiwan.

over material ones, and the development of a self-sufficiency model based on a closed economic system (Platonov, 2006b, 5).

Platonov regarded the Russian economy as mainly a moral category, in that economic activity aimed at self-provisioning, and that moral incentives played a more important role than material ones. He emphasized that Russia was the only country in the world (even at the beginning of the twentieth century) that was close to autarchy in economic terms: it provided itself with all the necessary goods and consumed almost everything it produced. It was economic autarchy that allowed the Bolsheviks to withstand the Western blockade, to consolidate power and then to implement what he saw as an anti-Russian social experiment: anti-Russian, because by relying on the exports of raw materials, it broke with the tradition of autarchy (Platonov, 2006b, 24–25).

Referring to the *narodnik* economist Sergei Sharapov and other Russian populists of the late nineteenth century, Platonov accused the Western nations of having grown rich on the resources delivered by less developed countries (Platonov, 2006b, 29). This accusation repeated those that were often put forth by Western left-wing groups and anti-globalization theorists.[15] Platonov's main policy conclusion was that Russia should strive for economic independence, because otherwise the country would turn into a simple provider of raw materials for the West. The concrete measures he suggested included the introduction of a state monopoly on foreign trade, a fixed ruble exchange rate based on purchasing power parity and – in close co-operation with other emerging markets – political engagement to achieve a system of fair international trade.

Such proposals in the spirit of Latin American revolutionaries (*a la* Chavez) and radical Islamic leaders were quite typical for Russian nationalists. At the same time, Platonov argued in an unusual way when suggesting that Russia in principle would be able to achieve Western standards of material achievement. If Russia proved unable to do so:

> It is not because we cannot work well or create advanced technology, but because high Western standards are to a great extent provided by unpaid labor of the people of other countries. This would be incompatible with the Russian civilization and contradicts the economic model of Russia (Platonov, 2006b, 34).

Russia's task was therefore to break away from Western-style globalization, where 'the world order of money comes into conflict with Christian globalization and becomes the main source of destruction of human society' (Platonov, 2006b, 168). According to Platonov, autarchy did not necessarily mean complete isolation from the world. However, in order to profit from international trade, it would be necessary to create a powerful economic system that would allow the dictation to Western countries of Russia's own conditions of economic partnership, including setting the level of world prices.

---

15 They include environmental exploitation of the third world, the debt burden imposed on them, transfer prices of transnational corporations, excessive consumption of resources, and manipulation through dollars as a world currency. The same accusations against the USA are set forth in Platonov's famous book *Why America will Perish* (Platonov, 1999).

In conclusion, the author spoke of two major implications arising from Russian economic thought. The first one was that any measure of economic policy must take the particular Russian model into account, and must be based on the labour mentality of the Russian people. Secondly, as Western consumptive societies would, not least because of ecological problems, lead into a dead end, Western standards of economic development should not be taken as benchmarks for the Russian economy. As a result, Platonov argued that the Russian economic model with its orientation towards autarchy, as well as its capacity for self-restraint, offered one of the few survival options for mankind (Platonov, 2006b, 37).

Conclusion

A belief in the superiority of the Russian model of social and economic order is typical of Russian nationalists, and this belief has a long history in Russian thinking. It first appeared in the fifteenth century after the fall of the Byzantine Empire: Moscow was then considered to be the Third Rome. The first and the second Rome had fallen because they had abandoned Christianity, which had been preserved in its original form only in Russia. In the Soviet era, this idea was transformed into the conviction that the Soviet Union was ahead of all other nations on the road to the classless society predicted by Marx. In the current post-communist period, this communist dogma has returned to its traditional form. The Russian model was considered to be superior because only in the Russian Orthodox tradition have Christian values been preserved in their original form.

The 'Third Rome' ideology, along with the 'Holy Russia' slogan in modern Russia, is certainly intellectually archaic, and it is not the mainstream of contemporary Russian economic thought. However, the old Slavophile idea of the strong specificity of Russian economy and society, according to which general theories do not apply (as in Kirdina's ideas), finds more and more adherents among Russian academic economists. The adherents of the view that Russia represents not just a country, but also a unique civilization, usually proclaim the latter as the real global alternative to the West. In spite of the collapse of communism they refuse to recognize the fact that non-market societies (or isolated national markets) are doomed to failure in world economic competition.

The current surge of nationalism in modern Russian economic thought is probably connected with what often is referred to as a 'value gap' between Russia and the West. It is nearly impossible for the majority of Russian people and the majority of the power elite in particular, to admit the superiority of the West in economic, military, civil and legal terms. This causes the growth of a psychological defence mechanism, which manifests itself as declaring a special way as the dominant contribution of Russian culture, that is its non-affiliation to the outside world (Dubin, 2004, 29–30).

Nationalism in today's Russian economic thought plays three important roles. First, because the original domestic economic theories had little in common with present-day internationally recognized economics, it makes it difficult to evaluate the professional level of university teachers and researchers. Being accused of a lack of theoretical understanding, Russian economists can argue that they belonged to a different and allegedly superior theoretical current.

Secondly, 'original' economics gives university teachers the possibility to continue teaching in the old way that they were familiar with in the Soviet period. For instance, Kirdina mentioned that the theory of institutional matrices was transformed into such courses (Kirdina, 2004, 98). In this and other similar cases the value of the studies for the students was limited by the narrow basis of their teachers' views.

And, finally, it will be no exaggeration to say that Russian nationalism in political economy represents an attempt to reflect the present Russian political regime's demand for nationalist ideology. The methodological individualism of Western mainstream economics was alien to rising nationalism and etatism. Nationalism and holism better suit the newest Russian 'resource nationalism' of massive state intervention in the oil and gas industries, the use of energy supplies as the means of pressure on European consumers, and attempts to restore economic and political dominance over the former Soviet geographical area. This is why there may be predicted in the immediate future some attempts to further develop 'national economic theories' as ideological tools for strengthening Russia's bureaucratic authoritarian rule.

References

Abalkin, L. (2001). 'Rossiiskaya shkola ekonomicheskoi mysli: poisk samoopredeleniya', *Voprosy ekonomiki*, no 2: 4–18.

———. (2002). 'N.Ya. Danilevsky o Rossii, Evrope i Slavyanskom Edinstve', *Voprosy ekonomiki*, no 11: 122–28.

Avtonomov V. (2001). 'Istoriya ekonomicheskoi mysli i ekonomicheskogo analiza', *Voprosy ekonomiki*, no 2: 42–47.

Bessonova O.E. (2006). *Razdatochnaya Ekonomika Rossii*: *Evolutsiya cherez Transformatsii*. Moscow: Rossiiskaya politicheskaya entsiklopediya.

Danilevsky, N.Ya. (1869). *Rossiya i Evropa*. Saint-Petersburg.

Dubin, B. (2004). '"Protivoves": simvolika Zapada v Rossii poslednikh let', *Pro et Contra*, no 3: 23–35.

Ekonomicheskaya Nauka, (2001). 'Obrazovanie i praktika v Rossii v 90-e gody', *Voprosy ekonomiki*, no 1: 84–95.

Glyn, A. (1987). 'Marxist Economics' in: J. Eatwell et al. (eds). *The New Palgrave: A Dictionary of Economics*. London: Macmillan: 394–95.

Kirdina, S.G. (2000). *Institutsionalnye Matritsy i Razvitie Rossii.* Moscow: Teis.

———. (2004). *X- i Y- Ekonomiki: Institutsionalnyi Analiz*. Moscow: Nauka.

Kulkov, V. (2004). Natsionalnoe v ekonomicheskoi teorii i v ee vusovskikh kursakh. *Rossiskii ekonomicheskii zhurnal*, no 4: 60–71.

Nureev, R. and Latov, Yu. (2002). '"The Fruits of Enlightenment" (The New Russian Economic Science at the Threshold of the Third Millenium)', *Problems of Economic Transition*, vol. 44, no 9–10: 22–57.

O'Hara, P. (ed.) (1999). *Encyclopedia of Political Economy*, vol. 2. London, New York: Routledge.

Osipov, Yu. et al. (eds) (1998). *Ekonomicheskaya Teoriya na Poroge XXI veka* – 2.

Moscow: Yurist.
Platonov, O.A. (1999). *Pochemu Pogibnet Amerika*. Moscow: Russkii Vestnik.
———. (ed.). (2002). *Svyataya Rus. Bolshaya Entsiklopediya Russkogo Naroda. Russkoe Gosudarstvo*. Moscow: Entsiklopediya Russkoi Tsivilizatsii.
————. (2006a). *Russkaya Ekonomika bez Globalizma*. Moscow: Algoritm.
———. (ed.). (2006b). *Svyataya Rus. Bolshaya Entsiklopediya Russkogo Naroda. Russkoe Khozyaistvo*. Moscow: Institut Russkoi Tsivilizatsii.
Ryazanov, V. (1996). 'Kakoi byt bazovoi ekonomicheskoi distsipline v vuzakh?', *Rossiskii ekonomicheskii zhurnal*, nos 11–12: 76–84.
Schumpeter, J.A. (1954). *History of Economic Analysis*, New York.
Sorokin, D. (2001). 'Politicheskaya ekonomiya dlya Rossii', *Rossiskii ekonomicheskii zhurnal*, no 2: 78–84.
Zaostrovtsev, A. (2005). 'The Principle Conflict in Contemporary Russian Economic Thought: Traditional Approaches Against Economics', *HWWA Discussion Paper*, no 329.
Zemlyakov, D. (2000). 'Distsiplina "Natsionalnaya Ekonomika": metodologo-teoreticheskie i metodologicheskie osnovy', *Rossiiskii ekonomicheskii zhurnal*, no 9: 75–83.

Chapter 13

Conclusion

Vincent Barnett and Joachim Zweynert

After progressing through all the chapters of the volume, the reader should now be in a much better position to understand both the development of aspects of Russian economics over time, and also the diversity of its content and results. It should be immediately recognized that the topics presented for analysis here make up only a small fraction of the total contributions made by Russian thinkers to economic concerns broadly considered. Both of the editors (and most of the contributors) have written extensively on Russian economic ideas elsewhere, and hence a more comprehensive understanding can be obtained by starting from these previously issued works.

Even so, some general observations can be made using many of the economists discussed in this volume. Firstly, that the progress of economic ideas in Russia was (and still is) inextricably connected to matters of economic policy and also to issues of governmental control. The destruction wrought on Russia's finest economists at the beginning of the 1930s has been well publicized for a long time now, but the fact that this sort of rough treatment was not unusual centuries before Stalin's rise to power might come as rather more of a surprise. The emigration of Russian economists can consequently be seen as one way of escaping from this type of governmental wrath, as was a straightforward conformity to (ever shifting) doctrinal orthodoxy.

But for some individuals, avoidance proved impossible to secure, perhaps due in part to the fact that such treatment was initially considered too horrific to be thought possible. The case of Nikolai Bukharin (1888–1938), once considered the 'darling' of the Bolshevik party, although not discussed in this volume, is indicative. On the very eve of his execution, after experiencing an Orwellian campaign of mendacious slander directed against him by his own former comrades, he still expressed a firm belief that everything would turn out perfectly well for the Great Socialist Fatherland. Perhaps the shock of fully comprehending that the October revolution had degenerated to such a base level, and hence that all of his political efforts had been drowned in a totalitarian corporate quagmire, would have destroyed him just as surely as Stalin's pen actually did. In the twenty-first century, those individuals who were subject to the Stalinist terror might rest a little easier in their graves with the knowledge that it is Stalin's legacy that currently lies in shreds.

In case it is believed that, at the start of the twenty-first century, this sort of treatment for those critical of government policy is a thing of the past, it is well to be reminded of recent developments in Russia characterized by a tendency toward the 'state capture' of key branches of the economy, increasing restrictions on political liberty, and a low conviction rate regarding serious crimes against persons critical of the Russian government such as journalists. Even if no cases, so far, have been reported of economists being subject to direct political pressure, it does not take much imagination to conceive of such a case in the near future. Although a continuous and important link between economic ideas and economic policy cannot be denied in the development of (say) British and American economics, in Russia this connection has sometimes been raised to quite extraordinary degrees of proximity, and with quite tragic consequences. American economists who have fallen foul of political orthodoxy have sometimes lost their jobs, or have even committed suicide under critical pressure, but none have been deliberately assassinated. Only leading American politicians have been so treated.

Secondly, the question that was raised in the introduction regarding the existence of a 'Russian school of economics' can now be reconsidered in the light of the individual chapters that have been presented. Both of the editors consider this conception of the subject (in the main) to be mistaken, as the diversity contained within the chapters of this volume will support. Both editors have argued elsewhere that within Russian economics there has been a definite tendency to focus on specific themes and topics over a considerable period of time, for example on the progress of business cycles and industrialization strategy. In tackling these topics, Russian economists have employed a wide variety of ideas and tools of analysis, many of which were adapted from overseas. The specific mix of the adaptation regarding the balance of Western and native Russian ideas was invariably unique, but this does not quite constitute the existence of a 'Russian school' of economic thinking, as is implied in other geographically-focused phrases such as 'Austrian school', 'Cambridge school' or 'Chicago school'. Russian economics was frequently more diverse in methodology and approach than the economic analysis of these more accepted types of school invariably displayed.

Thirdly, it might be surprising to some readers how little the 'doctrinal trinity' within Soviet-style economics of Marx, Engels and Lenin have been mentioned within this volume. Russian economics had a long and distinguished history before 1917, and in the second half of the nineteenth century, Marx was considered by non-socialist economists in Russia (if at all) as a very minor post-Ricardian indeed. Although Marx's ideas were frequently discussed more vividly by Russian socialist economists than by socialists in other European countries, he was by no means a dominant figure in pre-revolutionary Russian political economy. It was only after 1917 that the crimson shadows of Soviet interpretations of Marx could be seen being cast forcibly across every nook and cranny of Russian history. Now, in the early twenty-first century, Marx is of course very much a 'dead dog' within many Russian intellectual circles, just as Hegel was in Germany at the time of the publication of the first volume of *Capital*. Perhaps in the near future some coquetting with Marxian terminology might consequently be in order. In truth, what winding avenues Russian economics will explore in the future is of course unknown, but what is certain is that it will be building upon (or reacting against) a rich tradition of analysis, that deserves to be further explored by both historians and economists alike.

Name Index

Subject Index

Modern Economic and Social History Series

General Editor
Derek Aldcroft, University Fellow, Department of Economic and Social History, University of Leicester, UK

Derek Aldcroft
Studies in the Interwar European Economy
1 85928 360 8 (1997)

Michael J. Oliver
Whatever Happened to Monetarism?: Economic Policy Making and Social Learning in the United Kingdom Since 1979
1 85928 433 7 (1997)

R. Guerriero-Wilson
Disillusionment or New Opportunities?: The Changing Nature of Work in Offices, Glasgow 1880–1914
1 84014 276 6 (1998)

Barry Stapleton and James H. Thomas
Gales: A Study in Brewing, Business and Family History
0 7546 0146 3 (2000)

Derek Aldcroft and Michael Oliver
Trade Unions and the Economy: 1870–2000
1 85928 370 5 (2000)

Patrick Duffy
The Skilled Compositor, 1850–1914: An Aristocrat Among Working Men
0 7546 0255 9 (2000)

Roger Lloyd-Jones and M.J. Lewis with the assistance of M. Eason
Raleigh and the British Bicycle Industry: An Economic and Business History, 1870–1960
1 85928 457 4 (2000)

Ted Wilson
Battles for the Standard: Bimetallism and the Spread of the Gold Standard in the Nineteenth Century
1 85928 436 1 (2000)

Andrew D. Popp
Business Structure, Business Culture and the Industrial District: The Potteries, c. 1850–1914
0 7546 0176 5 (2001)

Bernard Cronin
Technology, Industrial Conflict and the Development of Technical Education in 19th-Century England
0 7546 0313 X (2001)

Geoffrey Channon
Railways *in Britain and the United States, 1830–1940: Studies in Economic and Business History*
1 84014 253 7 (2001)

Sam Mustafa
Merchants and Migrations: Germans and Americans in Connection, 1776–1835
0 7546 0590 6 (2001)

Robert Conlon and John Perkins
Wheels and Deals: The Automotive Industry in Twentieth-Century Australia
0 7546 0405 5 (2001)

Michael Ferguson
The Rise of Management Consulting in Britain
0 7546 0561 2 (2002)

Scott Kelly
The Myth of Mr Butskell: The Politics of British Economic Policy, 1950–55
0 7546 0604 X (2002)

Alan Fowler
Lancashire Cotton Operatives and Work, 1900-1950: A Social History of Lancashire Cotton Operatives in the Twentieth Century
0 7546 0116 1 (2003)

John F. Wilson and Andrew Popp (eds)
Industrial Clusters and Regional Business Networks in England, 1750-1970
0 7546 0761 5 (2003)

John Hassan
The Seaside, Health and the Environment in England and Wales since 1800
1 84014 265 0 (2003)

Andrew Dawson
Lives of the Philadelphia Engineers: Capital, Class and Revolution, 1830–1890
0 7546 3396 9 (2004)

Anne Clendinning
Demons of Domesticity: Women and the English Gas Industry, 1889–1939
0 7546 0692 9 (2004)

Armin Grünbacher
Reconstruction and Cold War in Germany:
The Kreditanstalt für Wiederaufbau (1948–1961)
0 7546 3806 5 (2004)

Joseph Harrison and David Corkill
Spain: A Modern European Economy
0 7546 0145 5 (2004)

Lawrence Black and Hugh Pemberton (eds)
An Affluent Society?: Britain's Post-War 'Golden Age' Revisited
0 7546 3528 7 (2004)

Marshall J. Bastable
Arms and the State: Sir William Armstrong and the
Remaking of British Naval Power, 1854–1914
0 7546 3404 3 (2004)

Robin Pearson
Insuring the Industrial Revolution: Fire Insurance in Great Britain, 1700–1850
0 7546 3363 2 (2004)

Ross E. Catterall and Derek H. Aldcroft (eds)
Exchange Rates and Economic Policy in the 20th Century
1 84014 264 2 (2004)

Till Geiger
Britain and the Economic Problem of the Cold War: The Political Economy and
the Economic Impact of the British Defence Effort, 1945-1955
0 7546 0287 7 (2004)

Julian Greaves
Industrial Reorganization and Government Policy in Interwar Britain
0 7546 0355 5 (2005)

Timothy Cuff
The Hidden Cost of Economic Development: The Biological Standard of Living
in Antebellum Pennsylvania
0 7546 4119 8 (2005)

Derek Aldcroft
Europe's Third World: The European Periphery in the Interwar Years
0 7546 0599 X (2006)

James P. Huzel
The Popularization of Malthus in Early Nineteenth-Century England: Martineau, Cobbett and the Pauper Press
0 7546 5427 3 (2006).

Richard Perren
Taste, Trade and Technology
The Development of the International Meat Industry since 1840
978-0-7546-3648-9 (2006)

Roger Lloyd-Jones and M.J. Lewis
Alfred Herbert Ltd and the British Machine Tool Industry, 1887-1983
978-0-7546-0523-2 (2006)

Anthony Howe and Simon Morgan (eds)
Rethinking Nineteenth-Century Liberalism
Richard Cobden Bicentenary Essays
978-0-7546-5572-5 (2006)

Espen Moe
Governance, Growth and Global Leadership
The Role of the State in Technological Progress, 1750–2000
978-0-7546-5743-9 (2007)

Peter Scott
Triumph of the South
A Regional Economic History of Early Twentieth Century Britain
978-1-84014-613-4 (2007)

David Turnock
Aspects of Independent Romania's Economic History with Particular Reference to Transition for EU Accession
978-0-7546-5892-4 (2007)

David Oldroyd
Estates, Enterprise and Investment at the Dawn of the Industrial Revolution
Estate Management and Accounting in the North-East of England, c.1700-1780
978-0-7546-3455-3 (2007)

Ralf Roth and Günter Dinhobl (eds)
Across the Borders
Financing the World's Railways in the Nineteenth and Twentieth Centuries
978-0-7546-6029-3 (2008)